Pulci's *Morgante*

# Pulci's *Morgante*

## POETRY AND HISTORY
## IN FIFTEENTH-CENTURY FLORENCE

*Constance Jordan*

Folger Books
Washington: The Folger Shakespeare Library
London and Toronto: Associated University Presses

Associated University Presses
440 Forsgate Drive
Cranbury, NJ 08512

Associated University Presses
25 Sicilian Avenue
London WC1A 2QH, England

Associated University Presses
2133 Royal Windsor Drive
Unit 1
Mississauga, Ontario
Canada L5J 1K5

The paper used in this publication meets the
requirements of the American National Standard for
Permanence of Paper for Printed Library Materials Z39.48-1984.

**Library of Congress Cataloging-in-Publication Data**

Jordan, Constance.
    Pulci's Morgante : poetry and history in fifteenth-
century Florence.

    "Folger books."
    Bibliography: p.
    Includes index.
    1. Pulci, Luigi, 1432–1484. Morgante.   2. Pulci,
Luigi, 1432–1484—Contemporary Italy.   3. Florence
(Italy)—History—1421–1737.   I. Title.
PQ4631.M4J67   1986        851'.2        85-45572
ISBN 0-918016-89-4 (alk. paper)

Printed in the United States of America

*For*
*C. M.*
*in memory of*
*L. H. M.*

# CONTENTS

# PREFACE

THIS book began with my belief that to ignore the historiographic dimension of the Italian epics on the Orlando story was to misread them. The error, I think, originates with Tasso's *Discorsi*. In defending his own *Gerusalemme Liberata* as an epic written with due regard for what he considered Aristotelian proprieties, Tasso had deliberately emphasized the romance character of the earlier and enormously popular *Orlando Furioso* and repeatedly criticized its neglect of a high seriousness. His argument tended to obscure the extent to which Ariosto's poem was engaged in examining not only the status of historical narrative but also the role of the epic poet as historian, in his case one who was patronized by a powerful nobleman with a stated interest in evolving for his family an impressive lineage and history. As Margaret Ferguson's study of poetic defenses establishes, the *Discorsi* record Tasso's experience of reading the *Orlando Furioso* as a text of intense personal meaning which evoked memories of the later poet's father (and Ariosto's contemporary); Tasso's criticism of Ariosto needs to be interpreted accordingly. What has not yet been made clear is that the struggle properly to formulate historiographic norms is registered—in different ways and at different levels—throughout both the *Orlando Furioso* and its precursor Italian poems on the "matter of France."

The most fundamental exercise of the historicist imagination is revealed in the *Morgante*. Luigi Pulci inherited a subject hallowed by literary tradition and in the popular historical imagination of Florentines for whom Carlo Magno was a kind of founding father. He was celebrated as such in virtually all the fifteenth-century histories of the city, even those, like Bruni's *Historiarum Florentini Populi Liber,* that betray a sympathy for republican forms of government. The notion of a Florentine empire and of the city's ancient connection to the French monarchy was, moreover, an important factor in the foreign policy of the Medici in the latter half of the century; they counted on the support of Florentines to forge sometimes costly alliances with Milan and the house of Anjou against Venice and Naples. Pulci's *Morgante* was one of a number of works sponsored by the Medici that were intended to further relations between France and Florence. Its problematic form, especially evident in the differences in style and theme between Parts 1 and 2, and its powerful (if also tardy) development of an authorial voice, reflect the actual political pressures its poet confronted in the course of its composition. Pulci's was not a life of easy courtiership. Having begun the poem as a Medici protégé, specifically of Lucrezia Tornabuoni, he was later dismissed from the palace by Lorenzo, who sought to establish there an intellectual ambience conducive to the kind of philosophical activity exemplified by the exercises of the so-called Platonic academy headed by Ficino. The effects of Pulci's changing relationship to the Medici are registered in various ways throughout his poem.

It was a fruitful coincidence that Pulci's departure from Florence occurred about the time at which he changed sources for his poem and began to write what would become Part 2. There he had to confront, in a way he had not earlier, the question of the credibility of his sources. In particular, he was forced to come to terms with the judgment of Dante, whose decision to place the Emperor in paradise served to illuminate for the later poet the problems of interpretation of historical events. By contending with this judgment and with narratives that provided him with what he considered historical evidence, Pulci was able to evolve a notion, however rudimentary, of the self-critical discipline necessary to the historian. It is no accident, I think, that this discovery was made in a period in which Pulci was himself comparatively free from the obligation to conform to the social norms Lorenzo had endorsed. One can say that for him the crisis of authorship is closely bound up with a political crisis; in his struggles to survive and yet to continue to function politically he could discern suggestive analogues to his efforts to develop a creative independence while at the same time remaining within an established literary tradition.

When Pulci began writing his poem, he did not realize, I think, that he was in possession of all the elements with which to articulate the central concerns of historiography. How he did so is in part my subject. In a real sense his poem is both traditional and innovative. It tells an old and popular story, transcribed and transformed fully to represent Medici preoccupations with a propaganda of empire; yet it also subjects this material and mode of narration to a critique that, while not systematic, is nevertheless sustained. The interest of the poem chiefly lies in the dialectic between representation and revision.

In the pages that follow I have not attempted to comment on aspects of the *Morgante* that have already received careful attention from its many Italian critics during the last several decades. It would be difficult and perhaps presumptuous for anyone whose experience has largely been comparative to try to improve on their rich and suggestive studies of Pulci's style and his transformation of the medieval themes and topoi he found in his sources. Rather I have chosen to consider the poem *as a narrative* and to focus on its complex structure, its use of perspective as both a formal principle and a figure of thought, and its representation of the poet as historian. I have been guided here largely by what I take to be the poet's concern with the status of his poem as a record of a past that is also intended to be a model for the future. This approach implies (and it is in fact the case) that I believe the poem has a serious side and engages issues that Pulci's contemporaries judged decisively important to their age. It does not mean that I rule out the value of regarding the poem as facetious or underestimate the importance of its burlesque elements. The *Morgante* is clearly a humorous poem. Its fantastic characters, especially Morgante and Margutte, are consistently droll; its chivalric characters frequently verge on the ridiculous. While Pulci was not a master of irony in the sense that Ariosto would be, he nevertheless delighted in demonstrating that the typically serious matter of France could be treated in a ludicrous manner. But if our knowledge of the popular culture of Pulci's Florence, to which the poem itself is much in debt, permits any kind of generalization, it is certainly that a comic treatment of a social ideal—such as Pulci's of the chivalry of Charlemagne's court—does not indicate that this ideal was held to be superfluous. On the contrary, the stylistic doubleness of the *Morgante*, so characteristic of Renaissance culture as a whole, provides a way of testing social values in order that they may be more clearly understood and, when appropriate, reaffirmed.

In my discussion of chivalric behavior I have made use of a term in Italian which is in my opinion difficult to translate: *virtù* or heroic strength, skill, and courage, particularly as it is to be distinguished from virtue, a moral quality. I have also referred to the Italian "fama" by the Middle English (and especially Malorian) term "worship"; in the context of chivalric romance "fama" means not so much "fame," that is, reputation (whether good or bad), as the glory owed to a knight who performs great deeds, a notion more accurately covered by the term "worship." When "fama" is to be understood in a negative sense, or ironic, it is generally clear from the context in which it is used. I have similarly referred to the Italian "compagnia," as in a company of knights, by the English word "fellowship"; this will, I hope, convey that to belong to a company of knights is to enter into a relationship of mutual trust.

All translations from Italian and Latin works in this text are my own, unless otherwise noted. When quoting passages from early editions I have spelled out words abbreviated by printer's marks and, where the original punctuation is confusing, I have altered it for clarification.

All quotations of Pulci's *Morgante* come from the text edited by Franca Ageno (Milan, Ricciardi, 1957). I have used texts in the Loeb Library series for quotations of passages from Vergil, Ovid, and Statius.

Portions of Chapters 1 and 4 have appeared in *Studies in Philology* and the *Romanic Review* respectively.

# ACKNOWLEDGMENTS

I am happy to acknowledge the assistance and support of various friends in writing this book. I thank Lorraine Daston, Margaret W. Ferguson, Robert W. Hanning, Amy Johnson, Walter Oakeshott, David Quint, Richard Sacks, and Laura Slatkin for reading portions of the manuscript in draft, and Donald Lyons of Associated University Presses for his expert editing; I have been sustained by their encouragement and enlightened by their observations. I also received valuable advice from Joan M. Ferrante, Jonathan Goldberg, Andrée Hayum, Daniel Javitch, William J. Kennedy, Richard McCoy, James V. Mirollo, Stephen Orgel, and Edward W. Tayler; speaking at crucial moments, they saved me hours of labor and vexation. I am grateful to the staffs of the Columbia University Libraries and The British Library for facilitating my research in Renaissance mythography and Florentine history; and to my friends in London, John and Susan Martin Gray, and Robert Oakeshott, for their hospitality during the spring of 1981. To my sons, Wilson, Andrew, and Geoffrey Kidde, I owe a special debt; without their affection, understanding, and companionship this book could not have been written.

# Pulci's *Morgante*

# INTRODUCTION

To read the *Morgante* as a poem celebrating the life of the Emperor Charlemagne, a figure who for Renaissance audiences was both historical and legendary, inevitably leads to questions concerning its intention. Writing on historical subjects is generally understood to be apologetic in more or less specific ways, and works in the generic category to which the *Morgante* belongs, Renaissance epic-romance, are perhaps outstandingly so. Their elaborate dedications, their ceremonious commemorations of lineage (more often than not fanciful), their references to events that actually occurred as well as to those that most certainly did not, usually indicate the pressures of patronage, and frequently a patron's demand that a dynasty and therefore a particular form of government be established as legitimate.[1] But a reader's interest in the rhetorical context of a work on a historical subject can justify a survey of a larger field of inquiry than that outlined by the circumstances of patronage—a field in which such a work is considered in relation to the aspirations and values of the culture of which it was a part. Given the characteristic elusiveness of determinations of this sort—ideological in the most general sense—satisfactory answers to questions about particular works can be difficult to discover, but this is not a reason not to search for them. In the case of Luigi Pulci's epic-romance, readers do well to begin by being informed not only of the various myths and historiographic traditions upon which the poem draws for its plot and representation of causality, but also of the politics of Florence and the details of the poet's life from 1461 to 1481, the years in which it was composed.

Among the *literati* of a fundamentally humanist training that Cosimo de'Medici had attracted to his palace at the via Larga, Pulci, a poet of the *volgare* exclusively, was a distinct exception. It is therefore not surprising that he was patronized by a woman—Lucrezia Tornabuoni, Piero de'Medici's wife, Lorenzo's mother, and Cosimo's daughter-in-law—nor that his subject, which he says was her choice, was popular, deeply implicated in the folk traditions of Italy, and of little apparent interest to the new scholarship.[2]

He must have recognized from the outset of his enterprise in 1461 that Lucrezia's choice had political implications, if not a political motive. What he claimed in the very first octaves of the poem—that the roots of Florentine nobility were in the court of Charlemagne—was in fact an element in an important myth of the origins of the city. In a poem about Charlemagne Lucrezia's contemporaries could scarcely have failed to see a reference to this myth and by extension to whatever in their city's history they could imagine as a fulfillment of an imperialistic destiny. How deliberately the Medici, and especially Cosimo, sought to promote an ideology of empire to give an attractive coloration to their own activities both within the city and throughout northern Europe is and perhaps will remain debatable, but the evidence is suggestive. Pulci certainly began his poem in social and political circumstances that would have made him aware of its potential as propaganda; moreover, as he continued to write it, he appears to have seen this potential more clearly and with greater concern for its possible effects.

### The Idea of Empire in Florentine History

In the fifteenth century, the history of Florence was sustained by two myths of origin that were in theory incompatible but in fact intertwined in the popular imagination: the myth of an imperial past and the myth of a republican past.[3] The latter was associated with the city's link to republican Rome, the former with its almost miraculous restoration by the Emperor Charlemagne.

Early in the century several Florentine humanists, principally Lionardo Bruni and Coluccio Salutati, had advanced the notion that Florence had enjoyed at its foundation a republican form of government. They declared that the city began as a colony of pre-imperial, republican Rome, and from this they concluded that its first government had been by representation rather than despotic.[4] The position is fully articulated in Bruni's *Historiarum Florentini Populi Liber*, which includes both a denunciation, first expressed in his earlier *Laudatio Florentinae Urbis*, of the imperial government of Rome (an opinion he bases on his reading of Tacitus) and the account of the founding of Florence by the soldiers in Sulla's army that he found in Salutati's *Invectiva in Antonium Luschum Vicentinum*. To his picture of the city's origins he adds a description of the free, powerful, and learned Etruscans, a people who before the rise of Rome dominated the Italian peninsula although they were themselves respectful of liberty.[5] Those of Bruni's contemporaries who championed the merits of a government responsible to the people were encouraged by the belief that the Florentine constitution, which stressed *ius* and *libertas*, was not a product of generations of political struggle but the simple birthright of all citizens of the city.

The work of these scholars affected not only political but also intellectual life. It encouraged Florentines to regard critically the Petrarchan notion of the superiority of the *vita contemplativa* and to consider favorably the concept of the Ciceronian *vita activa* as a more useful guide to life in a republic. The work of humanists like Bruni, Salutati, and later Palmieri turned the attention of educated citizens from questions relating to the moral status of the individual to those posed by the well-being of the city as a whole; and ethics became what they were for Aristotle, subordinate in function and importance to politics.[6]

But however supportive of republicanism in theory, the myth of the city's republican past also served in this period to screen a political reality of a different order. Despite a constitution that appeared to allow for a representative government, decisions affecting the life of the city were, in the first half of the century, always (and increasingly) the prerogative of those citizens whose financial affairs had flourished; to them, the common belief in the constitutionality of Florentine government, difficult to challenge because a general prosperity made the government popular with many citizens, proved a convenience. The oligarchy retained control of the city because, as Martines notes, they were protected by the illusion that power "was truly distributed according to constitutional forms."[7] The actual hollowness of the republican ideal provided a space for the concentration of power in the hands of relatively few persons who, after the return of Cosimo in 1434, were increasingly identified with the Medici.

The erosion of the representative government provided by the constitution can be traced by reference to the activities of a single group of men known as *accoppiatori*, elected officials who in turn supervised all city elections. From 1434 and for several extended periods thereafter, the *accoppiatori* exercised the privilege of determining who would be a member of the Signoria, a body of nine citizens without whose assent no law could be passed. These powers were in a sense extralegal, for according to the constitution such determinations were to be made by lot. Under Cosimo's influence, the *accoppiatori* generally considered for this office only persons sympathetic to the Medici. The *accoppiatori* were not, admittedly, all Cosimo's clients, much less his tools: Rubinstein describes them as " 'representatives' of the inner circle of the regime."[8] But their interests coincided for the most part with those of the Medici. Cosimo, enlisting others to do his business, held political office infrequently.

A constitutional crisis occurred in 1458 and it resulted in a further and more open consolidation of power in the Medici circle. Rubinstein notes a consistent republican opposition to the practice of election by choice of the *accoppiatori* from 1434 to 1458. Nevertheless, when the Parlamento convened in August of that year, this opposition was not strong enough to win the vote. Various persons strenuously advocated a return to constitutional government, notably Girolamo Machiavelli, but in the aftermath most of them were exiled. Cosimo, the real winner of the struggle, retired to his palace, and from then until he died in 1464 the *accoppiatori*, deciding as before whom to include as candidates for election, met there and not in the palace of the Signoria. Pius II, visiting Florence in 1459, stated that affairs of state were discussed in Cosimo's house and cited this as proof of his control of the city.[9]

The nature of Cosimo's hold over Florence during this period is difficult to determine precisely. It was the power of a grey eminence who stood behind not a monarch but what appeared to be a representative government. Historians remark on Cosimo's protestations of weakness and cite the experience of Pope Nicholas V, who, when he preached a crusade in 1463, learned that Cosimo thought of himself merely as a citizen in a "free and popular republic," and accordingly believed that there were limits to what he could promise and perform.[10] Such a self-characterization does not do justice to the real power of this merchant banker. It is quite possible to identify among his supporters various persons who sought power themselves, who disagreed among themselves as well as with him. Yet it is also the case that these tensions were contained within the party itself and, more important, that they were not available for exploitation by a political opposition. Guided by Cosimo, the party sought to present a united front and to discourage any impression that among its members dissent could lead to serious division.[11] Certainly Medici interests were becoming increasingly difficult for any citizen of Florence to ignore. The economic strength of the city as a whole was becoming progressively more dependent on the spread throughout Europe of Medici commercial activities; these were in turn linked to the establishment of political alliances, which often entailed expenditures for military operations, both in Italy and to the north.

The second myth of origin Florence cherished was chronologically older and also the more popular. The notion that Florence was an imperial city was early connected to associations with Rome and later with Charlemagne. More important, it was fused with the related notion of a return of the past, especially of empire as a recurring phenomenon and therefore in some sense a continuous entity—a *translatio imperii.*

The most important of the early histories of Florence stress its renascence in the sixth century following the barbarian invasions and associate this with an imperialistic destiny. The anonymous author of the first of these, the thirteenth-century *Chronica de origine civitatis,* insists on the essentially Roman character of the Florentines, which he sees in successful rivalry with that of the "barbarians" of Fiesole and later of the north. Colonized by the Romans in the time of Julius Caesar, then destroyed by Totila, Florence, he declares, was *rebuilt* by the Romans. He pictures the city engaged in a periodic struggle against the enemies of civilization—a struggle marked by an extraordinary energy that led to reconstruction and revival.[12] A similar kind of optimism, clearly inspiring a vision of empire, is evident in the inscription that was carved on the Palazzo Popolo in the middle of the century:

> She [Florence] strengthens, acquires, and destroys castles,
> She controls the sea, the land, the whole world,
> In this government all of Tuscany rejoices,
> Like Rome, she endures always, a leader in triumph. . . .[13]

The fourteenth-century history of Villani adds an important element to the history described in the early chronicle: it credits Charlemagne with reviving the city. After Totila had razed the city, Villani declares, the Emperor sent troops there to assist the Romans.[14] Then, conflating imperial and republican traditions, he further asserts that the Emperor instituted a free citizenry in a free commune, which "established a government on the Roman model, that is, by two consuls and the consent of a hundred senators. . . ."[15]

Villani's association of independent Florence with Charlemagne, so important to later Florentine historians, probably reflected the rise of Angevin power in Italy during the two previous centuries, a development that had also inspired fourteenth-century prophecies predicting a new Empire under a new French king Charles. Known as the Second Charlemagne prophecies, these accounts foresaw that the king would descend into Italy, renew its political and cultural life, and eventually conquer the Holy Land.[16] As Florence became involved in defending itself from Milanese aggression, the popular conception of its past came to include this prophetic strain.[17] A fourteenth-century Florentine manifesto against the Visconti characterizes their conflict with Milan as a war for control of Italy: Milan, "il serpente," wishes to take over all Tuscan and Lombard cities and so to obtain the "crown of Italy to make its tyranny respectable with the splendor of a title." But, the Florentines declare, "our existence will prevent Italians from falling into slavery"; in effect, a comparably imperialistic declaration and perhaps a deliberate echo of the inscription on the Palazzo Popolo.[18] A fifteenth-century Florentine prophecy, the so-called "Bridget prophecy" because it was (wrongly) ascribed to St. Bridget of Sweden, substantially repeats these assertions, and, in a postscript to one manuscript, declares that this war of liberation will occur between 1460 and 1470.[19]

Fifteenth-century histories of the life of Charlemagne and his court, including those of several of Pulci's contemporaries, continued to give color and immediacy to the Florentine claim that he had played a decisive part in their past. Donato Acciaiuoli's *Vita Caroli Magni* not only repeats all previous accounts of Charlemagne's restoration of the city; it also attributes to his example and guidance the future greatness of Florence: "For that we live free in our own land, that we have magistrates, laws, a state *(civitas)*—all these things that we have received must be seen to derive from Charlemagne. His memory, so welcome, ought to be celebrated with everlasting testimonials. . . ."[20] These compliments may have had an ulterior purpose. Acciaiuoli, representing the city of Florence, offered the work to Louis XI of France on his accession to the throne in 1461, a time in which Cosimo was vigorously pursuing a pro-French policy against the interests of the Aragonese in Naples. In any case, it pictured the Emperor as more than ever the source of Florentine civic *virtù* and gave explicit formulation to the notion that Florence had been connected to the French monarchy for centuries.

Palmieri concludes his *Della vita civile* (1538) with a pious story of the Emperor in which he reveals his particular concern for Florence. A young Florentine soldier, who has died in the war against the Aretini in Casentino, tells Palmieri's "Dante" of meeting "Carlo Magno" in heaven. The young man praises the Emperor for ridding Italy of barbarians, *barbari*, whereupon the Emperor declares: "I still so love *virtù* that when it is cherished by mortals below I am their friend, united (to them) by a single will; moved by it, and having seen that you died for love of Florence where I lived while on earth, I descended to you, to show you the glory that awaits one who, when alive, understands it *(virtù)*."[21] Palmieri's dramatic account of how Dante came to know of the Emperor's salvation makes the latter's ties to the city explicit, and critical to his image as a Christian. Canonized by Pope Pascal III under the direction of Frederick Barbarossa, Charlemagne achieved a place in paradise as a defender of the faith; to Dante's compatriots he was also a civic hero.

Ugolino Verino's *Carliade*, probably begun in 1468, is certainly the most elaborate of the Florentine panegyrics to Charlemagne. Its political purpose is beyond doubt and one can even speculate that it may have had political effect.[22] Composed in a period when the Medici were continuing to foster an alliance with the French, it was finally dedicated to Charles VIII in 1493 when he acceded to the throne. To this fanatical monarch, already committed to establishing a cult of Charlemagne that might justify French imperialism, the Florentine poem may well have seemed the signal he was waiting for; the following year he invaded Italy, terrorized Piero de'Medici into surrendering Florence and its tributary cities, and was in turn cowed into submission by the Florentine

Signoria. These events appear to be an ironic realization of the imperialistic dream—the more so, perhaps, because they finally resulted in the expulsion of Piero and the Medici from Florence, and the reestablishment of the city's constitutional government.

Like other Florentine historians, Pulci sees Charlemagne's court as the source of the city's greatness and the model for her development. In canto 1 he alludes to the Emperor's sojourn in Florence and, in a few lines, conflates both the mythic and prophetic traditions concerning him:

> E tu, Fiorenza, della sua grandezza
> possiedi e sempre potrai possedere:
> ogni costume ed ogni gentilezza,
> che si potessi acquistare o avere
> col senno, col tesoro e colla lancia,
> dal nobil sangue è venuto di Francia.

(1. 7)

And you, Florence, possessed and always can possess his greatness; every gentle habit that may be acquired or had by wit, wealth, or arms, has come from France through noble families.

The prophetic strain here is muted but important because it gives to the poem a presumptive purpose: by illustrating the *virtù* of Carlo's court, the poem will prescribe a moral program for the future of Florence. The passage tacitly assumes that history is, in some sense, cyclical, that the continuum of passing years is punctuated by events that are or seem to be repetitions. It therefore exemplifies *in nuce* the theory of history that the poem itself will later illustrate: that the perception of continuities in history is intimately connected with the idea of renascence. To Florentines, this vision of the future as a re-presentation of the past was well established; in Pulci's poem they were to find it expressed and at last also questioned.

Of the two myths of origin available to Florentines, that of an imperial past was clearly the more popular, especially in its associations with French chivalry. This preference was exploited by the Medici who demonstrated their enthusiasm for an imperialistic rather than a republican culture by their sponsorship of the various public festivals that took place in the city on great feast days. At the beginning of the fifteenth century, the forms of communal celebration exhibited (perhaps predictably) a certain tension. Citizens could perceive in *armeggerie*, jousts and tournaments, relics of a feudal, northern (French and Teutonic) Europe; in processions of persons devoted to the welfare of the people, the clergy and government officials, they saw manifestations of civic authority. As Trexler notes, "the former activities were aristocratically, familially, and individually oriented; the latter, publicly and popularly."[23] They thus appealed to the Florentines' sense of a dual allegiance—to the idea of a republic, to the image of an empire. But as the century progressed and the Medici increased their hold on the city, aristocratic and feudal forms of public celebration came to dominate those which honored the city as a whole.[24] Cosimo moved with characteristic discretion. He refrained, for example, from challenging the civic character of the feast of San Giovanni, but he made ample use of the festival of the Magi, celebrated on the feast of the Epiphany, to reinforce the notion that a society which observed distinctions between commoners and a nobility acquired a certain magnificence.[25] This festival was organized by the Confraternity of the Magi, a brotherhood to which Pulci belonged in 1467; their procession began by honoring the secular authority of "Herod" at "Jerusalem" and ended at the "Bethlehem," actually the Medici church of San Marco. The symbolism of the event is obvious: in the splendid paraphernalia surrounding the figures of the Biblical kings, Florentines saw represented the results of Cosimo's commercial activities. The riches brought to the Christ child were, in a sense, reflections of what the Medici had brought to Florence.[26] The procession appears to have assumed the character of a ritual obeisance.

It was the youth Lorenzo, however, who during these years seemed most vividly to symbolize Medici pretentions to a chivalric and imperialistic past. Cosimo sent him on his first embassy, to Jean of Anjou in 1454, at the age of five; he was splendidly dressed in a suit designed "à la française."[27] In 1460, he was the leader of a group, a *brigata*, of participants in a joust. The anonymous observer who gives us a verse description of the occasion relates that he saw Lorenzo, a boy of ten years, "young in age and old in wisdom," who had "great power"; he was the "son of Piero and grandson of Cosimo" and the "gentlemen" there "made him lord."[28] In subsequent years he frequently participated in similar events, notably in 1469, in the *armeggeria* celebrating his marriage to Clarice Orsini, an event Pulci celebrates in his poem entitled *La Giostra del Magnifico Lorenzo de Medici*.[29] The chivalric combat that was supposed to constitute the *raison d'être* of these aristocratic *armeggerie* was purely formal. It involved no antagonism other than the symbolic one implicit in the display itself—the assertion of political power of one person or family over the spectators and the community to which they belonged. Yet despite their essentially dramatic nature, such displays appear to have helped create and enforce actual relationships of authority and subordination.

How vital this dream of empire might have been to Cosimo—a dream he had in many respects already realized—is apparent in what are reported as his words on his death bed.[30] Counselling his son Piero, he envisages an aggressive foreign policy, aspiring to the domination of Italy, to be pursued through coercion not war. He insists that Piero set an example with "just laws" and cultivate "honorable acts." Yet he also imagines that by these means his son will create a unified Italy under the control of Florence, and he terms it the "Tuscan empire" ("l'impero toscano").[31] His words suggest that the concept of empire was for him not an image in a nostalgic fantasy but a determinative element in his vision of Europe.

Cosimo's direction of Florentine diplomacy from the early 1450s to his death in 1464 relied for public support on the city's ancient connection with the French, a connection kept alive in popular histories and by the imagery of public festivals. This diplomacy was largely predicated on maintaining an alliance with the Sforza in Milan against Venice and the kingdom of Naples. To strengthen his hand Cosimo repeatedly sought the support first of Charles VII and then of Louis XI. In this venture he was backed by his fellow citizens.

Enthusiasm on the part of ordinary Florentines for things French was especially keen during the period in which Pulci was beginning the *Morgante*. This was in part a reflection of actual diplomatic maneuvers during 1460 and 1461, critical years for Cosimo's pro-French policy. Ferrante of Aragon had succeeded his father Alfonso on the throne of Naples and had thus successfully defeated the claim to that throne of Jean of Anjou, who six years earlier had entertained the child Lorenzo. In 1460 the Signoria voted a sum to help Jean; the frugal Cosimo persuaded the Signoria to withdraw it. This was not a popular decision. When Louis XI succeeded Charles VII in 1461, Cosimo had to defend and to an extent to mask his neutrality by promises of support to France. In fact, when Francesco Sforza, hoping to break relations with France over Naples, asked Florence to raise money to lend him, Cosimo refused; he had found that popular opinion was too pro-French to tolerate actions that would threaten Florentine connections with France, even were they to prove costly in the short run. He knew, in any case, the extent to which Florentine commerce was tied up with French interests.[32] It may well have been that the *Morgante* was to have been an element in a Medici policy with regard to France and Louis XI. Contemporary diplomacy was conducted by a variety of means and one of them was certainly literary compliment—of the sort Donato Acciaiuoli had offered Charles VII (the *Vita Caroli Magni*) and that Ugolino Verino was later to offer the sinister Charles VIII (the *Carliade*). Pulci's poem could have been designed for the same royal audience. Such a diplomatic purpose would have further enhanced its potential value to Cosimo.

In sum: when Pulci entered into the Medici circle in 1461, the inevitable consequences of the centralization of power achieved by Cosimo's policies were beginning to be felt. The shape of government was being altered; from a city run by its patriciate where no family had power immune from attack, Florence was being transformed into an autocratic state. In pursuing both domestic and foreign affairs, the images of chivalry, of feudalism, and especially of empire were clearly manipulated to further Medici interests, not least by those protégés of the family who discharged their obligations to Cosimo by creating for him the imperial image he desired. Landino, Ugolino Verino, Naldo Naldi, to name a few, had specifically eulogized Cosimo as imperial patron, a Maecenas, an Augustus, in the years preceding his death.[33] Pulci himself may not have been fully aware of the dynamics of Florentine political life when he accepted Lucrezia's commission, but by writing a history of Charlemagne he became in some sense an apologist for a more conservative and at the same time more nationalistic and therefore modern form of government than the constitutional republicanism advocated by the humanists of the early fifteenth century.

The closest parallel to the kind of propaganda the *Morgante* represents is to be found in the processions and *armeggerie* of the Florentine festivals. Clearly facetious yet evoking an ideal of conduct, they reflected a popular awareness of civic life as determined by both requirements of a high moral order and a readiness to perceive these requirements realistically, as a kind of comic game. In their rituals of authority and submission Pulci would have discovered the elements of a chivalric drama comparable to the one he was about to compose. Moreover, in both the participants and the spectators of the annual round of public celebrations, he had a prospective audience for his poem. Admittedly he never indicates that he writes for them especially. (His letters do, however, show how intensely he disliked certain humanists, notably Ficino.) But the fact is that he was writing a poem to which the Florentine people at large could respond because it depicted the kind of action they were accustomed to interpreting. Its humorous passages, which so frequently in the first cantos of the poem concern chivalric combat, need to be understood in the context of the shows and entertainment in which the citizens of Florence saw the manifestations of actual political power. In neither case were the readers (or spectators) supposed to mistake the artistic representation for the real thing. Both burlesque and ritualized gesture, indicating the safe encounters of a world of play, were clearly ways to test, mediate, and validate political and social realities.

The fact that Pulci was virtually alone among the poets and historians of the Medici circle in writing in a popular vein was probably in his favor. He appears to have symbolized the link between the intellectual life of the palace and the artistic life of the piazza, where the people still flocked to hear the *cantimbanchi,* itinerant poets, recite the legends of chivalry in verse. His presence at the palace, indicating a reciprocity between the two cultures, popular and learned, was, I think, an element in a deliberate Medici strategy to create an ideology that would help to sustain their increasingly autocratic politics. The intellectual temper of the Medici circle promoted what Ramat has termed a "civil culture," or culture of the state;[34] this was represented on the one hand in the work of humanists like Palmieri and Donato Acciaiuoli, but also in Pulci's *Morgante,* written probably for the benefit of the less educated and in large measure patronized from a shrewd assessment of its value as propaganda.

### *Pulci and the Medici*

Such was the ambience in which Luigi Pulci began his poem. Its effect on the poet was, I think, profound. But one must also acknowledge that, whatever Pulci's opinions on Florentine politics were, he was not, in 1461, in a position to decline an offer of patronage from a member of the Medici family. The year he entered service at the via Larga palace may have been the first of his adult life in which he enjoyed a relative financial security. His father, Iacopo di Francesco, a man of a noble but impoverished family, had died in 1451 in debt to the commune and, despite a career in public service, proscribed by law from voting or holding political office. He left the care of his wife and two daughters to his twin sons, Luigi and Bernardo, both nineteen, and to their elder brother, Luca. The family did not prosper and supplying the daughters with dowries involved it in fresh debts. In 1458 Luca went to the Arrighi bank in Rome, but his service there did not alleviate his family's poverty.[35]

A year after Luca's departure for Rome, Luigi found employment as secretary to Francesco di Matteo Castellani, who had further helped him by giving him books, among them a copy of Vergil. Bartolomeo Scala, at that time a secretary to Pierfrancesco de'Medici, began a series of lectures on the poet in Pierfrancesco's house in Florence, and it was for these Pulci wanted the book. One can imagine that he regarded the venture with a certain diffidence. He was twenty-eight, probably already a poet of popular lyrics, and untrained in the study of classical authors. He knew some Latin but no Greek and, more important, had little time to devote to humanistic pursuits. When Castellani introduced him to the Medici circle in 1459, it was logical that he be asked to write a poem on a popular and medieval subject.

Pulci's letters from 1461 to 1469 reveal that he felt himself an intimate of the family and especially of Lorenzo. He visited their several villas; he hunted with them. To Lorenzo he wrote letters in praise of the young man's *brigata*, among whom he counted himself; he read aloud the *Morgante* and, in 1465, sonnets ridiculing Scala. The latter were in part inspired by Pulci's dislike of scholars, but they may also have been motivated by professional jealousy. When Scala was appointed chancellor that year, Pulci wrote Lorenzo a letter alluding to the event as a joke.[36] Pulci may have hoped for a public office at this time (in 1470 he was to ask Lorenzo for a magistracy); by the end of 1465 he was certainly in debt and consequently in difficulty with the law. Luca Pulci's business had failed, and both Pulci and Bernardo were banished from Florence because of their brother's obligations. The economic outlook in general was poor. Piero de'Medici had begun his career as effective head of state by calling in the vast debts owed his bank and as a result many Florentines had suffered bankruptcy. Pulci went to a farm his family owned in the Mugello where, in 1466, he wrote several letters begging sixteen-year-old Lorenzo to intercede with the authorities of the city to allow him to return. Lorenzo acceded to the request eventually, and Pulci was once more part of the Medici circle.

Yet the incident also has its dark side. Pulci's letters from this brief period of his banishment show that the harmony of his early years in the Medici circle was finally flawed. Because he was always fearful of poverty, he attached himself to Lorenzo with a certain violence that had something of the bully behind it. At the same time he never lost his defensiveness. The bantering tone of his correspondence barely covers his anxiety. He requested help urgently, yet he saw himself as reprehensible, doomed, and even allied with diabolical forces. His first letter from the Mugello is worth quoting at length because it illustrates so well the tone of desperation, the effusiveness, even the self-pity that in general characterizes his correspondence with Lorenzo. He writes:

> I am very distressed that at the height of your friendship and benevolence I am thus dismissed: I advise you that from now on I am entirely yours, that this injustice is done to you. It seems that I am a criminal in chains, in distress, to be blamed; but what have I done . . .? But by my good faith I deserve that you love me. Love me then extremely, so that I will still be grateful and profess my loyalty. . . . And yet I was hoping you could help me one way or another. I can't do any more. Never would I be able to arrive at a plan whereby fortune did not spoil in an hour what I worked years for. I was born like the hares and other more unfortunate animals, to be the prey of others, and through my indebtedness I love you greatly and am with you hardly at all. The more I long for you the more I am separated

from you. But heaven does not have enough force so that I am not with you in one way or another: I see you always, I speak with you constantly. And thus you are still afflicted with my poor and unfortunate muse. I will make you part of my nonsense. And when I am in Mecca I will send you verses in Moorish; then when I am in hell I shall send them up to you by some spirit. Finally I say in closing, Lorenzo, that if only I feel that you love me I am more than happy, in the woods or wherever I am. Heaven has left me nothing but you. Don't take yourself away.[37]

To these requests he evidently had a negative answer; in his last letter of this period he accused Lorenzo of neglect for having gone off to Rome without him. He begged to accompany his patron and vowed not to be an embarrassment. He supposed that there was an easy way to raise collateral. And he closed on a familiar note: "[I]ndeed I am not wrong to trust you alone because I am yours alone. . . . If you don't help me I have no other hope. What ought I to do? Give myself to thirty thousand devils?"[38] Letters such as these, written in a period of distress, obviously cannot indicate the temper of a friendship which endured for a number of years. Nevertheless, their high passion, uncontrolled by rational reflection, reveals a person who saw life in terms of stark contrasts, who found compromise uncongenial, who chafed at delay. They contain the seeds of his eventual loss of favor.

The events of 1465 and 1466, however serious in their implications, were without further immediate consequences. From 1467 through 1470 Pulci travelled on diplomatic missions to Pisa, Foligno, Rome, Camerino and Naples. In 1467 he was present at a meeting between Lorenzo and Galeazzo Maria Visconti in which a campaign against the Venetians and the Marchese of Ferrara was deliberated. During that year he also attended a reception for the Duke of Calabria in Pisa. His letters to Lorenzo, never without a certain jocularity, report the news that came his way.

His general well-being can partly be gauged by the progress of his poem. By 1462, after a year of work, Pulci had written to canto 14, octave 53—the portion of the poem that is closest to its source. By 1468, though certainly distracted by the misfortunes of his brother, he had advanced to canto 18, octave 179. But during the next four years he wrote much less: by March, 1472, he had completed only to canto 19, octave 173. And from then until 1476, he worked sporadically—the first part of the poem was not finished until 1478.[39] One needs to look, therefore, at events during the year 1469 and immediately after; evidently they constituted some kind of crisis. Two are of especial moment. Lorenzo came to power in 1469 at the death of Piero, and Pulci's financial situation, never sound, became again precarious in 1470.

From 1470 to 1474, when he entered service with Sanseverino, Pulci's life was complicated by embarrassments of several kinds. Late in 1469 or early in 1470, his brother Luca again went bankrupt and was imprisoned. Pulci and Bernardo, though not themselves involved in Luca's business, were implicated in his failure. Pulci, applying to Lorenzo as he had done before, described his affairs as hopeless, himself as Lorenzo's slave, and his devotion beyond the power of fortune to change.[40] The poet's self-portrait here is similar to those he paints in other letters. He generally saw the solution to his difficulties in a twofold process: first, a profession of loyalty to Lorenzo and of his own innocence, and second, an admission of absolute helplessness. His condition of subservience anticipates that of the weakest of sixteenth-century courtiers and could well serve to illustrate the dangers of the office Castiglione was to define in the next century.[41]

In 1470 Luca died and left his wife and children in the care of his brothers. Pulci and his twin Bernardo did not in fact go to prison and Pulci himself undertook business for Lorenzo at Camerino and Naples while continuing his efforts to extricate himself from his brother's debts. From Naples he wrote to Lorenzo of that city's projected crusade against the Turks, of hunting excursions, but also of further losses, sustained in trying to get a "few crumbs of bread for Luca's children." The diffidence of his brother Bernardo annoyed him: "It's true my Bernardo is made of milk, for I told him and wrote him on March 6th to go quickly to you, so that you would in some way help him: he is so timid and churlish that he does nothing."[42] The following year found him still harping on the subject of his financial responsibilities, especially with regard to Luca's family: from Folengo he wrote a jesting letter to Lorenzo, requesting the office of magistrate in the city so that he might strike his own name from its list of debtors. "You would do well to give me that magistrate's hat on my return and shove it down on my head to my nose, because my father used it 20 times and was in 39 the head of Colle di Valdes and in 50 Captain of the mountain of Pistoia."[43] Lorenzo denied this request, and in his next letter Pulci insisted that he was not angry about the matter of the magistracy, praised Lorenzo for all his help over the years, and repeated his request for money. The conclusion of the letter conveys how difficult it was for Pulci to accept Lorenzo's indifference or to imagine that other resources might be available to him. He saw himself attached to the Medici by historical bonds and imagined himself in the guise of a feudal retainer, offering services to his lord and deserving his protection in return:

Recommending myself to you, I hope you will help me; and I have for a long time wished that you might be able [to do this], both for your own security and that of your dear servants of ages past and of your father's time, for it seems to me that I am one of those. Help me, therefore, if you are able, and my poor descendents for whom I wear myself out will live for you. Without your help, to speak candidly, I am in more trouble than you would imagine.[44]

The passage recalls the emphasis Pulci placed on the mutual obligations of vassal and lord in the *Morgante,* notably in passages of his own invention; but the concept itself he did not invent. An essential element in the ethos of mock feudalism so cultivated by his patrons, it had sustained the social order—chivalry—he was supposed to be celebrating. He was not therefore perverse in drawing his own service to Lorenzo's attention or in suggesting that it had earned him the right to ask for protection. But he was naive. Entirely absent from Pulci's correspondence of this period is any conception of politics as a sophisticated science. He seems to have been unable to appreciate the needs of a ruler of Lorenzo's type or to take account of the manipulative side of Lorenzo's public character.

Pulci's standing at the Medici palace also changed as Lorenzo acquired more control of the city. The actual effects of his alterations in policy are manifest by 1473, when the cultural and intellectual style Lorenzo fostered assumed a character more in keeping with his increasingly autocratic mode of government. Poliziano had been entrusted with the palace library (two years later he was to become tutor to Lorenzo's children), the monk Matteo Franco had entered the household as chaplain, and Ficino, who was to become Pulci's most formidable opponent in his struggle to retain Lorenzo's favor, had accepted Lorenzo's patronage. Pulci's morals were criticized, his religious orthodoxy questioned. Nannina, Lorenzo's sister, reported that he received Easter communion very devoutly (possibly at her suggestion) and in September he took minor orders.[45] Franco, who served Lorenzo's religious interests as Ficino was to do later and with much more brilliance, became Pulci's harshest critic. With unrestrained animosity, he ridiculed in bad verse Pulci's attempts at conformity, drawing attention to Pulci's financial difficulties and even Luca's bankruptcy: "Tu n'andrai a pie zoppo/A trovar Luca tua, ladro di zecca,/ Che per te serba un luogo alla Judecca" ("You will go with a game leg to find your Luca, a thief, who keeps a place in prison for you").[46] Pulci defended himself and mounted a counterattack with other verses.

In many respects, theirs was a battle fought over the suppression of one kind of culture in favor of another. The cause of the innovators was championed by Ficino and represented in the activities of the so-called Platonic academy. Its emphasis fell on the more sober disciplines of the mind, philosophy and religion, but it can be argued that it indirectly affected the social and political life of the entire city. The relative popularity of pastorals during the 1470s, signalled most notably by the circulation in 1474 of Lorenzo's *Altercazione,* a poem praising the merits of rural over urban life, was itself a political phenomenon. Seeking to make the *vita contemplativa* once more the preferred solution to the challenge of a moral life, and reversing most of the response to this question since Bruni had urged the advantages of the *vita activa* early in the century, Lorenzo attempted to make attractive the sort of civic quietism that would most directly work in his favor. He followed the spirit of Landino's *Disputationes Camaldulenses* written during the same year. Probably fictitious, Landino's dialogue records the discussions that took place between Ficino, Alberti, Lorenzo, and others during the summer of 1469, and thereby demonstrates the existence of a political component in neoplatonic thought. The case for the citizen's participation in public life was no longer made as creditable as it had been. Instead the dialogue enjoins the conscientious man to fix his attention on the permanent truth beyond temporal vicissitudes. It is no coincidence that this year saw the passage of various laws governing the freedom of Florentines to enjoy certain kinds of pleasures. Lavish dress and games of chance were prohibited.[47] Lorenzo, inspired by Ficino who was finally readying himself for the priesthood, was convinced it was his duty to regulate in all respects the cultural life of the city.

Pulci had not the slightest chance of fitting into this program of reform. He had neither the temperament nor the training for such a life. His early encounters with Scala had evidently prejudiced him against humanists and his dislike of Ficino appears to have been almost instinctive. In 1473 he lashed out at the academicians in several sonnets, certain of which evidently came to Lorenzo's attention and brought about some sort of reprimand. In a letter from Bologna of August 1473, Pulci writes to Lorenzo that, contrary to what Lorenzo imagines, he is *not* reluctant to associate with the academy and, moreover, that he will triumph over them for Lorenzo's sake, an event he seems to think will please his patron:

> You said I hastened my departure in order not to find myself with the academy. Let them come here and you will hear how I have flayed some of them for you. I know they will fall into my hands, and we will find out from them how the Muses are doing. If I had not been in a great hurry, I would have satisfied you there but I shall do you more honor here and many shall hear of it.[48]

Orvieto associates this letter with one of the most plaintive of Pulci's sonnets, also, he believes, of 1473.[49] In "Sempre la pulcia muor, signore, a torto" ("The flea always dies unjustly"), Pulci defends himself from detractors who take a single sonnet of his much too seriously, and he asks his reader to overlook his work if it fails to please.[50] Which of his sonnets Pulci refers to here is uncertain, but he wrote several against what he considered abuses of religion and in particular Ficino's new Platonic theology. His sonnet "Costor che fan si gran disputazione" ("Those who offer such a long argument"), ridiculing the immortality of the soul, addresses the subject on which Ficino had already circulated writings and was perhaps the poem the philosopher found most offensive.[51] This sonnet was answered by five others, written at the request of Lorenzo, probably by Feo Belcari. Recorded in the *Cronaca* of Benedetto Dei, Pulci's lifelong friend, they tiresomely defend the doctrine of the soul's immortality as Plato defined it and assert that the opposite view is "nonsense" ("e una frulla"), and worthless to the learned ("presso a' dotti o·nnulla vale").[52]

These are the sonnets to which Pulci refers in the most desperate of his letters, written to Lorenzo from Milan on February 14, 1474. He states that he received copies of the verses that Matteo Franco had circulated and he immediately denies the validity of their charges:

> I write this to you with my hand trembling with fever because today I received sonnets forwarded to me by my relations where there were jibes, and accusations, and many other things I didn't recognize. I was so grieved by this that I caught a fever from it in the piazza. Cino came to treat me and he said you had told him about the matter. I beg this of you, that you give me leave to see you, for I would have come now were I not shivering, and that you hear your servant before you judge him with anger and by the word of others who in their fashion pursue me like an animal.

He reports that he has sent a "messer Marsilio" to inform Lorenzo that he had been "tricked by the priest," and that he was sure Lorenzo would clear him.[53] He adds that he has almost finished his verses on the tournament celebrating Lorenzo's marriage, *La Giostra,* and claims that Cino could vouch for the fact that he had composed other verses praising Lorenzo. He concludes with a pathetic comment:

> I see that the good has not been reported to you but God will report it; and when you are no longer angry you will recognize that I love you perhaps more than those that daily accuse me before you. Finally do with me what you will; I will go today when and wherever you tell me, to any punishment; I believe it would be good if I took up a staff and together with my unfortunate wife, who is here this evening on this jolly occasion, journeyed on a pilgrimage; for I am hateful to God, to you, to the world.[54]

Orvieto notes that the phrase "hateful to God" ("odio a Dio") is one which Ficino used to describe Pulci in a letter he wrote to Bernardo Pulci and concludes that Pulci repeats it here deliberately. It echoes similar condemnations of the poet in several other of Ficino's letters of this period. Representative is a letter written in the early part of 1474, in which Ficino criticized Lorenzo specifically for tolerating flatterers, "adulatores," and critics, "obtrectatores," and warned him against persons who encouraged him in idle pastimes, "supervacuis ludis."[55] Franco, certainly sympathetic to Ficino at this time, wrote a scurrilous letter condemning Pulci and accusing Lorenzo of tolerating a scoundrel.[56] By October 1474, Lorenzo, asserting that the friendship of Ficino had made him forget all others, was ready to acknowledge the philosopher as his mentor in all things.[57] His letter complimenting Ficino and professing his loyalty to him can be taken to mark the end of his friendship with Pulci.

Lorenzo proceeded to establish another kind of relationship with his former protégé; he continued to rely on him in matters of state and in a manner more confidential than had been the case up to that time. In this sphere of activity Pulci was less likely to antagonize the academicians; presumably ordinary diplomatic relations were of little concern to persons whose minds were fixed on a higher reality. The evidence from the correspondence of the two men suggests that early in his period of exile Pulci was able to regain Lorenzo's confidence. It may even be correct to say that, in a sense, he had never quite lost it, that in arranging to have Pulci occupied with business outside Florence Lorenzo was merely shifting him from a situation in which he might be disruptive to one in which he was likely to be useful.

Pulci had made the acquaintance of Roberto di Sanseverino in 1473, and in 1474, almost certainly at Lorenzo's instigation, he became the intermediary between this condottiere and the city of Florence. Sanseverino, a nephew of Francesco Sforza, had been made Duke of Caiazzo by Ferdinand of Aragon in 1461.[58] His connections to the Dukes of Milan were predictably close: he received from them various territories and an entree to the Medici circle. At the request of Galeazzo Maria Sforza, he was given a contract by Florence in 1467; other contracts followed.[59] In effect, Sanseverino served both cities. His actual importance to the military balance of power in Italy is revealed by the mention he receives in Lorenzo's correspondence—between 1474 and 1479 no other condottiere is so often the subject of Lorenzo's concern.

In 1474, evidently to maintain good relations between Sanseverino and Lorenzo, Pulci travelled to Milan, Pisa, Bologna and, as an unpublished letter indicates, to Lyon, where Sanseverino was trying to arrange a contract with Louis XI.[60] The king was not interested in what

Sanseverino proposed, and the negotiations failed, but this did not make Sanseverino any more amenable to the terms Milan continued to offer him. In April of 1476, negotiations between Galeazzo Sforza and Sanseverino threatened to break down altogether. Had they done so, the condottiere would have been free to make new arrangements, conceivably less agreeable to Florence. Lorenzo directed Pulci to Milan to patch up the alliance, but, having heard that Sanseverino was dissatisfied with Pulci's arrangements, also warned Jacopo Guicciardini in Milan that his power over Sanseverino was no more than moral.[61] That at this time Sanseverino was mindful of Lorenzo's interests—and the possibility of further contracts with Florence—is to be attributed to Pulci's constant influence.[62] Where Pulci's loyalties were is most difficult to determine. He was presumably in Sanseverino's employ during these years—that is from 1474 on—yet, to judge from their correspondence, he appears to have been remarkably responsive to Lorenzo.

After the murder of Galeazzo in 1476, Sanseverino's position in Milan became even more precarious. Pulci quickly wrote to Lorenzo that Sanseverino would remain loyal to Florence in any case, an assurance that, if welcome, was not wholly borne out by future events.[63] Throughout that year, Lorenzo worried about Sanseverino's career in Milan, writing letters to Tommaso Soderini, one of his agents at the Sforza court, insisting on Pulci's role as his representative, complaining to Pulci himself that he had not received letters from him—Soderini, actually under instructions from the new Duchess, had intercepted them—while also professing his loyalty to Sanseverino.[64] Throughout these negotiations Lorenzo appears to have wholly trusted in Pulci's representation.

The precise nature of Pulci's service during the next two years, from 1477 to 1478, can only be a subject of conjecture. If he remained with Sanseverino, who was accused by the Duchess of conspiring to murder the Duke and exiled from Milan, he would presumably have seen something of the revolt in Genoa, in which Sanseverino participated, and been party to the condottiere's attempts to secure a contract from Venice. Lorenzo's letters of this period do not mention Pulci—Lorenzo himself gave assurances to the Duchess through her ambassadors that, as a consequence of the Genoa affair, he dissociated himself from Sanseverino, and that he would arrest Sanseverino were he to come on Florentine soil.[65]

In the war between the Papacy and Florence, an aftermath of the events following the Pazzi conspiracy and the murder of Giuliano de'Medici, Sanseverino served the Pope and his ally Ferrante of Naples. A letter of Pulci, dated May 14 and assigned to the year 1479, suggests that Pulci participated in Sanseverino's occupation of Tuscany and had had occasion to see Lorenzo. The letter asks for an extension of the loan

Lorenzo had made him at the time of his marriage and expresses grati-
tude for past favors:

> For although I opposed you a short while ago, know that I am always
> with you and more than ever yours, and of that I am certain and
> capable; and I will place my goods and my life at your disposal. I saw
> you completely taken up with strange thoughts and I did not know
> what to offer you. But of this much you may be sure, that I have not
> forgotten so many good offices from your father and you, and I know
> that you have not served an ungrateful person, for I have engraved
> everything on my heart.[66]

Pulci's profession of loyalty in this instance echoes his earlier promises
even to the use of similar terms: he offers unqualified support and
speaks of inherited obligations. One needs to notice, however, a slightly
different tone. Here Pulci speaks with an assertiveness missing from his
earlier pleas for help. In the five years of serving Sanseverino and
Lorenzo's interests outside Florence, Pulci had apparently found within
himself a sense of purpose. Lorenzo's correspondence reveals that the
Magnifico did not consider him merely a buffoon, nor did he refuse to
entrust him with serious diplomatic business. If Pulci had aroused the
ire of Ficino in Florence, Lorenzo appears to have responded to the fact
that he did not have a similar effect on persons outside that city. However painful Pulci's exile, it provided him with options he would not
otherwise have had; letters he wrote after 1479 indicate that, while he
retained his affection for Lorenzo, he also contemplated living in a
region other than Tuscany.

In 1481 he had hoped to gain a position as Captain in Val di Lugana in
Lombardy, a fief of Sanseverino, and he wrote to Benedetto Dei in Milan
declaring that he had become a Lombard and would remain so as long as
his patron lived.[67] But, when the appointment was not forthcoming, he
wrote to Dei again to say that he could never be a Lombard: "If I do not
come in a dream to Lombardy or [am not] carried like witches by a
fantasy, I shall not come again into that country; and it would not grieve
me were it not that your master, Guasparre, kept you so far away." He
closes this letter by announcing that he hopes for an appointment in
Florence: "I still have friends here and someone will help me," and he
asks Dei to write Lorenzo.[68] Pulci's vacillation—is he a Florentine or a
Lombard?—reflects his perception of the chances of soliciting patronage.
At the same time, it reveals a kind of independence. His interest in
Lorenzo is no longer exclusive of other forms of protection.

His new attitude and the conditions in which it emerged illustrate
some of the paradoxical features of Renaissance courtiership. When the

political interests of a courtier whose livelihood depended on awaiting and fulfilling the commands of his lord were identified with a single court, he enjoyed a certain security but his real autonomy was neglible. As Castiglione's Federico was later to state, the courtier's most self-regarding act in situations in which his conscience will not allow him to obey his lord might be to leave (the security of) that court.[69] On the other hand, when a courtier developed what we might call mixed allegiances, his chances of enjoying a relative autonomy of a certain scope were improved.

While in the service of Sanseverino yet answering also to Lorenzo, Pulci himself appears to have understood something of this kind of courtiership; certainly he seemed to be prepared to exploit the rapid shifts of allegiance that complicated the politics of those on whom he was dependent. His last letters to the Magnifico are a case study in ambiguity. Despite the fact that Sanseverino had been in the employ of the Pope against Lorenzo, Pulci is obliged to relate, on two occasions in 1484, that the condottiere is wholly well-disposed toward Lorenzo: "I have only to tell you of signor Roberto whom I found so well-disposed to you and your children that you all might be either Medici or of Sanseverino's own family."[70] If he was aware how hollow the recent political entanglements of his patrons rendered this profession of loyalty, he gives no indication of it.

Pulci's removal from Florence temporarily exacerbated his hostile relations with Ficino. In the second part of the *Morgante* (actually begun in 1476, before the first part was completed), he would openly declare himself an enemy of the so-called Platonic academy and covertly, as Orvieto shows, of Ficino, whom he masks in the figure of Marsilio, the Spanish king. In sonnets written after 1474 he continued his energetic attack against certain forms of religious life and the discipline of theology. The sonnet to Benedetto Dei was written in 1475 on the occasion of the Jubilee and mocks the pilgrims who came to Rome. And in a sonnet to Bartolommeo dell'Avveduto he tells of finding a Hebrew book in which the miracles of the Bible are all proved to be fictitious.

Despite (or perhaps because of) assurances he had received from Lorenzo, Ficino kept up his criticism of Pulci. He could not have known of the offensive passages in Part 2 but he responded vigorously to the sonnets which he considered sacrilegious. Over several years he wrote letters against Pulci to various members of the Medici circle: notable is that to Lorenzo and Giuliano de'Medici, dated the end of 1476, which demanded that Pulci be dismissed from the Medici circle and that Lorenzo show, in Ficino's words, his unwillingness to permit whatever was "sacred" and his "own" to be given to the dogs to tear or to the dogs' fleas, *canum pulices*, to bite.[71]

Two more letters sum up the conflict. Pulci's letter of September 1476, confirms that Lorenzo no longer sought his company and reveals that he imagines his former place to be occupied now by Poliziano. He adds: "Remember me when you are with Baccio for otherwise I do not think you will, for, whether because I have had the pox or gotten fat, it has been a while since you took notice of me."[72] And in a letter to Cavalcanti in 1477, Ficino relates that the Medici intervened in his dispute with his "adversaries" who indulged not only in criticism, *correptio*, but also invective, *invectiva*.[73]

The anti-Ficino passages in the *Morgante* suggest that Pulci was never reconciled to the philosopher. What is remarkable is the part Pulci has the character "Marsilio" play: by casting him as a traitor to Charlemagne, his feudal lord, Pulci identifies his own quarrel with Ficino as a matter of politics, and, by implication, he makes Lorenzo, masked in the duped Carlo, a participant in it. Pulci's case against Ficino had an elementary logic behind it. Ficino had criticized him for being dissolute, sacrilegious, and for holding heretical opinions. It was also widely known that Pulci had practiced magic—a topic Franco had labored. But Ficino was himself not immune from similar charges. Pulci almost certainly knew of Ficino's interest in the occult sciences; he also knew of opinions that were, by the traditional criteria of the church, heterodox.[74] It must therefore have appeared unjust that he, Pulci, was criticized for practices his critic had indulged in with impunity.[75]

Whether or not Ficino—in his function as priest rather than protégé of the Medici—had valid religious grounds for complaint against Pulci is, in my view, extraordinarily difficult to determine.[76] The question of Pulci's religion has been raised frequently and received different answers. The available evidence, yet to be examined fully and with due consideration for the contexts in which it appears, falls into four main categories. First and most important are the confessions of past errors that Pulci inserts in the *Morgante* and also in his *Confessione*, where he speaks of his conversion. Second are the brief allusions to magic in his letters, all dated before 1467. Third are the sonnets that treat certain questions of doctrine in a facetious manner, and fourth are the passages in the *Morgante* addressing matters of theology which are given to the infidel king, Marsilio, and the devil, Astarotte. The nature of the evidence is thus various and must be evaluated accordingly. The statements Pulci makes about his own religious practices obviously need to be considered apart from the statements on doctrine he assigns to characters in his poem. The latter, on which the most extensive studies of Pulci's religion are largely based, are controversial and provocative, but they are also expressions which occur in a dramatic narrative of immense scope and temporal unfolding. One needs to ask who is speaking and where.

The confessional passages in the *Morgante* refer most directly to Pulci's practice of magic. In canto 24, he announces that, while he made the "mountain of the sybil" his muse for a time and took pleasure in the work (actually astrological) of Cecco d'Ascoli, he now understands his error and asks to be excused: "Convien che al gran Minosse io me ne scuse, / e ricognosca il ver cogli altri erranti . . ." ("I ought to ask pardon of the great Minos for it and acknowledge the truth amidst falsehoods," 24. 113; see *Inf.* 5. 4–6). Elsewhere in the poem is abundant proof that Pulci knew something about the practice of magic. Earlier in the same canto he has Malagigi claim that all magic falls into the myriad operations of nature; that is, he distinguishes it from supernatural operations, presumably the function of God or angels. And in the next canto, he has Astarotte identify as deceptive the actions of "spiriti folletti" ("wild spirits") who cannot be constrainted in water or glass but wander through the air (25. 160; see also 21. 46, 22. 102). Even without the admissions in canto 24, these passages would indicate his acquaintance with certain terms and phenomena associated with the occult sciences.

Pulci also mentions magic briefly in five letters to Lorenzo, referring to "Salay," evidently a spirit whom he thinks he has in his control. In two letters from 1466 he declares "here I rule myself with certain little trees and counsels of Salay," and "I can only think of you (i.e. Lorenzo) and Salay."[77] In 1470 he writes of visiting the grotto of the sybil at Norcia.[78] No letter after this mentions anything to do with the occult sciences. This may indicate that by this time Pulci had abandoned his interest in them. Three years later, when he took certain steps—communion, holy orders—to bring himself into line with religious orthodoxy, Matteo Franco accused him of having practiced magic for twenty years, that is, since 1453, and sarcastically urged him to confess not to God but "Sallai."[79]

But to interpret the religious significance of Pulci's magical arts is a more doubtful enterprise than to determine that he practiced them. Interest in astrology and hermetic philosophy as well as magic was common among the intelligentsia in Florence in the last decades of the fifteenth century. Much of it went unremarked by the clergy. Pulci may in fact have been forced to be scrupulous about his activities for social and political rather than religious reasons. He never appears to have been out of favor with the Medici women, Lucrezia Tornabuoni, Nannina Rucellai, or Clarice Orsini, all of whom were rigorous in their devotions. (Clarice, for example, dismissed Poliziano as tutor to her sons because he failed to instruct them sufficiently in religion.) And he was never expelled from the confraternity of the Magi, as he presumably would have been had his interest in "Salay" been perceived as heretical. By 1473 he had probably come to believe that his magic was sinful. But, for the years in which he was actually involved in it, there is no record of such a judgment against him, by either Lorenzo or his peers.

His sonnets are highly facetious works that cannot be read as straightforward statements of religious principle. In the first and most often cited, "Costor che fan si gran disputazione," Pulci asserts that the soul is no more than a pine nut in a hot white pan, or a coal in a cracked pan; whoever thinks otherwise is a fool, etc. And he closes the poem by telling his listener, "Pandolfo," that they will go to the Valley of Darkness together without hearing more Allelujas. The poem is obviously intended to be an insult, first to "those who argue," that is, Ficino, and second to those who ridicule such arguers, that is, the poet and his listener "Pandolfo." Pulci's early letters are replete with declarations and denunciations (often of himself) of this sort, composed, it would seem, to gain attention, to exhibit a comic bravado, to excite and appall an audience. The sonnet "Costor" is a poetic statement made to a similar end.

Pulci's other religious sonnets share this intention and thus offer unreliable evidence of the poet's heterodoxy. In the sonnet against miracles, for example, "Poich'io partij da voi, Bartolommeo," ("Since I left you, Bartholomew") the reader learns that Peter walked on ice, Samson tore down a summer house, etc., and that therefore the Bible lies—statements obviously blasphemous in content.[80] What makes the poem memorable, however, is not its blasphemy but its verbal wit, its energetic and explosive diction. It obviously proposes to provoke, perhaps to anger, its reader. Like "Costor," it cannot be read simply as a credo. In fact it points up what is characteristic of many of Pulci's most controversial statements on religious matters. They are assigned to questionable speakers, here in "Poich'io" to a Jew; and in the *Morgante*, to Marsilio, an infidel king, and to Astarotte, one of the damned in hell. At the very least this ought to give the reader pause. Unless it can be determined that the poet identifies himself with the speaker, these objectively shocking statements ought to be understood as more or less ironic.

It is also the case, of course, that a highly orthodox and devout Christian could not have written "Costor" or any other of Pulci's sonnets that touch on religion. But whether the reader must infer from this margin of deviance, as it were, a truly heretical stance is quite uncertain. Febvre and others have wisely cautioned against perceiving instances of "free thought" in the restless and expansive yet fundamentally orthodox statements of Rabelais.[81] He has argued lucidly for the pervasive influence of Christianity over all aspects of Renaissance life and has indicated how difficult it was for anyone living in the fifteenth or sixteenth centuries to have divorced himself from the system of belief instituted by the Catholic Church. Pulci simply did not have a philosophical mind, much less the passion for theology necessary to the reformer. In general his poetry suggests that discussion of religious matters engaged his attention only when he felt under pressure to conform to the norms of his society or to defend himself from his accusers.

Critics have interpreted his *Confessione* as evidence both for and against his "conversion" from some form of irreligion to true belief. The positive case is strengthened by his own remarks in the *Morgante,* where he tells a hypothetical listener that his faith is as true as anyone's, and by a passage in the *Confessione* where he states that he has been led to the Virgin by one "distinguished" ("segnato") with her name, a Mariano from Ghinazzano.[82] This implies not only a conversion but also a re-education. The negative case is based on the fact that the *Confessione* is a formal work, without appreciable religious feeling. Neither case is, I think, especially strong, again because the circumstances in which these statements were made are so difficult to determine. The banality of the *Confessione* itself proves only one thing—that Pulci could not write devotional verse, although for some reason he felt compelled to do so in this instance. It is altogether likely that the poem is (like his communion and holy orders) yet another effort to demonstrate that he was qualified to receive Lorenzo's support.

Despite the *Confessione,* the church regarded Pulci as a heretic evidently because of the sonnets, and he was buried without a service, "ob scripta prophana prophano in loco."[83] The truth of the matter is more complex. Pulci's letters and literary works demonstrate that he took human relations seriously. His largely invented portraits of Gano and of Antea, his bizarre creation of Margutte, reveal a concern with social virtues and vices. And his supposed impieties—dismissal of the soul as a definable entity, of miracles, of the sacrament of penance—have greater reference to the *behavior* of the faithful than to articles of faith themselves. He ridiculed those who carried on disputations, busied themselves in pilgrimages, or tried to explain miracles. Like many reformers of the next century, he appears to have been disillusioned with the intellectual and ritualistic aspects of Christianity, and to have considered them open to abuse. He defends himself at the conclusion to the *Morgante* by declaring that if ever he wrote "vane cose" ("trifles", 28. 43), he was only attacking hypocrites, that is, those who in their actions betrayed their profession of faith and the significance of ritual. Pulci probably did not hold heretical views, largely, I think, because he was not interested enough in theological doctrine to develop them. At the same time, he was not a religious man. His discussions in the *Morgante* of such matters as free will, grace, and repentance refer principally to questions of human and divine agency in history rather than to the means to salvation.

The years immediately preceding Pulci's death brought him recognition as a poet of epic-romance: he published the first part of the *Morgante* in 1478 (an edition now lost), and in 1481 and 1482 four other editions appeared. In 1483 he published the entire poem.[84]

The following year Sanseverino appointed him his agent, *procuratore*, in Florence at an annual salary of fifty ducats, a post certainly more to his liking than the captaincy at the Val di Lugano he had failed to obtain three years earlier. Before allowing him to take up his new duties, however, Sanseverino insisted he be in attendance at meetings in Venice. He died of a fever on his way to that city.[85]

To credit Pulci with an awareness of a political identity without fixed parameters, developed in the course of writing and serving his patrons, is perhaps further to grasp the nature of the differences that forced him from Florence in 1474. As Gramsci has argued, no intellectual of any period is exempt from the control exerted upon him by those in his society who hold economic power.[86] The Medici's protection of such writers and scholars as Argiropoulo and Ficino, Landino and Acciaiuoli, as well as of Pulci himself, needs to be examined in this perspective. Each of these persons was implicated in the process of the massive acculturation of their society undertaken by the Medici, their patrons—not, the evidence suggests, to pursue the truth with disinterestedness and detachment but for such immediate goals as an end to effective constitutional government. Merely to leave Florence and the palace at the via Larga would, therefore, have created for Pulci an occasion not only for self-doubt but also for a reassessment of the political and economic conditions in which he had been employed. To have been free of them would in turn have been to be free of the intellectual constraints they entailed. Shifting into the orbit of Sanseverino, Pulci would in effect have acquired a second set of obligations which he might play off against the first. In regard to his life in diplomatic service, there is nothing to suggest that he actually did so. But in his poem the effects of his dissociation from the Medici are discernible and result not only in a new view of his subject but also of the possibility of its representation.

# 1

## THE FORM OF THE NARRATIVE

PULCI states his complicated intention in the first octaves of his poem. He proposes to write a history, *istoria,* of the Emperor Charlemagne, for (he claims) no existing work is adequate: "as I see it, this history of Carlo has been poorly understood and worse written" ("è stata questa istoria, a quel ch'io veggio, / di Carlo, male intesa e scritta peggio", 1.4). But because his patroness must always be obeyed (1.4) he is also committed to representing *her* view of the subject, implicit in the notion of an Italianate (and particularly Florentine) Charlemagne dear to the Medici. His double obligation—to the history and to his patroness—is clarified in his complaint against Carlo's indifferent chroniclers in the octave. He refers to Bruni's assertion that were Carlo to have had a suitable historian rather than a mere Turpino or an Ormanno, he would have been "a divine man" (1. 5). This is not what Bruni said about Charlemagne, but for the reader's perception of the status of the poem the attribution establishes again how complex a role the poet proposes to play.[1] He must be the better historian, that is, supply the kind of evidence that will instruct his readers in the truth of the past. Yet the account he must give is in the main already determined; the subject of his history is a hero of superhuman abilities and accomplishments. In other words, while writing as a historian, he must honor the generic requirements of epic. Earlier accounts of the matter of France, whether in *chansons de geste* or chivalric romances, had not generally made explicit the differences between the purposes of epic and those of history because they were yet to be perceived. In the case of the *Morgante,* however, such distinctions were to be forthcoming.

Pulci further admits to having for his representation of Charlemagne an authority who stands impressively outside both the cycles of popular poetry and the Florentine histories describing events in the Emperor's life. For him it is *Dante's* not Bruni's vision of Charlemagne that will be decisive. The fact that Dante placed the Emperor in paradise will come to constitute, for the later poet, the most formidable and fruitful challenge to his completion of his poem:

> ("dopo la dolorosa rotta quando"
> nella sua *Comedia* Dante qui dice,
> e mettelo con Carlo in Ciel felice).
>
> (1. 8)

in his *Commedia* Dante says "when after the grievous defeat," and puts him [Orlando] in heaven with happy Carlo.

This confession, indicating that the *Morgante* will engage problems of intertextuality, anticipates the conflict the poet will face as he writes. He will discover that Carlo's history, as it is reported in the sources on which *he* is forced to rely (whatever were those that Dante drew on), cannot be reconciled to Dante's judgment of the Emperor as a Christian hero in the *Paradiso*. He must then decide whom to believe and where to put his confidence. Pulci articulates his epistemological distress in his conclusion to the *Morgante* when he emphasizes that because Dante's estimation of Carlo must be correct—"not without reason did he place Carlo and Orlando in heaven" ("non sanza cagion nel Ciel su misse / Carlo et Orlando")—he continues to trust him "even at this point" ("ancor molto qui", 28. 40), in other words, after having reported so much evidence that has tended to call this judgment into question. It is from this apparently unenviable position that the real concerns of the poem will have been generated. In the course of writing, Pulci will make of his methodological problem a thematic virtue. He will emphasize rather than seek to hide the discrepancies between the history he writes and his obligation to represent Dante's case and, calling attention to the variety of sources upon which he has drawn, he will address the question of truth in history.

My understanding of the role Dante plays in the development of the poem's subject is predicated on the assumption that Pulci did not consider Dante's judgment of Carlo to be a subject for parody and that he did not engage in retrospective revision, at least in regard to this point. My evidence is entirely in the poem itself and is largely based on the poet's tone and what I have gathered from a comparison of the text of the *Morgante* with its sources. When Pulci refers to Dante in cantos 1 and 28, in both cases in passages of explanation and not in connection with events in the narrative, he is respectful (if at last also anguished). Compared to the strictly narrative portions of the poem, in which the Emperor is presented as foolish, although never the subject of burlesque (unlike the paladins), Pulci's exposition and reassessment of his subject is generally serious, especially when he entertains the significance of Dante's portrait of Charlemagne. When he strikes a parodic note, the object of ridicule is not Dante but persons who represent the historian. In theory, of course, Pulci might have returned to canto 1 in order there to depict Dante as an infallible authority—and thus to heighten the irony with which he colors the concept of authority later—at any point after which he had begun to realize that Dante's judgment was going to present him with difficulties.[2] That is, Dante's function as the poet's authority for his poem may itself have been the product of the poet's reflection on the poem. But if so, this would only make Pulci the more self-critical a poet, since it would reveal his willingness to explain his predicament rather than to gloss it over by ignoring the real differences between what Lucrezia had requested (and such other Florentine historians as Dati and Acciaiuoli had produced) and the poem he himself had written. I should add that I consider the case for retrospective revision of any sort is generally weakened by the fact that the *Morgante* as a whole has the stylistic and tonal texture of a patchwork, its discontinuities reflecting both the poet's changing sources and, as I will argue later, also his changing treatment of these sources. It is, in other words, a poem that exhibits in its form what I take to be a record of the processes by which it was composed. It seems unlikely, although again not wholly impossible, that Pulci should have conceived of his poem at its beginning as the formally inconsistent work it turned out to be, however interesting he was to find it at its conclusion.

In fact, Pulci's emphasis on Dante's authority, his insistence on the historicity of his poem, and his epic pose—established in his invocation to an angelic muse here and in the opening octaves of all remaining cantos—provide its actual matter with an anomalous if provocative introduction, for the *Morgante* proves to be neither a history nor an epic in the ordinary sense of these terms. Neither an account of the past nor the life of a saintly crusader, it is rather a self-reflexive work that in the course of its unfolding explores the nature of the process by which history is written and historical judgments, whether or not incorporated in epideictic poetry, can be made.

A brief sketch of the action of the poem indicates why this is so. The first twenty-three cantos of the *Morgante* relate the successive and parallel adventures of the Emperor's chief paladins, Orlando and Rinaldo. As part of a poem extolling Carlo these cantos are, however, strangely unsatisfactory; the Emperor himself is a weak figure who is praiseworthy only insofar as his paladins are triumphant over forces which threaten the survival of his court. Pulci pays little attention to realistic detail and the interest in actual causes that, however rudimentary, characterizes chronicle or history. His mode of narration is chiefly *alle-*

*gorical,* lightened by moments of self-critical burlesque. Pulci writes in extended metaphors about the temporality and finally about the writing of history that represent an experience of continuity and change. In the figure of Carlo Mano, who is neither heroic nor magnanimous, is reflected a fear of change and a failure to understand temporality. The last five cantos of the *Morgante,* in contrast, do describe an epic conflict and evince an interest in *historical* questions, preeminently the problem of determining causality.[3] But they are also pervaded by a sense of the poet's despair. He recognizes that he has committed himself to a judgment of the past and of his principal character that the evidence itself cannot support. Throughout the *entire* poem the reader recognizes a disjunction between the point of view the terms of the poet-patron contract entail on the one hand and the opinions the matter can be construed to signify on the other.

To recognize in the poet's interest in historiography the basis of the poem's significance is also, paradoxically, to confront one of its most obvious weaknesses as a literary work: its lack of formal unity and structural coherence. The question of the unity of the *Morgante* was first addressed by Pio Rajna who, in the middle of the last century, discovered that Pulci's source for the first twenty-two cantos was the anonymous fifteenth-century poem, the *Orlando.*[4] Comparing texts, Rajna showed that Pulci at first followed the *Orlando* closely, rephrasing and amplifying the material of his source but not changing its plot, its characters, or the sequence of its episodes. As the *Morgante* progressed, he altered its sources more freely, but apart from the Astolfo and Margutte episodes, he made no major changes or interpolations. Material from the *Orlando* appears through canto 22. Because the conclusion to the anonymous poem is lost, it is impossible to say whether this forms part of canto 23 but critics have assumed so. To Rajna, it seemed obvious that Pulci stopped writing at canto 23 because he ran out of a source.

Searching for a comparable source for the remaining cantos, Rajna discovered that Pulci drew mainly on two texts describing the battle of Roncisvalle: the *Spagna in rima,* and the *Spagna in prosa.* His indebtedness to these sources is far less extensive than his earlier debt to the *Orlando,* but Rajna regards Pulci's method of composition throughout the entire poem as essentially redactorial. He concludes that the *Morgante* is actually two poems not one: "The connection between the first and second part remains purely external and accidental."[5] He formally divides the poem in two, calling Part 1 the "Morgante" and Part 2 the "Rotta di Roncisvalle." He terms the entire poem a version—or "rifacimento"—of its several sources, and concludes that to search for its formal unity or structural coherence is a mistake.[6]

Rajna's research has served to preface most of the criticism the *Morgante* has received. Since his identification of it as a twofold representation of earlier poems, it has been frequently perceived as a creative translation and its readers have concentrated on matters of style rather than on plot, character, or theme. For many critics the poem has been chiefly interesting as a brilliant example of the creativity of late medieval modes of rhetoric, a work in whose tropes and colors the effects of the poet's transformative imagination are registered. Getto's study, for example, stresses the poem's aesthetic nature: although Pulci lacks narrative ability, his poem has immense philological vitality. Its charm consists in its evasion of traditional schemata, in what Getto terms the poet's "skill in alteration" (literally "in deforming").[7] A decade later another of the poem's critics, Domenico De Robertis, summing up its critical history, notes that the poem as narrative is uninteresting and observes that the poet lacks a "vision of the whole," and "does not succeed in establishing a single tone, a single temporality."[8] Paolo Orvieto, whose recent study in fact does much to demonstrate the considerable coherence the poem achieves as an expression of the poet's own preoccupations with the cultural politics of Lorenzo's court, also recommends a stylistic analysis of the poem. He argues that it is "absolutely unconnected with factual reality" and rather represents a reality "purely literary, constituted by amplifications, elaborations, and tinkerings of tradition—a literature about literature."[9]

These remarks indicate an aspect of the poem—its redactional character—that is of undeniable critical importance. To read the *Morgante* as extended revision of its immediate sources (De Robertis) or as a richly inventive composition drawing on a grammar of medieval tropes and conventions (Orvieto) is to take pleasure in the most lyrical expression of the poet's talent.

But the *Morgante* is not only a literary *rifacimento*. It narrates a series of stories, the last of which, the story of Roncisvalle, it offers in several different versions. Before deciding that the poem has little interest as narrative and that it lacks a "historical" dimension, we will need to consider how this series of stories is conceived and what effect its internal order has upon the meaning of the poem. We need principally to ask what such a series gains in being arranged so that its stories appear in some way to echo each other, to show certain more or less precisely repetitive features. The question cannot be answered satisfactorily without a close look at the narrative itself; at this point I shall anticipate my discussion of the matter by stating that these repetitions are not the result of the poet's compulsion simply to retell the adventures in his poem as if no single version of any of them could be adequate. Were this the case, the narrative would not show at a thematic level a dialectical progression; that is, its matter would not be developed by repetitions that reveal an ever more complex and comprehensive view of the subject of the poem. In the *Morgante* repetition does not call the subject into question; it actually constructs it. What it does call in question is any representation of the subject that stands alone and unqualified by further representations. Repetition in the *Morgante* is in fact a constitutive element of the principle upon which the poem evolves. Together with the element of difference—the repetitions are not parrotings—it produces what I shall call the poem's perspectivism. This is both its principle of structure, the way it organizes its matter, and also, finally, an important aspect of its significance. By perspectivizing the history of Carlo, the *Morgante* establishes the fact of its own historical contingency. It reveals that what is known of the past, as history, is discovered not as some glimpse of a bygone time but rather as the product of a continuous process of re-vision. Whatever its subject, a history will, and must inevitably, indicate something about its own timeliness.[10]

It is, moreover, important to notice that Pulci's manner of recomposing his sources also contributes to the impression of historicity the poem gives. While it is obvious that Pulci amplifies his sources in a manner typical of medieval writers, he clearly does so, in most instances, to heighten the matter of his tale, to make it more dramatic and memorable, rather than substantially to extend it by supplying it with additional incidents. Both kinds of amplification are common in medieval narrative. The first, producing interpretative embellishments, is derived from classical rhetorical practice; the second, adding to the narrative episodes and incidents to motivate its action, is the compositional basis for the great narrative cyles of Arthurian and French romance.[11] Pulci generally exploits the first mode of amplification, producing a single narrative which is alternately dramatic and allegorical, and avoids the second, which would in practice have resulted in a complex narrative of interlaced stories. Indeed, by *joining together* in the *Morgante* two (Italian) fragments of the French cycle (the *Orlando* and the "Spagna" narratives of Roncisvalle) to form a continuous story of the Emperor and his special relationship to Orlando, Pulci stylistically dissociates his poem from the digressionary narratives of the cycle, each of which relates a portion of the matter of France, and shows that he intends to present it as a *single* narrative relating what he considers the major events in the Emperor's life. The fact that his actual telling of the story is problematic, especially in his determination of its conclusion, does not obscure this aspect of his intention.

Both Getto and Orvieto are sensitive to the syntagmatic aspect of the poem. Getto declares that the poem lacks "a center from which spring

. . . moving poetic images . . ." and a comprehensive plot. Yet he also admits that it displays an "extemporaneous" order in which events are made to appear in narrative "nuclei which are both discrete and interrelated." This order does not confer upon the poem a discernable structure but rather gives it a "rapid movement," the movement of the imagination itself.[12] The admission begs further questions: what are these discrete nuclei and how are they interrelated? For Orvieto the poem's structure is principally to be discovered in its intertextuality, the relations it develops as the poet's innovative imagination enunciates a particular story and draws for its constitutive elements on the vast "grammar" of the tradition of medieval narrative and chivalric romance in particular. Yet like Getto he also acknowledges that the poem possesses a narrative order of a certain kind. He discerns in it units of narrative, or "brani," each of which represents a discrete action and exhibits "a kind of conclusive circularity."[13]

Few readers can have failed to notice what Orvieto and Getto both point out—that the action of Part 1 is patterned, apparently composed of a series of similar narrative fragments more or less independent of each other, and that the action Part 2 is sequential. If a structural analysis of the narrative is in fact possible, as Orvieto suggests, it will need to begin by addressing the generically related differences between Parts 1 and 2.

### Part 1 (Cantos 1–23)

Narratives like Part 1—in which the relation of events rather than the description of character or scene determines content—invite a study of plot. The plot of Part 1 is complicated but also logical. It consists of *nine* separate and related stories or adventures (Orvieto's *brani*), each of which depicts the survival of a monarch and his court. These adventures begin by representing a court in danger of dissolution and conclude by representing its reconstitution as a center of political and social order. The pattern is absolutely clear:

i)   Carlo's court is threatened by Orlando's madness and restored to order by the paladins.

ii)  The abbey of the Chiaramonte (an ecclesiastical court) is threatened by Morgante and his brothers and rescued by Orlando (Morgante's conversion).

iii) The abbey is threatened by Brunoro and rescued by Rinaldo (Brunoro's punishment).

iv)  Merediana's court is threatened by Manfredonio and rescued by the paladins.

    v)   Forisena's court is threatened by a dragon and rescued by Rinaldo.

    vi)   Carlo's court is threatened by Rinaldo's ambition and is restored to order by the paladins.

    vii)   Chiariella's court is threatened by the Sultan and rescued by the paladins.

    viii)   Marsilio's court is threatened by a wild horse and restored by Rinaldo.

    ix)   Filisetta's court is threatened by a monster and rescued by Rinaldo.

These adventures are further complemented by *three* others in which the court does not appear as the central image: a) the Princess Uliva is captured by giants and restored to her father by Orlando; b) the Princess Florinetta is captured by giants and restored to her father by Morgante; and c) Gano is captured by a witch and rescued by the paladins. Finally this series contains a *single* adventure that, although modelled on the dominant pattern, is clearly parodic; d) Filiberta's court, which her husband has usurped from its rightful monarch, is restored to her by Rinaldo. This inverts the legal logic upon which all earlier action is based; every adventure except Filiberta's shows forces representing a civilized order prevailing over chaos and disorder. Gano's adventure represents a special case; the traitor, substituting for the endangered ladies of Pagania, is rescued by the paladins because (as I shall discuss in Chapter 3) at this point in the narrative the principal agency in the poem is not any human character, behaving according to reason, but a Boethian Providence mysteriously working through fate to incorporate an apparent evil in its divine plan.

    Considering the dynamic elements of these adventures abstractly, one can detect in each the same fundamental opposition of conditions: the action moves from a condition of deficiency—a court in political disorder or vulnerable to some form of illegitimate power—to an opposite condition of sufficiency—a court ordered in itself and secure abroad. The first condition is expressed either in the menace of internal dissension or civil war or in the threat of usurpation or an invasion of foreign or hostile forces. The latter condition is manifest in the preeminence of a legitimate in contrast to a revolutionary or usurping authority. The opposition deficiency——sufficiency links one adventure to the next by virtue of the fact that the second term of the opposition—the condition of sufficiency—is always problematic and so generates the condition of deficiency from which the next adventure is motivated. Each adventure can

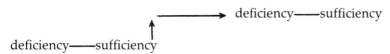

therefore be said to *reflect upon* the previous one and the series as a whole to assume a gyre-like configuration:

The plot of Part 1 is further complicated by the subordination of some adventures to others. The adventures I have listed—in the order in which they occur in the narrative—are not of equal length nor are they simply sequential. The adventures concerned with the political order of Carlo's court, i and vi, embrace, like the outermost box of an enveloping series of Chinese boxes, the other adventures—a configuration which suggests that the welfare of Carlo's court is more important than that of all other courts. (These differences are registered most obviously in the distinction between Carlo's court as Christian and all others as infidel.) Other adventures are further subordinated. Thus adventure i embraces ii through v; v is subordinate to iv; the completion of iv is the precondition of the completion of i; and i is concluded after ii, iii, v, and iv. Adventures vi through viii show the same kind of subordination as i through v: viii is the precondition for the completion of vii, vii of vi, and vi is concluded after vii and viii. i and vi are similar in being longer and more comprehensive adventures, embracing others, and also in being motivated by the disruption of the political hierarchy at Carlo's court, expressed by the rebellion and absence of his two principal vassals, the paladins Orlando and Rinaldo. And they are further motivated, in the later portions of their stories, by the effects of this disorder; in both adventures invasions led by infidel monarchs attack the defenseless Emperor. The return of the delinquent paladins in response to these threats is conceived as a consequence of their moral education in Pagania; logically, therefore, i and vi conclude with the restoration of political order in the Emperor's court, expressed by the paladins' allegiance to him. i and vi are therefore alike not only in being primary, but also in being bipartite. The second half of the action that is described as part of these adventures occurs after the completion of the secondary adventures they embrace: so i' should appear after v, and vi' after viii. Because iv and vii embrace v and viii respectively, they should also be represented as iv and iv', vii and vii'. (They are not, however, bipartite in the way i and vi are; the action they describe does not fall into two opposing movements.) A complete outline will include adventures a and b in place in the sequence after viii, although they occur before vii is concluded, and similarly c and d in place in the sequence after vii' but before vi':

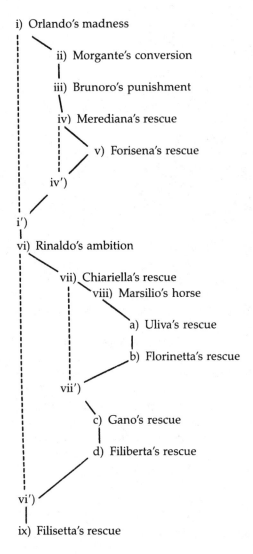

i) Orlando's madness

ii) Morgante's conversion

iii) Brunoro's punishment

iv) Merediana's rescue

v) Forisena's rescue

iv')

i')

vi) Rinaldo's ambition

vii) Chiariella's rescue

viii) Marsilio's horse

a) Uliva's rescue

b) Florinetta's rescue

vii')

c) Gano's rescue

d) Filiberta's rescue

vi')

ix) Filisetta's rescue

Emended in this way, the action of Part 1 divides into two major sequences: i–i', and vi–vi', each beginning with rebellion at Carlo's court and ending with a restoration of its order. Adventure ix is unfinished and highly digressive, but insofar as it holds together at all it forms a third sequence. Each of the two major sequences builds to a climax with action that restores political order in Pagania, and moves to a conclusion with the reconstitution of Carlo's court as a model of feudal hierarchy. The action of the climax then foreshadows that of the conclusion.

All three sequences are unified by their persistent focus on a single political theme: the continuity of chivalric society as a center of civility.

The action of adventures i and vi is realistic and relatively easy to read; it imitates the actual conflicts of chivalric life. The most important threat to Carlo's court is always internal. It is experienced as a divisiveness at the heart of chivalric society, generated by the norms of chivalric behavior. (Hence a certain underlying pathos to the poem as a whole, however comic or even parodic certain of its passages.) In the very process of acquiring fame, *fama*—the attribute that in the English romances is termed worship—the paladins become rivals and the order at court is jeopardized. The chivalric desire for unusual distinction, implied in the act of setting forth on a quest, is revealed at its most destructive in the traitor Gano, who incarnates the spirit of discord. In Part 1 he initiates division among the paladins, or the allies of Carlo, by encouraging jealousy and exposing to ridicule or disbelief the bonds, essentially acts of good faith, that knit together chivalric society. The action of all other and secondary adventures, describing the restoration of order in infidel courts, is conceived in different, symbolic terms. Infidel courts are imperiled by figures who emerge monstrously from the wilderness or assault without honorable cause virtual bastions of propriety. In each adventure the apparently external enemy embodies or exemplifies a moral weakness that actually afflicts the paladin confronting it. The adventures are therefore allegories of chivalric education and serve as tests to strengthen moral virtue; their successful completion guarantees moral regeneration. Between primary and secondary adventures, therefore, there develops yet another kind of relation: action concerning Carlo's court is represented realistically and imitates historical narrative; action in Pagania is allegorical and refers to spiritual conditions.

If one examines the relationship between primary and secondary adventures in order to discover the basis on which certain adventures are subordinate to others, one finds a principle of organization that might lend itself to a structural analysis of the entire narrative of Part 1. In both sequences, i–i', and vi–vi', the narrative is organized in terms of the same series of eight operations or functions—a complete action which has both been caused by an earlier action and results in a later action, that is, a complete action which has a place or function in the logic of the plot:[14]

| | | | |
|---|---|---|---|
| I | Disobedience | V | Obedience |
| II | Exile | VI | Return |
| III | Test(s) | VII | Test(s)' |
| IV | Confirmation of virtue | VIII | Social and political order |

In the first sequence, the first and second functions are expressed in the opening octaves of the first adventure which concludes with the fifth, sixth, seventh, and eighth functions. The second function is in fact an act, leaving the court and journeying into Pagania, but its importance is felt rather as a condition which obtains through the fourth function, "Confirmation of virtue." The third function is manifest problematically in the narrative. In the first sequence certain portions of the narrative are divided in a double and interlaced story line: the function of testing the hero is really expressed in several adventures, i.e. ii, iii, iv, and v. The second sequence is comparably organized; vii, viii, a, b, and c constitute tests preparatory to the successful completion of vi. Adventure d is, as I have indicated, intentionally parodic and contributes to the problematic conclusion of vi which, in turn, generates ix.

Furthermore, if each of these secondary adventures is analyzed in terms of functions, an even greater multiplication of the function "test" and the function "confirmation of virtue" is evident. Several of these adventures are punctuated with tests of various degrees of importance which result in the repeated confirmation of the virtue of the hero. For example, within adventure viii, itself a test, Rinaldo encounters a second test: to save the virgins of King Vegurto's kingdom from a dragon. By completing it successfully, he receives confirmation of his virtue: Vegurto supplies him with forces to help Chiariella. But whether or not this test is qualitatively different from others, it cannot be said to affect the logic of the plot. It adds to the reader's perception of the significance of the narrative, but its function as a function, gauged in relation to questions of cause and effect, is negligible. It is theoretically possible to analyze and diagram the functions in all the secondary adventures but the perception of the form of the narrative that one would then have would not be essentially different from that supplied by lumping all the tests together to comprise a single function, however strung out and internally repetitive.

If one accepts the simple picture of functions for each of the sequences, i–i' and vi–vi', one can perceive that these sequences are bipartite and that this form relates to their thematic content. Functions I and VII–VIII take place in France and refer to an historically determined social order; the remaining functions take place in Pagania and refer to a timeless moral order. Function IV describes the action at the climax of both of the primary adventures and takes place at that point literally farthest from France, namely at the infidel court itself:

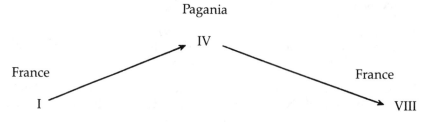

Seen in functional terms, the form of each of the primary adventures indicates the moralization of chivalry. Carlo's two principal vassals move from a state of political chaos, represented realistically in the Emperor's rule, to the hypothetical ground of moral testing and psychomachia, and return to rectify the state they had earlier abandoned.

Of crucial importance to any analysis of the form of the narrative is an understanding of the purpose of repetition. This will reveal more exactly how Pulci's sense of perspective contributes to the significance of the narrative. Here we can ask what advantage he secures by repeating the same series of functions in both sequences. The action of Part 1 as a whole repeats the sequence of functions in different contexts:

$$I\text{———}IV\text{———}VIII; \quad I'\text{———}IV'\text{———}VIII'; \quad I''. \dots$$

A narrative organized in this way makes interpretation especially demanding. To read such a narrative competently is to perceive, identify, and remember the relations between its various narrative units. This is a fairly complicated task and goes well beyond the simple determination of cause and effect, which in Part 1 is of no real interest to the poet. The continuous act of remembering what has happened and associating it with what is happening, of registering similarities and differences, of recognizing with each repetition of an action the new ground or level upon which it is being played, requires a reader particularly sensitive to the logical (in contrast to the psychological) relations the narrative develops. Truly perspectival narratives—like the *Orlando Innamorato,* the *Orlando Furioso,* and *The Faerie Queene,* not to mention the brilliant parody, Don Quixote—do much more than exploit point of view. Unlike narratives devoted to the development of a notion of the subject, or more generally of subjectivity—and one thinks of such works as *What Maisie Knew* or *As I Lay Dying*—a narrative composed as a series of a perspectives always engages the reader in an experience of *extensiveness.* It forces him to have in mind ever more comprehensive portions of the past (or history) that the narrative creates in the process of its unfolding. In a certain sense, the form of the narrative of the *Morgante*—in Part 1— introduces the subject of the poem covertly, by requiring the reader to undergo, in reading, the particular condition of the historian. Like the historian who pieces together a picture of the past from a variety of sources, the reader of the *Morgante* is asked to look again and again at certain characters and types of action (rebellion, revolution, and so forth). He is forced to reassess them in light of changing circumstances, both those depicted in the narrative and those determined by his own experience of reading.

An analysis of the narrative based on the sequences of functions in the arrangement of its adventures demonstrates its perspectival character at its most elementary:

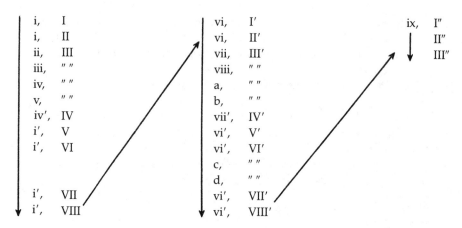

Clearly all similar functions invite comparison. But the nature of a comparison between functions in the first sequence is going to depend on a narrower range of interpretative experience than a comparison between those which occur in the second sequence. Of central importance is the fact that functions are repeated within a continuous story (Part 1 as a whole) in which the plot also shows major (i and vi) as well as minor redundancies (ii and iii, iv and v, and iv and vii). The attentive reader will begin to understand that the meaning of the narrative is in part in the interpretation of these repetitions. Because of its formal characteristics, Part 1 is something of a structural paradox; its dynamic forward movement is constantly caught in an act of recoiling upon itself in order to advance the next step.

At this point I must indicate what I do not claim for any of my outlines or diagrams of the narrative action or plot of Part 1; that is, that they represent its structure, substructure, or second level of the text. They are merely analytical versions or abstractions of this narrative action or plot and are designed to provide the reader with an idea of the arrangement of stories in this portion of the poem. It is important to make a distinction between the exposition of the structure of a narrative and what I have actually set forth—a series of schemes of the plot of a narrative—because without it certain of the most obvious limitations of my analysis are in danger of being overlooked. No reader of the Part 1 can fail to notice how much that is important to its action I have left out. Crucial to an understanding of its concept of chivalry is, for example, the changing role of Malagigi, the white magician, who intervenes to guide, protect, and save the paladins. He does not appear in all adventures, nor does he act in a functional manner. Yet the nature and frequency of his help is an index to the stability of chivalric society. The criteria by which I have omitted Malagigi's part in the action of Part 1 are not logical but rather strategic. My analyses are based on a decision to examine Part 1 as part of a distinct corpus of late medieval narrative and therefore to consider those of its features that most closely exemplify this kind of narrative. Its concern with the fate of a Christian court which depends on the maintenance of political order is characteristic of narratives relating the matter of France; its circular plots are typical of Arthurian romance.[15] These considerations—not anything latent in the narrative itself—determined the nature of the analyses I offer above. One could certainly develop other schemes by which to illustrate the importance of Malagigi to the action of Part 1, but they would center on other kinds of considerations (for example, the role of the poet's persona, his narrative voice) and not on the concept of the court as the origin of the action of the narrative.

The partial or subjective nature of my analysis justifies my unwillingness to elevate it to the status of a demonstration of structure. Critiques of structuralist interpretations of narrative are now numerous. In my view they render theoretically indefensible both structuralist methodology and critical programs designed to produce objective analyses.[16] They generally advance the same kinds of objections, none more fundamental than that against the structuralists' division of the text into two levels: a superstructure which is the level of the narrative itself and then a second level which is understood to inhere within or to underlie the first. This is the level at which the structure of the narrative is said to become apparent. To discern this is therefore also to discover, at least in theory, the essential elements of the narrative by which it is unified and made significant. The difficulty with this approach is, however, clear: there is no way to sustain the notion of such a second level apart from the act of interpretation itself. This second level cannot be proved to exist in the sense in which the narrative itself exists; it is, inevitably, the product of the reader's judgment. In fact, the reader and critic are always concerned with a single level of narrative, the text they actually read, whether this is the original text or some radically simplified version of it. The second level is no more than a formularization of an aspect of the narrative, but the formularization evolves by means of the "humble technique of paraphrase."[17] The so-called metalanguage in which the formularization is expressed as the second level of the narrative thus has no sure linguistic status. It designates a set of terms the critic has chosen to use for which no clear or certain measure of objectivity exists.

But in fact the terms and models evolved by structuralist critics to analyze complicated narratives are useful critical tools. To illustrate the repetitive quality of Part 1, I have chosen to make use of the structuralist concept of the function, because it has been used to advantage in analyzing narratives of a similar type. Like narratives of folklore, Part 1 is relatively weak in the depiction of character and psychological motiva-

tion, and correspondingly emphasizes the event. It therefore invites an
analysis based on the concept of a unit indicating causal relationships.
The function, initially demonstrated by Propp with regard to Russian
folktales (and more recently adapted by Dorfman in his study of French
and Spanish medieval romances), is such a unit.[18] More sophisticated
units and models have certainly been proposed by other critics for
narratives where description and authorial point of view count for more,
notably Barthes's model for Balzac's *Sarrasin*, which analyzes narrative by
reference to a unit he terms a "lexie"; Todorov's grammar of the *Decameron*; and Genette's study of chronology and achronic structures in
Proust's *A la Recherche*.[19] (And in fact these analyses do propose to
provide a reader with what the critic considers the structure or substructure.) But for a narrative like the *Morgante*, the virtue of an analysis of
functions over those based on other concepts of a narrative unit is clear.
It establishes what a reader of these narratives most needs: the general
nature of its plot, what its principal and secondary story-lines are, and
where the turning points of each story occur. When Ariosto, in the
*Orlando Furioso*, and Boiardo, in the *Orlando Innamorato*, warn their
readers how difficult it is to remember portions of the stories they have
already narrated, they indicate, however facetiously, the extent to which
these plots bear the burden of signification. Understanding such a plot
gives the reader an elementary object lesson in literary interpretation.
Theorists of narrative have drawn attention to the act of reading as a
memorial synthesis; they see that the determination of meaning in a
narrative depends on the reader's ability to understand a given passage
in relation to earlier passages. As Segre notes, meaning is not revealed at
the end of a narrative but acquired in the process of reading it.[20] It
cannot be divorced from the notion of a process, an experience that takes
time. Late-medieval romances, by exploiting the resources of plot so
fully, demand from the reader an unusually intense effort to achieve this
memorial synthesis. Unlike a novel of Balzac or Tolstoy, a narrative of
this type can hardly be approached through the examination of what the
critic may consider an important or typical moment. The critic of late-
medieval and formally related narratives is forced by their structural
intricacies to resort to analytical versions if he wants to appreciate a
dimension of their poetics that their authors deliberately emphasized.

### Part 2 (Cantos 24–28)

The narrative of Part 2 is, unlike that of Part 1, not patterned; its
storyline is single, its episodes unique, and the order of its events

chronological. At stake is the fate of Carlo and Christendom, and the conflict, involving the infidel opposition led by Marsilio, is essentially epic—an augmented version of Pulci's principal source, the *Spagna in rima,* itself a version of the *Chanson de Roland.* In contrast to its sources, Part 2 shows the Christian forces as twice victorious over the infidel. To the plot of the *Spagna,* which has a simple bipartite form—that is, the defeat of Christian forces at Roncisvalle under Orlando is followed by the victory of Christian forces in Spain under Carlo—Pulci adds two other episodes: Antea's invasion of France and her defeat by the paladins, assisted by the magic of Malagigi, and Rinaldo's return to France.

The first addition serves several purposes. Pulci bases his account of Antea's invasion on that of Balugante in the *Spagna* but he alters its order in the narrative, placing it before rather than after Roncisvalle.[21] It therefore alters the symmetry of the original plot and transforms the narrative into three major sections, of which it is the first and in a sense the preface: 1) Antea's invasion and defeat, 2) Orlando's death, and 3) Carlo's revenge. This gives Pulci's plot greater verisimilitude—Christian forces are more likely to be able to repel an infidel invasion *before* rather than after Roncisvalle where they lose Orlando—and reduces the *virtù* of Carlo, who after Roncisvalle is not obliged to repel an invasion as he is on his way to punishing Marsilio. Both these changes have thematic importance and affect the argument about Carlo's true place in history that Pulci inscribes in the last canto of Part 2. Pulci's second addition to the material he finds in his sources, an account of Rinaldo's return to France and participation in the battle of Roncisvalle, has primarily, I think, an apologetic purpose; it contains a veiled account of the poet's own errors and imagines a way to make amends by reconciling a wish for independence with an obligation to adhere to orthodox views. But it also modifies the plot by supplying an episode describing an instance of chivalric fidelity (Rinaldo's) to counter the episodes describing treason (Gano's). In so doing, it shifts attention from the Emperor as a Christian hero. Pulci's intention appears to have been to emphasize the cohesiveness and loyalty of Carlo's knights; in effect, however, the episode reveals more clearly the Emperor's own weakness in contrast to his vassals' strength and courage.

Part 2 is remarkable for its varied interpolations of non-narrative material. These occur in passages in which several characters question or argue with each other, sometimes at such length that it is appropriate to refer to their speeches as monologues. At other times the voice is the poet's own, commenting on his story or defending himself from accusations. As Part 2 progresses, the length and content of these disquisitions become more impressive. They halt the flow of the action entirely and create (in what would have been Pulci's audience) a strong impression of contemporaneity: they link the narrative directly to the poet's intellectual milieu. They less explain the action in terms of action, as, for example, a digression describing a causal event might, than contribute to the reader's understanding of the action as a manifestation of certain cultural values. And because the action in Part 2 is dramatic, these values are, in a sense, themselves under review. If the allegorical action of Part 1 is interpretable on the basis of certain ideological norms such as the chivalric code and the concept of a Providential history, the dialogue and drama of Part 2 provide occasion to question these norms.

To analyse the narrative of Part 2 in the manner employed for Part 1, in functional terms, is not therefore particularly enlightening. On the other hand, what does need special recognition are the progressively longer portions of text devoted to non-narrative material, particularly in cantos relating events that are not part of the Roncisvalle story: in canto 24, nine octaves; in canto 25, seventy-eight; in canto 27, fourteen; and canto 28, one hundred and twenty-seven (over three-quarters of the entire canto.) These passages obviously affect the form of the poem. With the exception of canto 25, substantially the story of Gano's treachery and the battle of Roncisvalle, Part 2 is a true *genus mixtum;* into an epic framework Pulci introduces scenes of drama and encyclopedic fragments of religious and philosophical knowledge. The narrative becomes increasingly a discursive meditation, opened up by the centrifugal forces of the poet's imagination analyzing his own work.

Much of the last canto is taken up with closure which, given the evolution of the poem as a progressively more self-reflexive text, is as one might expect: problematic. The narrative becomes repetitious and finally metaleptic, that is, it concludes by projecting the accomplishment of its intended purpose beyond the limits of epic and on to another kind of poem—pastoral—which is chronologically both earlier and later than it is. The temporal relations thus developed can be briefly summarized.

Having described Gano's death, Rinaldo's later exploits, and Carlo's death, Pulci twice recapitulates his life, first according to a source he calls "Lattanzio," and second according to an "Alcuin."[22] He concludes these histories by sketching the main events in the life of Carlo's son Ludovico, who, he asserts, will be the subject of his next poem. He then reverts to a description of the character of Carlo based on the work of "many authors" (28. 119–128). The chronological range of events the *Morgante* refers to is enlarged with each of these histories. Parts 1 and 2 follow the chronology of Carlo's life from middle age to death, 1. 12 to 28. 51; events described in "Lattanzio's" account, 28. 53–66, begin with Carlo's youth, and those in "Alcuin's" account, 28. 67–114, in the reign of his father Pepin. With Pulci's anticipated history of Ludovico, 28. 115–18, the timeframe of the poem extends forward:

i)                          Carlo's maturity and death      (Pulci)
ii)                   Carlo's youth, maturity and death      ("Lattanzio")
iii)   Pepin's reign, Carlo's youth, maturity and death      ("Alcuin")
iv)                                          Ludovico's reign (Pulci)


The poem concludes with Pulci's entertainment of the idea of a pastoral that will revive in the historical present of Florence—the time in which he lives and writes—the golden age of poetry and the Heliconian spring of the Muses. It is actually unclear to what corpus of writing he refers here; that is, whether at this late stage he wishes in some way to redefine as a pastoral the poem he is about to complete or whether he states that he will write pastoral in the future.[23] But in any case, he now proposes to substitute the mythical time appropriate to that genre for the generally historical time of the *Morgante*. He thus appears to frame the *Morgante* in a temporality more extensive than that he first gave it: his pastoral verse will recreate a time before chivalry (the golden age) in a time in which chivalry is a thing of the past (Lorenzo's court). To the extent that the history of Carlo—the poem just written—is recognized as different in tone and temporality from pastoral, it functions to separate the past of archaic pastoral, invoked allusively in Pulci's last octaves, from a future pastoral that is, according to the poet, either (strangely) mirrored in Carlo's history or the subject of a promised work that serves to conclude that history:


golden age pastoral  /  *Il Morgante*  /  new pastoral (?)
        (myth)                (history)           (fantasy)


Pulci's interest in pastoral is obviously crucial to the significance of the poem as a representation of history inasmuch as it implies his new willingness to treat time by reference to an ahistorical model and suggests his dissatisfaction with his narrative as history.

Were one asked to characterize the differences between Parts 1 and 2 as narrative, reference to the two principal types of late-medieval narrative would serve as an obvious starting place. Like many chivalric romances, Part 1 presents events as caused by other events through allegorical relationships developed and sustained for the entire length of the narrative. For this reason causality is generally clear, direct, and logically established. Each adventure poses a problem to be solved; this is presented at its outset where its solution is also in some way implied. The entire story is then informed by its end. Part 2, on the other hand, has a complicated form. It derives its matter from *chansons de geste* or

epic, and, because it narrates a series of events which have no beginning
or end, it also resembles a chronicle or history, albeit one punctuated
with dramatic scenes. It begins by definition *in medias res* and ends, as I
have indicated, inconclusively. Its formal character is that of a fragment
of a larger narrative whose full scope is realized elsewhere, in other
narratives. The depiction of causality correspondingly alters. Events
acquire an historical character; that is, their causes become multiple,
diffuse, problematic. Is Roncisvalle caused by Gano's treachery, Marsilio's greed, Orlando's pride, Carlo's stupidity? If by all of them, in what
order of importance? Nor are events determined by the idea of a single
objective; Gano's treachery has various consequences. Events of moment—they are of a miraculous nature—are ascribed to the agency of
God, not man. Lesser events, caused by such human feelings as jealousy, revenge, affection, are presented as part of a Providential plan, as
elements in a story known only to God.

Yet these distinctly different narratives also have characteristics in
common. In her article on medieval narrative, Vitz writes that its two
principal modes, which she terms "story" and "chronicle," show in
practice a certain interrelatedness. When the plot of a story becomes
vague, when incidents occur without a clear sense of the human agents
involved in them, it assumes the problematic character of history. Conversely, when a narrative imitating chronicle, relating events that pre-
tend to have a basis in historical fact, is also structured in terms of a
problem and its solution, then the narrative acquires the clarity and
comprehensibility of a story.[24] Parts 1 and 2 of the *Morgante* show in fact
such a hybridization. The allegorical story of Part 1 acquires the character
of a chronicle in its last cantos, where events are not explained either in
rational or symbolic terms. Correspondingly, the recognizably historical
events of Part 2 are linked in a story. Pulci presents the treachery of Gano
and the death of Roland as problems for Carlo to solve; Carlo's invasion
of Spain and the death of Marsilio are his solutions. The treachery of
Gano seems to entail Carlo's punishment of him and Marsilio. This
hybridization of the distinct types of narrative in Part 1 and 2 has the
effect of obscuring their differences and tends to unify the entire narrative.

The more one recognizes the importance of Pulci's attempts to give the
*Morgante* a historical character overall, the less likely one is to emphasize
its division into two parts of a formally different nature. The principal
advantage to distinguishing the *Morgante* as a historical narrative is not
that it confirms a perception of the poem as a work unified in a formal
way but that it supplies a context in which the question of the narrative
may be addressed with reference to other than formalist criteria. Crucial
to this enterprise is the reader's appreciation of the subtlety with which

Pulci presents his subject. The *Morgante* is not a work evincing a consistent enthusiasm for what it portrays. Pulci's voice is remarkable for its moodiness. He does not always affirm the same opinions and values, nor does he never deny what he has previously affirmed. These shifts in tone and point of view give the narrative a disputative quality. That his subject submits to revision becomes at a certain point a subject in itself. The poem becomes then not so much a history arguing a (political or legal) position, as a history manqué, which for its historical subject substitutes another of a different order: the writing of history itself.

The reader experiences this transformation of subject directly but also as the poet's loss of faith in the concept of authority. In Part 2 there is for Pulci no longer any point in maintaining what for him is now an illusion—that on a judgment of Carlo agreement is possible. Critics have faulted the last three cantos of the *Morgante* for being particularly formless, egregiously fragmented by interpolations. In a sense, however, these interpolations are perfectly consistent with the poet's ever more conscious and pointed attack on the idea that the *Morgante* is a true history of Carlo. Ramat argues that Part 2 is not successful as poetry because in it Pulci writes as if he were a compiler of anecdotes, not a poet.[25] In his haste to produce a poem that would restore him to favor, Ramat claims, Pulci overlooked the only really important element poetry ought to have—a language consistently adequate to the material it represents. Ramat discerns a style recognizably Pulcian only in passages where the poet's desire to accommodate his patron's learning is least in evidence, that is, in Part 1 where the transformation of the chivalric material into a bourgeois poetry mirroring the psychological and political realities of fifteenth-century Florence is unimpeded by the introduction of reflections on philosophy, religion, or science. But this is to overlook the possibility that in the discontinuities of Part 2 an equally compelling poetics is represented. The point is to recognize in the formal fragmentation of the narrative a paradoxical form.

It is as history and as a reflection upon history that the *Morgante* makes sense. The nearly repetitive narrative sequences in Part 1 and the digressions in Part 2 give the entire poem a perspectival form and enable the poet to examine the politics of chivalry and the concept of empire from a succession of points of view. The continuity of these social entities, how and on what terms they endure, is the matter that Pulci most persistently considers. Finally and inevitably, he must also examine the nature of temporality and the principles that provide the basis for the writing of history.

# 2

## MODELS OF CHIVALRY

THE *Morgante* expresses a theory of history from its very beginning—a theory that is bound up with notions of empire, feudal relationships, and the practice of chivalry as a moral discipline. The theory is implied in the way Carlo Mano's paladins fulfill their knightly obligations, pursue their adventures, and achieve their renown. As models of chivalry, they represent the agents or active principles in whose actions a divine purpose in history can be discerned. To speak of a theory of history in this poem is, then, also to speak of politics and morality.

The undertaking is complicated by the fact that the poem draws on varied sources in a literary genre notable for its diversity of styles and subjects; in other words, its picture of political life and its vision of the past are involved and in a sense evolutionary. A late example of a narrative on the matter of France—the cycle of stories on the battle of Roncisvalle, the youth and heroism of Orlando, the exploits of the Chiaramonte—the *Morgante* is indebted not only to earlier texts on these topics but also to the spirit and content of the second great subject of medieval narrative, the story of Arthur of Britain. That Pulci's poem exhibits a British aspect is partly reflected in the tension generated by the thematic differences in each of these cycles.

Broadly speaking, representations of the matter of France ought not to be seen as wholly divorced in the minds of their late-medieval writers and readers from what was understood as history and experienced as the abiding pressure, however attenuated by the passage of time, of past events on the present moment. The historical character of narratives concerning Charlemagne's court is most directly felt in those which approach the form of chronicle and focus on the epic struggle of Christian and infidel. Questions of credibility aside, their contemporary readers would have perceived in images of this strife a general correspondence to real conflicts for control of the Mediterranean from the time of the historical Charlemagne. Central to these accounts is the concept of loyalty—to the faith, to the Emperor, to the brotherhood of his paladins—which entails the recognition at some level of the necessity of observing social order. If Gano's treachery represents the most egregious kind of violation of this order, Orlando's pride, which in the *Chanson* is associated with his *prouesse* and the fact that he is *preux*, is a subtler threat to the empire. Political issues here are clear-cut and dramatic: the integrity of chivalric society depends on the willingness of its members to honor the feudal hierarchy despite its failure to correspond to a natural order of things. This is the point, I think, of representations of the Emperor as more or less weak in real terms. Society is never to be sustained by him but only through him and by virtue of his subordinates who legally make over their strength and will to him. The underlying conflict in these narratives is between a natural social order that mirrors actual human potential and a traditional social order that reflects certain a priori assumptions concerning who governs and who is governed.

The matter of Britain is, in contrast, essentially ahistorical in nature. This is not to say that it is impossible to find an account of the kingdom of Logres in which King Arthur is represented as a figure in history but rather that these narratives in general create a different category of expectations in their readers. The temporality they exhibit is that of fantasy, of legend; typically it flirts with the possibility of a return of dead heroes and raises questions concerning the irreversibility of events, the linearity of temporal sequences. Human action is often qualified by contact with a spirit world that enables human beings to be healed of mortal wounds and enjoy an earthly immortality. And while chivalric society remains in the main what it was in stories of Charlemagne, the representation of chivalric loyalty is enriched by an additional factor, erotic love. To the fundamental relationship between lord and vassal is added a third element: the *midons*, the lady for whom a knight exerts himself in order then to sustain his king and his society.

The primary influence of the matter of Britain on narratives of the Charlemagne story has usually been restricted to the realm of the emotions between knights and their ladies. Paladins who exhibit the sturdiest of feudal loyalties in the *chansons de geste* come to devote themselves to serving their ladies, like their British counterparts, in later narratives. The great sequels to the *Morgante*—the *Orlando Innamorato* and the *Orlando Furioso*—exploit the theme of love to a degree unprecedented earlier; the *Furioso* elevates Orlando's erotic *furor* to epic proportions and contrasts its destructive power with the loyalty traditionally demanded of the hero. Pulci, too, includes episodes where the actions of the paladins hinge upon their experience of love.[1]

Chivalric romances relating the matter of Britain also confer on these later Italian narratives something of their representation of time, which is further registered in narrative form. Action in chivalric romance is typically expressed in individual quests conferred by the king on his knights, which begin and end at court. The court is then both the literal center of chivalric activity *and* an element in the form of the narrative, the place at which action originates and to which it returns. In her analysis of the form and thematic content of Arthurian chivalric romance, Tuve sees the figure of the king at court as the center of the interlacing threads of the separate stories that make up the work. Never taking action himself, the king is represented metonymically in the figure of his knights. They invest him with their vitality and he benefits from and is in a sense validated by it. They constitute his actual power, and he endures only as long as they form a collectivity.[2] The image of the court has thus both a conceptual and a structural function.[3] It generates the codes, the rules and conventions regarding love and war that, in being respected or transgressed, determine the fate of chivalric society, and it provides the digressive plots of these narratives with thematic integrity.

Political life in Arthurian chivalric romance is a reflection of this courtly paradigm. The fate of King Arthur's kingdom depends more upon the loyalty and strength of his fellowship than on the outcome of particular events. What might be termed historical factors—invasions, rebellions, acts of treachery—do not figure decisively unless they also possess an ethical correlative. The final great event in the Arthurian story—in fact an invasion, a rebellion, and an act of treachery—is also (and primarily) a self-reflexive moral act. Arthur is killed by Mordred, but Mordred is the child of his incest. The motives for their combat transcend ambition and become fused with divine justice. The last redactor of these stories, Sir Thomas Malory, appears to have attempted to unify the corpus of Arthurian chivalric romance into one continuous historical narrative in his *Morte Darthur.* But in general the corpus exhibits an ahistorical character, and presents the reader with moralized or satirical versions of chivalric life rather than a representation of particular moments in history.

Narratives of the matter of France present a different picture of political activity in the degree to which they reflect the concerns of the *Chanson* and are devoted to the portrayal of Gano and the Maganzese. Charlemagne's court, because it is represented in action that is epic and historical, has in the *Chanson* neither the conceptual nor the structural significance of its Arthurian counterpart. But in later narratives that relate other portions of the cycle (the life of Renaud or Rinaldo, the youth of Orlando), and these would include the *Morgante,* the epic and historical terms in which political life is depicted are modified by the inclusion of others expressing the moral and courtly concerns common to the matter of Britain.

The *Morgante*'s fusion of the narrative forms of history and romance, or chronicle and story, is matched by a corresponding mingling of conceptions of the social order. Gano's treachery is of course instrumental in the disaster at Roncisvalle, but behind this act and informing it are a series of impressive scenes in which narrative action becomes significant by reference to the vitality (or decadence) of Carlo's court. Like Arthurian chivalric romance, the action of the *Morgante* (and the source for Part 1, the *Orlando*), is centered on the court and the succession of dynamic portraits that begin the poem is seen against the backdrop of the troubled politics of Carlo's empire. Orlando represents the chivalric character in its most elementary form; Rinaldo and Uliviero represent refinements of it. The second and third adventures, focusing on Orlando and Rinaldo respectively, establish their fundamental complementariness. Orlando, in short, is Roland, a Christian martyr; Rinaldo, by contrast, is likened to Hercules, the hero of Florentine civic life and an exponent of rationality. In Orlando are invested the desires of the faithful for a future in paradise, in Rinaldo the needs of the citizen for a present enlightened by reason. The terms in which these desires are expressed and the ways in which they are realized alter in the course of the narrative, but the characters of the paladins, in their emblematic purity, do not.

### The Virtue of Temperance: The Rescue of the Princess Merediana

Gano accuses Orlando of usurping the functions of his lord, the Emperor, and Orlando leaves for Pagania in a fury. He arrives at an abbey belonging to the Chiaramonte which is besieged by giants, overcomes them, and converts the largest and most terrifying, Morgante, to Christianity. The abbot gives Orlando a quest: to deliver the princes Merediana, daughter of the infidel king, Caradoro, from her besieging lover, Manfredonio. Orlando and Morgante, now friends, travel to deliver a palatial wasteland from a mysterious malady. Rinaldo, accusing Gano of envy and bad faith, pursues Orlando with a company of paladins, including Uliviero. He arrives at the same abbey Orlando delivered, once again besieged by giants, and overcomes them. Orlando arrives at the seige of Merediana and vows to help Manfredonio. Rinaldo follows him and en route delivers the princess Forisena from a dragon. Uliviero courts Forisena, who dies when he leaves her. Rinaldo sides with Merediana, arranges to reveal to Orlando his presence, and together with Morgante they overcome Manfredonio. Merediana urges clemency in battle and patience to the defeated Manfredonio. (She falls in love with Uliviero and conceives his child.) Her father Caradoro pledges help to Carlo in the future. (Adventures i–v)

The existing text of the *Orlando* is missing its opening octaves and there is no way of knowing whether Pulci's representation of Carlo's court and the departure of Orlando is his own. The opening scene, depicting the court's celebration of Christmas, is, in any case, typical of a beginning of Arthurian chivalric romance: such gatherings on major feast days conventionally signal the beginning and the end of adventures, the giving of quests, the acceptance of worship. In this case, however, the ideal of a court festival is invoked but the sequence of events that usually follow it is not imitated:

> Era per pasqua, quella di Natale;
> Carlo la corte avea tutta in Parigi:
> Orlando, com' io dico, è il principale
> èvvi, il Danese, Astolfo ed Ansuigi;
> fannosi feste e cose trïunfale.

(1. 9)

It was the Christmas festival; all Carlo's court was in Paris: as I have said, Orlando was the first and foremost [of them]; the Dane, Astolfo, and Ansuigi were there, and they feasted and celebrated.

The first two lines of the octave remind readers of generic conventions that the poet will not in fact observe in writing the rest of the poem. The lines, which are recognized as ironic as the scene unfolds, present what will become a dominant pattern in the sequences that make up the plot. A social norm, here the giving of quests—also a narrative norm, inasmuch as the court functions as a thematic center about which revolves subsequent action—will be proposed and appear to be about to determine the action of the poem. Yet finally both norms will be subverted. In this case the ambiguous third line provides the clue to the disintegration that will follow. Is Orlando "first" at court or merely "first" among the other paladins? It is because this question is being asked, by the reader and in the next octave by Gano, that Carlo's court can be understood to be unstable. From the political conflict that ensues, the action of the entire *Morgante* is generated.

Pulci describes Carlo as "too happy" ("troppo lieto") and notes that fortune waits in hiding to spoil the occasion:

> Orlando governava in fatto e in detto
> la corte e Carlo Magno ed ogni cosa;
> Gan per invidia scoppia, il maladetto,

> e cominciava un dì con Carlo a dire:
> —Abbiàn noi sempre Orlando a obedire?
>
> (1. 11)

Orlando governed the court, Carlo Magno and everything else, in fact and in deed; the cursed Gano exploded with envy and began one day to say to Carlo, "must we always obey Orlando?"

The earlier reference to fortune is somewhat deceptive. Gano's envy does not need to be attributed to chance or Providence because it is adequately motivated at a realistic level. Obviously he reacts to the impropriety of Orlando's leadership. The actual politics of the three-sided struggle between Gano, Orlando, and Carlo that is initiated here and developed throughout the poem determines that Gano's hatred of Orlando is not entirely gratuitous. However inherently evil he later becomes, he is in part the product of this situation which not he but Orlando and Carlo created and tolerated.[4]

Gano's outburst has a double effect: Orlando rushes from court in a fit of madness, "pazzia" (1. 20), and Carlo remains with Gano at his side. The action becomes a paradigm for the action of the poem until the battle of Roncisvalle. Both Orlando and Carlo continue to exhibit the kinds of misjudgment that have here occasioned political disorder. Orlando's madness is expressed in later episodes as an heroic pride, a gigantic self-will that only in being obedient to God acquires legitimate goals. Carlo's association with Gano—he stands alone with him repeatedly—is finally also termed "pazzia" by his paladins; it produces the machinations that in turn lead to Orlando's death. I stress the complexity of the Orlando-Carlo-Gano relationship to indicate the subtlety of the conflict the poem describes. Roncisvalle is, in essence, a political tragedy, emanating from a crucial confusion in the hierarchy of imperial government.

The next three adventures (ii–iv) develop the characters of Orlando, Rinaldo, and Uliviero as models of chivalry. They focus at the same time on the terms upon which a court survives as a center of civilized life, by which it can be said to be have a history. A reader familiar with the culture of the Renaissance will recognize in these four adventures signs of what might be called the Proteus complex, the obsession with change and stability or continuity that affects so much of the art of the period.[5] A consideration of the factors which made for change in social institutions led poets and historians to search for ways to unify diverse and perplexing human experiences in comprehensive patterns of events, in short, for a theory of history. To judge from the *Morgante*, Pulci recognized three possible ways of representing the human experience of time.

I sketch them briefly here, since they are analyzed at greater length as they figure in actual passages in the poem.

The return of spring, the renascence of vegetation after its death in winter, offered a model of temporality in which change was only apparent and actually subsumed in a larger pattern of stasis. It is to this model that the vegetation myths of Ceres and Proserpina, and Venus and Adonis, refer, as well as the seasonal myth of Castor and Pollux. The more sophisticated statements of Plato and Aristotle reflect a similar conception of time as a paradoxical timelessness. Plato conceives of time as a reflection of eternity and therefore of the motion of heavenly bodies or time-markers as both forward and in reverse, the whole achieving a balance. Aristotle's concept of change as *physis,* the movement from being to nonbeing, and its converse, expresses a comparable sense of time as both an unfolding and an infolding.[6] Myths that exploit the image of a return from death that may or may not be fully realized (Hercules and Theseus, Orpheus and Eurydice, Hippolytus as Virbius) test the terms of the seasonal or self-renewing model of time against the human experience of events as unrepeatable and often present temporality ambiguously. They illustrate that the seasonal model is both attractive and pathetic. For, to human beings who cannot imitate the return of spring, the idea of natural time must also be ironic; it will remind them that the tree of life flourishes in a paradise closed to mortals. For this reason the images of the seasons are frequently perceived in conjunction with those of loss and death. Pulci's plots in Part 1 are all variations of myths of return; they explore the possibilities human existence provides for the restoration (always somewhat imperfect) of social order after periods of perturbation.

Familial relations provided a model of a second kind of temporality. Here institutions are preserved and society made stable by the renewal of *virtù* that takes place in successive generations. A son is like his father; he confronts the same or similar dangers, which he overcomes with the weapons, literal or moral, that he has inherited from his ancestors. Because it corresponds to the human experience of generation in families, this model has distinct advantages over the seasonal model; it eschews an easy and mythical consolation in favor of one more realistic. The prospects for stability and continuity it offers are not, however, exclusive of certain violent and sometimes gratuitous kinds of loss. Generation implies death as well as birth. This is the model of temporality Boethius has Philosophia offer the distraught Christian who asks about the role of Fate in human affairs. According to Philosophia, Fate comprehends being and nonbeing, unlike Providence which is timeless and conceives only of being: fate "sustains all things coming into being and dying through similar generations of young and of seed.

This even holds the fortunes of men in an indissoluble chain of causes which, because it originates in immutable Providence, is necessarily also immutable."[7] That is, things are sustained (made to have a certain continuity in time) through birth and death (change) *by* generation which is also, because of its connection to Providence, a form of immutability or stasis. Pulci refers to this model and also to what motivates it: erotic love. He generally depicts the paladins' victories over the forces of change as darkened by some form of jealousy or injury. The adventure of Merediana, for example, depicts her restoration to her throne but also her sexual violation.

The last model of temporality Pulci exploits is in a sense the simplest. Typically Christian, it avoids speculating on the possibility that events proceed in cycles or patterns that approach repetitiveness and it stresses the uniqueness of the particular moment. Historical meaning is then what it was for Augustine, essentially unknowable in history itself and only to be revealed when history, the record of the *saeculum* or human time, is completed.[8] For Pulci this model becomes important after he doubts his mission as a poet and when, confronting his inability to comprehend the form and direction of his history, he tries to rely on faith and doctrine.

None of these models is in any sense prescriptive or even dominant in the narrative as a whole. Pulci constantly shifts between them, his inconsistency the index of his developing interest in the epistemological aspects of the problem—how to write history—he has undertaken to solve. It is nevertheless important for the reader to have them well in mind, for the question of temporality is rarely far from the focus of the poet's attention.

Orlando's departure from Carlo's court poses the first threat to its stability and therefore to its continuity as a social institution, and it is logical to seek in this event some indication of the factors which Pulci perceives as causing social change. In this case it is the hero's anger, his "pazzia," that provides the motivation for his first adventure, which consequently assumes an educative function: his conversion of Morgante represents an initial control of his madness. Orlando, destined for martyrdom, must struggle against this debility, actually an exaggerated form of heroic pride; his affliction contrasts with that which will trouble Rinaldo, that is, a reason so acute that it becomes a kind of unreason, a temper hot with impatience at Carlo's habitual obtuseness. In displacing Carlo as the center of the court, Orlando exhibits to excess the trait that in the *Chanson* is termed *prouesse*, the attribute that makes him *preux* in contrast to Olivier who is *sage*. His failing links the scene of his departure from Carlo's court with later scenes describing his *virtù* and makes

comprehensible his reluctance to summon help at Roncisvalle. His madness expresses ironically that extraordinariness characteristic of the typical heroes of epic, who as demigods resist common definition; his death
and salvation conclude the process by which he accepts his human
status. The elements of this drama of self-defeat and self-recognition,
implicit in the opening events at Carlo's court, begin to be analyzed
when Orlando rescues the abbey of the Chiaramonte (ii).

By describing Orlando's journey to the abbey of the Chiaramonte, his
own family, as "riding in one wrong path (or in error) after another"
("cavalcando d'uno in altro errore", 1. 19), Pulci suggests the allegorical
nature of this adventure. The isolation of the abbey, besieged by three
giants and thus cut off from civilization, mirrors Orlando's own removal
from Carlo's court and its moral consequences. His conquest of the
giants is an obvious act of self-control and atonement; moreover, in the
terms of his conversion of Morgante there is a further, anagogical reference. While he kills Morgante's brothers, he is given Morgante as a
companion in a mysterious fashion. The giant is converted to Christianity and to Orlando's side by a dream in which he is saved from a
devouring serpent by Christ not "Macon" (1. 43). Orlando's conquest is
therefore twofold. Over the giants, a lawless enemy, it is moral, but over
Morgante, an image of spiritual pride, it is by grace, literally conveyed in
Morgante's ability to dream his way to the truth.[9] The iconography of
giants in medieval narrative draws on classical sources of the story of the
gigantomachia and frequently presents giants as emblems of a pride that
does not acknowledge any superior authority. Morgante's subordination
signifies Orlando's conquest, through grace, of his own tendency to
lapse into a titanic rebelliousness. Morgante's dream itself suggests
Christ's salvation of the soul at the time of death, the devouring serpent,
an action which Macon cannot perform.

Into this brief allegory is woven a second strand of meaning which
concerns the individual will. Even after his conversion, Morgante considers a vendetta on behalf of his dead brothers, but Orlando tells him to
accept what God has decreed. The statement conveys Orlando's understandable wish to discourage Morgante from taking vengeance on him
but it also illustrates his new humility and gives it more than moral
significance. According to Orlando, the history of the world is perfectly
just. God destroys evil and "remembers to restore the good" ("il ben
ristorar si recorda", 1. 50); that is, to divinity alone vengeance belongs.[10]
Because the course of events is divinely ordered, actions intended to
redress any particular wrong must be condemned. Morgante's conversion is thus illuminated by a vision of history which is Christian and
especially Boethian. As Orlando's prohibition of a vendetta suggests, the
definitive causes of events are divine not human; that they produce

certain effects must therefore be accepted not debated. This vision of God's justice working through time recalls Philosophia's words to Boethius on the impossibility of distinguishing good from bad fortune: the course of events in history, expressed as Fate, arises from divine wisdom, Providence, and consequently "all fortune is good." That this is not always clear to human beings is merely a consequence of their situation in time; were they to attain a divine perspective, the justice in history would not be in question.[11]

Orlando's theory of history as Providential—a story unfolding in the mind of God the justice of which must be accepted on faith—provides the continuing basis for all of Pulci's subsequent speculations on history. Once Morgante is converted, Orlando's career is perceived as an expression of God's will. (The fortune that hides behind the scenes at Carlo's Christmas court can now be identified as fundamentally benign, whatever her immediate effects.) As the basis for an interpretation of events, the theory has the advantage of guaranteeing the concept of a just God and of conforming to Christian authority, notably to St. Paul and Dante, both of whom insist that in history the justice of God is exemplified and correlatively to be accepted as such by the faithful.[12] But since the theory also requires that all rational activity on the part of the historian be informed, not to say replaced, by faith, it is constantly liable to modification of one sort or another.

Generally the theory is modified so that history is either made to appear just by the assimilation of humanly comprehensible moral factors into the sequence of events (a solution expressly prohibited by Boethius), or it is made subject to different kinds or levels of interpretation at only the most abstract of which is God's justice seen to be at work. The first kind of modification is obviously attractive since it can be employed to write histories that are overtly apologetic. Two of Pulci's most influential precursors write histories of this kind: Villani's *Istorie Fiorentine* asserts that the city is protected by God and events reflect divine judgment. And Goro Dati, in *Istoria di Firenze*, advances the notion of an "earned grace," that is, of a human *virtù* or *ragione naturale* that by God's grace is permitted to shape favorable events.[13] Thus the prosperity of the city is proof of the spiritual merit of her citizens. The second kind of modification leads to sophistry and a measure of intellectual freedom, for it limits the sphere in which it is proper to perceive divine justice and allows for rational and not necessarily conclusive debate in the interpretation of ordinary and mundane events. Landino's *Comento sopra la Divina Comedia*, a work roughly contemporary with the *Morgante*, is such a self-critical text. Landino sets forth Dante's vision of history as Providential, explains the subservience of fortune to fate and divine will, and endorses the poet's judgment of Brutus the tyrannicide.

But he also ventures independently to speculate on the poet's motives and concludes that in the case of Brutus Dante condemned only the man who murdered in Caesar the image of the state and certainly not the man who liberated his city from Caesar, the tyrant.[14] Landino thus restores to the province of the historian the question of evidence and the fact of controversy. Because he conceives of Providential history in the vaguest possible terms—he asserts that amoral fortune is somehow governed by Providence but he does not go on to offer explanations for why events turned out well or badly—he is at liberty to discuss in ways more detailed and concrete what actually happened, or what is presumed to have happened. Evidently sensitive to the difficulties Orlando's Boethian theory of history entails, Pulci (like Dati) elects to consider human *virtù* as an expression of God's grace. He shows not only how thoroughly history is Providentially ordered, an opinion dramatized in Orlando's departure from the abbey, but also, in Rinaldo's subsequent defeat of the besieging giants, that *ragione* is *grazia,* that to be right is to win. Only at the conclusion of Part 1 does he resume an interpretation of events that corresponds to that which his hero has endorsed.

The moment of Orlando's departure from the abbey raises political questions the more critical in this instance because without Orlando the monks are again vulnerable to attack. The abbey contains, however, the answer to its survival in the script narrating its own history: a set of murals depicting the actions of Milone, Orlando's father, who a generation earlier had also defended the abbey from giants. This Christian institution has been preserved through the successive efforts of father and son, a sequence of events in which is reflected the generational model of temporality, a paradigm of one way in which the poem will relate the experience of change to stability and continuity. The importance of the image of the family is further enhanced by a new set of relations when the Abbot reveals that he is also a Chiaramonte and in fact Orlando's uncle. The image of fraternity, conveying in this instance an ideal of social cohesiveness, a pattern of cooperation among brother clerics and knights, complements the earlier image of generation. Addressing Orlando on the Christian life, the abbot remarks on a unity of purpose transcending individual differences:

> Così sempre s'affana il corpo e l'ombra
> per quel peccato dell'antico pome
> io sto col libro in man qui il giorno e l'ombra
> tu Colla spada tua tra l'elsa e'l pome
> cavalchi, espesso sudi al sole e all'ombra;
> ma di tornare a bomba è il fin del pome.
> Dico ch'ognun qui s'affatica e spera
> di ritornarsi alla tua antica spera.

(2.8)

So the body and soul are constantly employed because of the sin of the old apple. I remain here with book in hand, night and day; you ride with your sword [gripped] between hilt and pommel, and you often sweat in the sun and in darkness; but the end of the game is to be home free. I say that here everyone works and hopes to return to your (his) heavenly sphere.

The octave (clearly indicative of Pulci's ideas about history since it has no source in the *Orlando*) gathers into a unified vision the events of man's loss and recovery of paradise, "quel peccato" and "tua antica spera." Its punning end-words harmonize the differences between the clerical and chivalric functions and provide a musical analogue to the theme of the verse: that concerted action is required of men in a postlapsarian world. The solution to the problem of change through and within history is here presented as a relative one. The image of continuity created by the diverse and complementary activities of a family, where differences are balanced by correspondences, provides a realistic alternative to the stasis figured by virtually changeless revolutions of the seasons.

Important to any theory of history, and especially to those which refer to generational models of temporality, is the place of an individual death, an issue that Pulci addresses in the last episode of the poem that exclusively concerns the relationship between Morgante and Orlando. Here they take part in events which demonstrate that the temporality Christians experience does not admit the possibility of actual renascences in time. The episode of the palatial wasteland—"un bel palagio in mezzo del deserto" (2. 19)—dissociates Christian history, conceived in terms of an end in divine judgment, from classical history, which admits the possibility that events may occur in repetitive cycles.

The episode is an allegory of Christian life. The palace, which provides an abundance of food but no exit, is actually a trap, an image of earthly life. It can be escaped if the tomb it contains is left open and the devil who resides there is allowed to fight those entering the palace, and also if those who partake of its food are baptized (in this case Morgante) (2. 35, 36). Together these images signify the nature of the transition Christians make when they leave this life for the next. The necessarily open tomb signifies that the Christian must experience death, that he cannot exchange one life on earth for a second; baptism guarantees that after dying he may elude the devils in the tomb and achieve eternal life in heaven. That this transition once made is irreversible is established by Orlando who then instructs Morgante, albeit allusively, in what baptism means. Morgante, having left the palace, proposes to return there in order to rout the devils and save the souls trapped in the underworld tombs of the palace: "Someone, I don't know who, went there to get Euridice; I'd have very little respect for the devils" ("non so chi v'andò per Euridice io stimerei tutti i dïavol poco", 2. 38). Morgante's ignorance of the name and the eventual fate of Eurydice's hero reveals the impossibility of the task he contemplates. Unlike Proserpina (the greenery of the earth), Eurydice, her human double, does not return to life. Morgante's wish to harrow hell expresses a desire to use his immense power to give the damned the chance of a second life on earth, a wish he must renounce. The incident emphasizes not only that Christian time is linear, not cyclical and therefore reversible; it also underscores a corollary truth—that events, in this case the harrowing of hell, are unique and unrepeatable.

Rinaldo's departure from court is, like Orlando's, marked by a revelation of his character and how its principal weakness affects Carlo's court (i). Carlo's protest condemning Rinaldo's angry outburst against Gano affects concerns beyond the social hierarchy (Carlo does in fact tell Rinaldo that he turns his court upside down and dishonors him, 3. 28), and engages the central question of the poem to date. When Carlo assures Rinaldo that he, Carlo, will find the right time to punish Gano— "I tolerate the difficulty of everything to some end" ("a qualche fine ogni cosa comporto", 3. 29)—his implied request for a delay actually masks an unstated wish for political stability. The dramatic relevance of the remark lies in its equation of the technique of temporizing with the practice of temperance. Carlo is confused about these two forms of behavior. His vague allusion to the "end" he envisages echoes in a negative key Orlando's confident assertions of a Providential history and suggests that there are situations in which faith in such a history is inappropriate. Rinaldo's accurate preview of the true end of Carlo's temporizing (or his false temperance), namely the death of Orlando (3. 30), not only heightens our sense of Carlo's unreasonableness but also adds to the poet's concern with history two further questions: the proper place of human agency; and the distinction between timely moral action or temperance, and opportunistic calculation or temporizing.

The episode also presents *in nuce* the issues that Rinaldo will continue to confront to the very end of the poem. He will always be engaged in attempting rationally to discover the truth in progressively more sophisticated ways. His search will be hindered by impatience, haste, anger. The moral quality he will cultivate is precisely the true temperance which in this episode he sees Carlo lacks. Carlo has mirrored Orlando's madness of excessive pride with his own kind of delusion, a feckless reliance on Gano, a refusal properly to rule in his own right. Here he matches Rinaldo's intemperance with his own form of that vice, passivity, a refusal to act at all.

Rinaldo's encounter with a second set of giants (who again threaten the abbey of the Chiaramonte, iii) illustrates the symbolic dimension of his character as an exponent of *ragione,* reason, and, by virtue of being a near repetition of Orlando's earlier encounter there, associates Rinaldo's reasonableness with the ability to perceive likeness and difference essential to the perspectivizing technique on which Pulci bases the structure of his narrative. Rinaldo here begins to assume aspects of the poet's own character and role, an identification that becomes more direct as the poem progresses.

On entering the abbey, now in the hands of Morgante's brother Brunoro who has imprisoned the abbot in revenge for Orlando's killing his brothers, Rinaldo identifies his company as knights errant who fight, like Hercules, for reason ("per la ragion come Ercul combattiàno", 3. 38). They have been successful in their adventures because reason prevailed ("la ragion pur ebbe suo misura", 3. 38). Brunoro, remarking on Rinaldo's commitment to reason (3. 57, 58), demands that he judge his vendetta against Orlando favorably. But Rinaldo also listens to the abbot who, by relating the story of Orlando's rescue, supplies Brunoro's case with a historical context that entirely alters its significance. Declaring that the abbot is right ("ha ragione", 3. 65), Rinaldo agrees to fight Brunoro as proof that his decision is correct (3. 106). Brunoro's defeat confirms Rinaldo's reasonableness, evidenced in this instance by his ability correctly to perceive and judge events in history. The incident comments on the notion of Providential history advanced earlier by Orlando when he dissuaded Morgante from seeking revenge. In this version, formulated by the abbot, a new element is introduced: history is not only Providential; it is also comprehensible in moral terms. Rinaldo wins because the Lord helps him who is right: "aiuta ognun c'ha la ragione" (3. 63), and, by extension, history is seen to provide demonstrations in moral logic.

This adventure, entirely Pulci's invention with respect to its treatment of history, marks the most thorough adaptation of the Boethian theory, modified to include a positive function for the human intellect, that the poet offers in the course of the poem. His emphasis on the role of *ragione* recalls Goro Dati's treatment of the virtue in his *Istoria di Firenze,* where Dati tells his readers that "force accompanied by reason must always conquer" and that such success may be associated with divine judgment: "For since no good can be obtained without God's grace, which is available to everyone who looks where it is to be found, and it lives with *virtù* and good deeds[11] ("le buone operazioni").[15] For both Italians, to possess reason, *avere ragione,* is also to be right, *avere ragione,* and therefore necessarily to earn grace. By contrast, Boethius's acceptance of the justice or rightness of history, in being predicated on the inability of human beings ever to perceive it as such, distinguishes between an essentially transcendent truth and the human ability to be reasonable.

Rinaldo's characterization as Herculean is also Pulci's addition—the poet of the *Orlando* never calls Rinaldo a Hercules—and draws further connections between the hero and the poet's association with Florence and Medici. Pulci elaborates the simple and conventional outlines of the figure he finds in his source—the popular renegade, the champion of the people, a Hercules because of what he does—with attributes that unequivocally declare his symbolic importance to the history of Florence. Hercules was the secular saint of the city; in the fourteenth century he was portrayed on the great seal of the Signoria, and early in the sixteenth century Cosimo I, celebrating his government of Florence, called on artists to represent Hercules as a sign of social and civic virtue.[16] For Renaissance humanists, the interest of the hero was fully established by Cicero, who saw in his labors the epitome of politically responsible life and inscribed this vision in the *De officiis*, the work that served them as a guidebook to the public conduct of private citizens.[17] Many of Pulci's contemporaries doubtless also knew Salutati's treatise, the *De laboribus Herculis*, an extended meditation on the role Cicero had sketched for the hero. Salutati particularly insists on his moral and intellectual qualities, characterizing him as a philosopher, a rhetorician, and an astronomer, and comparing him with such mythical exponents of intellectual courage as Perseus, and Aeneas in his descent to the under-world.[18] Insofar as Rinaldo assumes the attributes of the hero, he can be seen to be a foil to the hero and martyr Orlando. Hercules had tradi-tionally lent himself to the comparisons of this sort. Petrarch, for exam-ple, assimilates Hercules into Christian history by making him a type of Christ, but he also separates him from it by characterizing his qualities as human, not divine.[19] It makes logical sense for Hercules to be perceived in relation to a second and saintly figure. Together they represent the claims of the *saeculum* and eternity, human society and the company of the elect.

The complementarity of the figures of Orlando and Rinaldo produced by this use of imagery is enhanced by the effect of repetition in the plot; both leave court in anger, both deliver an abbey from giants. The nar-rative illustrates Pulci's method of amplification. Each repetition qualifies the significance of earlier portions of narrative and gradually constructs a perspectival whole—here an image of the chivalric character—that by its nature prevents a simple definition. Orlando possesses the fundamental traits of the hero; Rinaldo is, by contrast, merely human. Orlando must contend with his pride; Rinaldo must simply control his temper. Or-lando's history makes sense as a progress of the soul; Rinaldo's as the development of a social being. Throughout Part 1 Pulci creates a sense of perspective through near repetitions that also exhibit crucial differences. It is correct to say that in the first twenty-three cantos of the poem hardly a single image of any importance stands alone, without its counterpart, and unqualified by comparisons and contrasts.

The politicization of the figure of Rinaldo continues to be a feature of the *Morgante*. It is expressed allusively in the next episodes (which also appear in the *Orlando*): Rinaldo acquires a guide, a lion whom he saves from a dragon, and defeats a second dragon who threatens the Princess Forisena (v). The iconographic significance of a lion is particularly rich in the context of a Florentine work. The lion was the city's totem animal as well as an attribute of Hercules, the beast's legendary acuity of vision ideally suited to a hero who exemplified *ragione*. Both Hercules and the lion were associated with the sun, a connection Pulci respects here when the lion guides Rinaldo out of a dark wood (5. 36). The defeated dragon may have once had associations with Milan. In early fifteenth-century Florentine accounts of the war against the city, it was identified as the serpent-like creature who, on the shield of the Visconti, is about to swallow a human figure.[20] In Rinaldo's two victories over dragons for the relief of the lion and of Forisena, something of this old struggle (although resolved at the time of the *Morgante*'s composition) may be recorded.

Rinaldo's deliverance of the lady Forisena confirms his character as an intellectual hero. The adventure generally recalls Perseus's rescue of Andromeda (Forisena is to be an annual tribute) and, in several of its details, Hercules' rescue of Hesione, as well as his killing the hydra. The two heroes are closely connected in mythology—Hercules is Perseus's grandson, and in mythography—they each represent rational thought. Their common interest in dragons further unites them; dragons, serpents, and hydra (in short, water creatures) were conventionally held to represent error and to disappear before heroes who possessed the sunlike quality of reason. Like Hercules' victory over the hydra, Perseus's rescue of Andromeda is often allegorized as the triumph of virtue over vice through prudence or foresight. In Perseus's case prudence is figured in his shield, obviously an image of a reflected light, or the process of reflection.[21] And in fact Rinaldo conquers the dragon because he plans ahead: he fashions an iron glove by which Uliviero can grasp the beast's fiery head. Elements of the myth of Hercules' rescue of Hesione may be present when Uliviero plunges his arm deep into the dragon's throat (Hercules descends into the dragon's belly) and when Rinaldo gives Forisena to Uliviero (Hercules gives Hesione to Telamon). In any case, the action clearly recalls the main features of traditional allegorizations of these classical heroes of reason, and its conclusion suggests that Rinaldo's *ragione* has a political reference: the dragon pursuing Forisena has embodied the vengeful spirit of King Corbante's brother, murdered by the king himself, and by killing it Rinaldo effectively eliminates the vendetta from the sphere of a rational politics. The action thus corroborates earlier visions of a Providential history. Rinaldo orders the dragon's head to be placed outside the city walls as a sign to

future generations, "al secol nuovo," where it will function ap-
otropaically, to ward off its own spirit from the life of the city (4. 78).[22]

But Rinaldo's efforts to deliver the city from its dragon of error and
therefore to provide it with a future to be determined in a rational
manner are finally inconclusive, not in the perspective of his own life of
reason, but in a second perspective established by his foil Uliviero.
Rinaldo saves Forisena, but Uliviero kills her with unrequited love. Pulci
marks this shift in the context of his story by establishing a difference in
point of view: Rinaldo sees Forisena as a heavenly creature, "angelica,"
"modesta," but to Uliviero she is a creature who shines and burns. Their
shared passion is expressed in terms of the courtly tradition (especially
4. 79–88) and in parodic echoes of Dante's representation of the fatal love
of Paolo and Francesca (4. 80; cf. *Inf.* 5. 103).[23] When Forisena sees
Uliviero departing, she falls from her balcony, the victim of the blind
archer: "Amore è quel che lo consente" (5. 18).[24] This rather farcical
episode nevertheless has thematic importance as an exercise in perspectivism, for the limitation of Rinaldo's achievement by the effects of
Uliviero's love is presented in terms which suggest the passage of time.
Forisena is characterized as sunlike and her fall is thus in a sense natural.
Here the drama of love and death is closely synchronized with the
sequence of day and night. What threatens to undo Rinaldo's achievements is not therefore some force specifically inimical to reason but
rather one associated with temporality.

The adventure of Merediana (iv) relates thematically to earlier episodes which have created for Orlando and Rinaldo their significance as
embodiments of the complementary virtues appropriate to chivalry:
faith or humility before God's creations, the social order and Christian
history; and reason or temperance. These characters are now deployed
in an adventure depicting a struggle to achieve the most elementary
form of social order—agreement among friends and allies—in a political
situation threatened with violent change. The adventure is bipartite and
constructed to present a thesis and its antithesis. At issue is the safety of
the princess Merediana, who is rescued from destruction by acts of
concord exemplifying *philia* or fraternal affection, but subsequently lost
by acts of discord that have their basis in *eros* or erotic love. In the first
part, the paladins together foil Gano, who, as the embodiment of discord, opposes Merediana; in the second, Gano is the victor, triumphing
because Uliviero, in love with Merediana, violates the harmonious
bonds of fellowship. All the action reflects on the previous narrative or
the past of the story and its representation of the generational model of
temporality. It exposes the debilitating consequences of *eros*, the force
motivating acts of generation, and shows precisely how the literal heart

of human history is ambivalently constituted, its capacity for biological creativity limited by the destructiveness of passion. In a sense the adventure addresses the idea of history at its most fundamental level.

The action which results in an alliance between the paladins and Merediana is predicated upon the various ways in which she is perceived by them and by Manfredonio. To no one does she appear in the same light. To Manfredonio she is an oxymoron: she is "gentile" and elicits his love, yet she is also "cruda" because she rejects him. He persuades himself that he loves her in the courtly manner: "not because of her beauty, her actions or speech, but because of her virtues . . . through her I am made both noble and courteous" ("non per vista, per atti o per parole, / ma per le sue virtù . . . / per lei son fatto e gentile e cortese", 2. 68). By describing his love in the terms conventional to the *dolce stil nuovo,* Manfredonio ritualistically endows himself with the attributes of such a lover. But by the act of beseiging his beloved—"I will get her with my lance" ("colla lancia intendo d'acquistarla", 2. 65)—he explicitly betrays his courtliness and reveals the exploitative, combative, and essentially Ovidian character of his affection. At first Orlando uncritically accepts Manfredonio's interpretation of this love. He is delighted by the prospect of war and the chivalric gear—tents, horses, armor—in Manfredonio's camp. Hiding his true identity under the name of "Brunoro," he agrees to substitute for Manfredonio in a duel to win Merediana from whatever champion she can persuade to fight for her. Like Manfredonio, he disguises his sexual brutality in the trappings of courtly love.

To Rinaldo, on the other hand, Merediana appears as truly distant, regal, and in command of "every gentle act." He associates her with Diana and "Palla" (or Minerva), goddesses of chastity, the chase (the pursuit of fame), and wisdom, and thereby reflects his Herculean devotion to reason and to fame (6. 8, 9). Uliviero, by contrast, sees Merediana as a Venus, a second sun who brings to life inert matter and, like Forisena, burns more that she enlightens (6. 17, 18). These differences in perception suggest the direction the action must take. It is not until the paladins can agree together to support Merediana that she will truly be their ally and free from the danger posed by Manfredonio's misconceived passion. Here Pulci overtly exploits the image of perspective as a structuring device to define the subject of the adventure: concord, the reflexive intelligence through which disparate points of view are gathered into coherent patterns of meaning to make agreement among individuals possible. He begins by establishing radically different points of view but finally show them in meeting in a single point of concurrence.

Manfredonio's self-deception is obviously the result of his passion and indicates his intemperance, but the nature of his mistake is also conveyed in allegory. In realistic terms Merediana is emotionally ambivalent, but as a symbol her doubleness is the basis of her moral nature. It is fully revealed when Orlando, taking Manfredonio's part against Merediana's supposed champion who is in fact the lady herself, splits her martial helmet and allows her venerian golden hair to appear:

> anzi pareva di Venere iddea,
> anzi di quella che è fatta un allora,
> anzi parea d'argento, anzi pur d'oro.

> (3. 17)

thus she appeared the image of Venus and also of that lady who was transformed into a laurel [Daphne (whose chastity may make her a surrogate for the disdainful Diana mentioned in 6. 8)]; thus she seemed of silver and of gold.

To Orlando, Merediana appears as a *Venus armata*, a figure conventionally representing concord.[25] Her significance is augmented by virtue of her name—she is a sundial or, Janus-like, the point of midday. As a complex whole, she clearly represents the possibilities of reconciliation within time. Manfredonio's actions confirm that he has not interpreted this image correctly. He is attracted by Merediana's charm (Venus), yet he cannot respect her disdain (Diana); he fights her as an armed enemy (Diana) without appreciating her womanly weakness (Venus). He cannot unify these diverse impressions to form the idea of a single though many-sided character who requires a variety of responses. Orlando begins to be educated in the virtue Manfredonio lacks when, after seeing that he fights a lady, he walks away from the duel, but it is not until he meets Rinaldo as Merediana's ally that he abandons Manfredonio's cause altogether.

The significance of Rinaldo's perception of Merediana as an object of chivalric inspiration rather than desire is conveyed in two separate episodes, both of which refer to previous images and moments in the poem. To defend Merediana properly Rinaldo believes he must fight "Brunoro," whom Malagigi has identified to him as the erring Orlando. At the same time, he hesitates to fight his friend and ally, who knows him only as the "knight of the lion." The dilemma is resolved by the lion who, in the middle of the duel, breaks his cord and causes Orlando to call for a truce (6. 46). The poet of the *Orlando* attributes the lion's escape to divine will—Christ wishes to perform a miracle to bring the two paladins to recognize each other—but Pulci's additions supply the incident with a psychological reference. In the *Morgante*, it is divinely willed "that he [Rinaldo] *remember* their friendship [between him and Orlando]" ("perché de'suoi amici si ricorda", 6. 45). This is, of course, what Orlando, in his state of ignorance, cannot perceive. The episode's play on *corda* and its derivatives *ricorda, discorda* (actually a false etymology: *ricordare* etc. derive from the Latin *cor,* heart) emphasize the theme of social harmony and its dependence on acts of remembering or, more generally, on a sense of communal history. It is appropriate that the burden of memory falls here on Rinaldo. Not only does he represent rationality but, Pulci implies, he may be suffering from an excessive love of the worship, "fama," Merediana has inspired in him, and require a lesson in the exercise of reason, in this instance exemplified in the act of recollection. Rinaldo's truce with his enemy is the result of his willingness to put his desire for combat in the perspective of past relationships. This sequence of events as a whole conveys with particular clarity the association of images of perspective with concepts of time and history. Merediana promotes the welfare of the fellowship by providing the occasion for concerted action, but such action is only possible when the paladins are aware of the meaning of their histories, both as individuals and as members of a collectivity.

The truce of the lion (who has demonstrated his acute vision) then provides the context in which Rinaldo's reason, clarified by memory, can bring about Orlando's return to the company of the paladins. This depends on another mode of rational activity, the act of disclosing. Gano has written both Manfredonio and Caradoro to tell them they are allied with Christians. Caradoro discloses the contents of this letter to Rinaldo, who in turn summons Orlando to Caradoro's court in order to reveal to him that he, Rinaldo, is the "knight of the lion." The incident is climaxed by the symbolic act of removing helmets, which leads to a mutual recognition. Orlando calls his discovery of Rinaldo "graceful": " 'grazia è questa, ch'io t'ho qui trovato' " (7. 9). Once again in fellowship ("in compagnia"), Orlando perceives the true nature of Manfredonio's quest, and his allegiance shifts to Merediana. The episode as a whole illustrates the effects of Merediana's presence among the paladins. A logical extension of the use of perspective, it conveys the importance of acts of disclosure that open to each paladin a vista of relationships and enable him to see himself not as unique but part of a community of persons. It thus reflects constructively upon the social fragmentation that followed the angry departure of the principal paladins from Carlo's court and prepares for their return.

Now allied to Merediana and thus symbolically to her virtue, Orlando can reject Manfredonio and restrain his own martial impulses that this association symbolized. He does this paradoxically but nonetheless in keeping with the allegorical demands of the story: he curbs Morgante in their subsequent war with Manfredonio. The giant's only weapon is a bell-clapper ("battaglio"), a toy to play at battle ("battaglia"), and so equipped he appears to be the martial spirit incarnate, desiring agonistic encounters for their own sake, not for a military end. Orlando, asserting that "there is always harm in fighting" ("sempre è nel combatter danno", 7. 35), opposes the giant in this venture and finally, as Manfredonio is folding his tents and signals defeat, orders the giant to put his clapper down: "we have enough dead for one day" ("assai morti n'abbiàn per questo giorno", 7. 86). Orlando's words indicate that he has come to terms with the gigantic pride and self-will that have brought about his self-imposed exile from Carlo's court, a process that parallels Rinaldo's more prosaic experience of self-control.

Merediana's emblematic nature is most powerfully revealed in her reconciliation with Manfredonio, whom she convinces to return home. In the most telling point in her argument she expresses the essence of her double nature as temporality and temperance, and demonstrates how an acceptance of the condition and the virtue are one. She argues that all sorrow diminishes if it is accepted, and that he who would force an issue to his liking finds disappointment. Only time ("il tempo") can truly fulfill the wishes of a present moment (7. 77). She advocates a restraint that, because it imitates the measures of time, will find fitting rewards. She rejects the use of force because it violates a temporal order which is also a moral order. Even if the present, in being a time of loss, signifies the absence rather than the presence of gratification, it must be regarded as offering enough, for "heaven consents to give us no more" ("più oltre il Ciel non ci consente"). And finally she holds out the hope that he will return at a more auspicious time: "wait for both a better fate and circumstance" ("aspetta tempo e miglior fato e segno", 7. 78; see also 76). As a figure of concord, Merediana also establishes the moral conditions temporality imposes on the temperate. She symbolizes the temperance *in* temporality.

For Manfredonio, however, her words appear to have little meaning; nor do his guilt and despair seem dramatically inappropriate responses to his appalling situation. He dismisses her hope of a later meeting (7. 80), and his return to Soria, although it is compared to Menelaus's to Argos at the end of the Trojan war, is more desperate. Manfredonio's much reduced army does not even win its leader's "Helen" and his men accuse him of perverse desire (8. 6). The episode situates the image of Merediana in yet another perspective—one in which she seems curiously trivial and remote. Manfredonio is really beyond her powers of instruction. His grief is intractable.

The episodes describing Merediana's part in Manfredonio's defeat form Pulci's first major elaboration of the material of the *Orlando* and, more than any previous portion of the narrative, they convey the poet's concern that his poem be intelligible as a logically ordered sequence of events and not merely demonstrate his skill in manipulating the tropes of medieval rhetoric. Focusing on the figure of Merediana as an image of concord, he expresses what is only implied in the *Orlando:* that on the paladins' different perceptions of Merediana the motivation for the entire adventure depends. Her substitution for Morgante in the battle with the infidel, her final encounter with Manfredonio, his epic retreat are all Pulci's interpretative additions to his source. And in Manfredonio's skepticism he provides an affective link with the second half of Merediana's adventure, a dramatization of the way in which the paladins lose her as their ally.

### The Vice of Envy: The Violation of Princess Merediana

At Carlo's court and free from the restraints imposed on him by Orlando and Rinaldo, Gano writes the infidel king Erminion encouraging him to undertake a vendetta against Rinaldo and avenge the killing of Erminion's uncle, Mambrino. Caradoro pledges help to Carlo and sends Merediana and Morgante with a huge army to assist him. Beseiging Montalbano, Erminion loses his own kingdom which unites under a new leader, Faburro, who then forms an alliance with the paladins Rinaldo and Orlando. Erminion's most powerful knight, Leofante, deserts him and he finally admits to Rinaldo that his vendetta was wrong. Before Gano is forced into hiding for his part in this adventure, he reveals to Caradoro that Merediana is pregnant. Caradoro sends his ambassador, a giant Vegurto, to ask for Merediana's return, but she denies Vegurto's claims and Uliviero complains of the giant's rudeness. Morgante kills Vegurto; Carlo is secretly displeased because the giant was an ambassador and he himself apparently ungrateful to Caradoro. Gano returns to court and Rinaldo and Uliviero quarrel. Carlo banishes Rinaldo, who is joined in his exile by Astolfo, and together they become thieves. Carlo arrests Astolfo, but Orlando and Rinaldo save him from hanging. Orlando persuades Rinaldo to forgive Carlo. Gano returns to court, Orlando leaves in disgust, and Gano persuades Carlo to banish Rinaldo. Gano arranges to arrest Ricciardetto, Rinaldo's brother, but Rinaldo saves him from hanging. Carlo and Gano flee, Rinaldo is crowned Emperor. (Merediana is deserted by Uliviero and Morgante escorts her back to her father.) (concludes i; vi)

The paladins' alliance with Merediana symbolically guarantees their return to Carlo's court and its consequent though momentary stability.

She enables them to complete the restoration of social order that was predicated on their moral education in Pagania (i). This is literally represented in the action describing the most dangerous of Gano's acts to date, his instigation of a siege of Rinaldo's castle at Montalbano, a threat which Rinaldo and Orlando meet and overcome. In the process Gano is exiled, Carlo's enemy becomes his ally, and the court is at a point of equilibrium. At stake here is again the status of the vendetta, now perceived as the expression of a misguided human (rather than heroic) will, setting itself against Providence. Given the terms of the Boethian theory of history the poem has established as its norm, Gano's ruse and Erminion's attack on France appear to be acts of pride, a fact the chastened Erminion admits when, decrying his own ambition, he regrets trusting too much in fortune (10. 68). The story is formulaic, a version of the typical story of the fall of a famous man. In its evident triteness it is even disappointing, a confirmation too pat of a vision of history that, by virtue of Pulci's perspectivizing technique, is even now beginning to be felt as complex.

There are ways, however, in which the episode exhibits its own kind of ambiguity. This is virtually the effect of Pulci's irony, a mode of representation he adumbrates in the scene of Manfredonio's departure but here makes explicit as a property of his own analysis of the history he writes. Erminion himself touches on the irony of his case in the simplest terms: "[N]ow my horrible plan is revealed; the conclusion of everything shows us what it really is" ("Or si cognosce il mio bestial disegno:/ogni cosa ci mostra il fine aperto", 10. 68). That is, only through reflection is the real nature of human desires known. In the difference between the envisaged goal and the realized end is registered the historian's awareness that retrospectively attributes an ironic intention to the failed plan or program, which he then perceives as a "bestial disegno."

Such an awareness characterizes the entire conclusion to the adventure that begins with the paladins' departure from Carlo's court and ends with their return, that is, with the episode of Erminion's defeat. It is evidenced in the symbolic drama that is played out between Merediana and Gano, and in the more realistic drama of Erminion's fall. Both are brought into focus by the traitor Gano, whose function it is to bring discord where Merediana has established concord. At its most abstract, the opposition between the two characters is fairly simple: in Merediana's adventure the paladins espouse her cause, win her liberty and, by foiling the stratagems of Gano who embodies the spirit of divisiveness, make her their ally. Under her aegis they return to France in harmony. But in Erminion's episode these alliances are tested by Gano's machinations and at its conclusion they are actually undone. Gano triumphs, at least for a time. Like Merediana, Gano is associated with temporality, although in him its effects are negative. If Merediana stands for the power that brings about concord through respect for the past and, conversely, by a beneficial forgetting, Gano embodies a restlessness, a perpetual untimeliness—"he doesn't rest for a moment" ("non si posa un'ora", 8. 14)—that destroys all possibility of repose and reflection. The verses describing his behavior in general play with words containing the word bond, *corda* (see above on 6. 46), and attribute Gano's love of *discordia* to his lack of pity, *misericordia* (8. 17).

Erminion's fate hangs on this power of Gano to create discord. Pulci emphasizes that Merediana's father Caradoro lends his aid because he is remembering, *ricordare*, past favors (9. 55, 66), an act that ironically parallels Erminion's remembering past affronts. Moreover the irony in this case is double. Not only is Erminion's memory faulty—he later admits that his uncle's death was not the result of treachery—but he is himself made to suffer the effects of political discord. By allowing Gano to determine his course of action, he becomes Gano's victim. Besieging Montalbano, he loses his own kingdom which, uniting under a new leader, Faburro, forms an alliance with the paladins. Erminion himself is left totally isolated and without support. The act of remembering, presented in a positive light in an allegory of temperance, here has a negative effect. Erminion would clearly have done better to forget.

Gano is also the victor over the spirit of chivalric concord in a second and subtler conflict. By disclosing to Caradoro that Merediana's virtue is actually scandalous—she has become Uliviero's concubine—he effectively removes her from the poem. Caradoro protests that a trust has been violated and he becomes Carlo's enemy. He sends his ambassador, a giant Vegurto, to ask for Merediana's return, but she denies Vegurto's claims and Uliviero complains of the giant's rudeness (10. 140). Nevertheless the enormous ambassador seems accurately to figure the extent of Caradoro's insult and the grossness of the "errore" in love to which Uliviero has earlier confessed. When Morgante kills Vergurto he compounds these differences and increases the distance between infidel and Christian, Caradoro and Carlo, Merediana and Uliviero. The lady grieves for the ambassador; Uliviero is "too happy" at his death; and the emperor is secretly displeased because the giant was an ambassador and he himself apparently ungrateful to Caradoro (10. 153). Thus the moment of the apparent reestablishment of the stability of Carlo's court is brief and, more important, deceptive.

Gano's tactics are subversive of the very *means* by which social harmony is created. Throughout the adventure, images of revelation and disclosing have signified the possibility of concord. Gano's betrayal of Merediana's love, producing discord, is obviously a limiting case. In that this action, in its effects, conforms to the pattern of oppositions that her entire story exhibits, it can be said to fulfill a logical function and to be consistent as allegory. If Merediana embodies the complex concept of temperance in temporality, she must in theory submit to periods characterized by passion, ambition, envy. That she is made to exist in time means that, like her predecessor Forisena, she will suffer eclipses: that she does not always prevail is a limitation that perfectly illustrates her nature.

Gano's act of disclosure has a thematic function as well. It reveals that the premises of chivalric behavior are in some instances subject to contradiction. Actions which reveal a knight's identity or intention, often exemplified by a disarming, are celebrated as the foundation of chivalric society. In contrast, those which make his love a public matter are forbidden according to the convention of courtly love. Gano's violation of the code, a type of action popular in the tradition of chivalric romance, calls into question any simple evaluation of the quality of frankness and reveals how the complex ways in which a chivalric character is expected to behave are subject to exploitation by his enemies. By eclipsing Merediana, Gano demonstrates that his power to divide a fellowship is based on an abuse of practices, honesty and frankness, which in other situations strengthen it. The allegory itself suggests that this irony is a feature of temporal existence and that the transvaluations the apparently stable functions of remembering and disclosing have undergone are due not to Gano's ill-will but rather to time, whose character he has in some measure already assumed: "non si posa un'ora."

Pulci brings his first great sequence of adventures (i–v, i') to a close by an episode in which the hierarchy of Carlo's court is challenged by Rinaldo but maintained, although precariously, by Orlando, who in this way demonstrates that he is cured of his madness. It is paired with its opposite, an episode which initiates the action of the second sequence of adventures (vi–vi') and reveals the disruptive effects of Rinaldo's ambition. Both episodes, examining the nature of the contract between lord and vassal, introduce to the conception of the court as a locus of political order a new set of considerations.

The topic is common to the French romances of the Montauban cycle where it is often associated with the figure of Rinaldo, the type of altruistic renegade, a Robin Hood who defends the rights of the common people against the tyranny of lords and magistrates—he is a republican within imperial ranks.[26] The *Orlando*'s account of Rinaldo's ambition, the basis for the second episode, emphasizes this aspect of Rinaldo's character. But for Pulci, these passages in his source must have proved problematic in ways quite apart from his concern with historiography. The anonymous poet was content to sketch in his characters only their obvious features; his poem was therefore free from the threat of inconsistencies of character. But Pulci had given his Rinaldo certain well-defined traits and a moral significance in earlier cantos; in writing this conclusion to Carlo's adventure, therefore, he had to devise a way of deploying a character who exemplified reason and civic strength of Florence in actions originally assigned to a rebel. He attempted to solve the problem by adding an episode in which Rinaldo's rebelliousness, not entirely irrational in the *Orlando* where Carlo demonstrates a foolish irascibility and relies on Gano, is contained by the efforts of Orlando who restores Carlo to his throne. Pulci's addition precedes and, by showing Rinaldo as tractable, qualifies the portrait of this hero who in his source is merely rebellious.

Both episodes represent different and conflicting positions in an argument on the nature of imperial rule. Rinaldo's rebelliousness (vi), a manifestation of his own ambition, is dramatically expressed by his exile of the Emperor and his own coronation and can be justified by taking a republican position. Rinaldo's action is made to appear sympathetic by Orlando, the exponent of political order in the previous adventure (i'), who leaves Carlo's court never to return after Carlo, again showing a dangerous affection for Gano, has repudiated Rinaldo for a second time (12. 37). This would seem to indicate a sympathy for the idea of government based on some sort of reciprocity between ruler and ruled, and it recalls the position on tyrants voiced earlier in the century by Bruni's fictional "Niccoli," a speaker in his *Dialogi*. Niccoli punctuates his dislike of tyrannical government by qualifying Dante's decision to condemn Brutus and Cassius; he states that Dante's condemnation is acceptable only on theoretical grounds, for, he claims, Dante could not have condemned one who had been praised by the Senate as a "restorer of liberty" ("recuperator libertatis"). He adds that Dante's "Caesar" is *not* the person represented in historical record but rather a political entity, a figure who wielded royal power and was worthy of respect for this reason.[27] On the other hand, Orlando's loyalty to the Emperor and all that it entails (i') suggests a position that would have found favor with such friends of Lorenzo's as Landino, who, while he accepted Bruni's criticism of Dante, also took seriously the notion of empire and judged it to be part of a Providential plan. As a defense of imperial rule, however, Pulci's depiction of Orlando's compassion and devoted loyalty to Carlo is felt to be weak. It hinges on a concept of time that the poem has already implicitly discredited—that events in history are in some way repeatable. It actually uses a plot of a mythical return: Carlo plays the part of Virbius, or *vir bis*, returning from the dead as if he were one of the fairy kings of romance, defined by tradition as an immortal restricted to a life in time.

The temptation to think in such terms was, admittedly, inherent in what we might call the imperialist position. It was a theoretical advantage to historians arguing against republican government that they could point to the phenomenon known as *translatio imperii,* the succession of empires from (as Dante would have it) Crete, to Troy, to Rome, and then to modern Rome. For thus the empire was both coextensive with time and recreated in time. The phenomenon suggested that such a state was part of the divine order of things, whether or not it could also be considered a vehicle for the fulfillment of God's purpose in history. Augustine's distinction between the *civitas terrena* and the *civitas dei* did not rule out the possibility that in the former society saw its best opportunity to organize its pilgrimage through this world in a manner conducive to a spiritual Christendom. It merely prevented any direct identification of the purposes of the two states. On the other hand, historians apologizing for republican government had to contend with the evidence that pointed to the instability of states which depended on a constitution designed to control the behavior of rulers as well as ruled. Until a notion of the natural rights of citizens and of a contractual form of government was developed (as it was in the seventeenth century), no notion of universality could be made easily to fit a defense of such states.

Carlo's behavior in both episodes is predicated on what we might call an obsession with empire—a ruler's intense longing for a stability so profound that it would prevent change of any sort. In Carlo's case this obsession has a tragic consequence. Because it is further determined by an uncritical (but human) fear of change and by the corollary perception that Gano is in some sense an index of his own ability to survive in time without change, it conduces to its ironic opposite. Carlo's wish for stability is deceptively met by Gano's nearly continuous presence at court; actually it is frustrated by his treachery. By creating for Carlo a semblance of stability Gano effectively discourages the moral attentiveness that prevents (inevitable) change from becoming catastrophic. Carlo's misunderstanding of Gano is in effect a misunderstanding of the nature and challenge of temporality. In the first episode this failing is compensated for by Orlando's *virtù,* which successfully returns Carlo to his throne and gives a dramatic reality to the notion that the history of empire can be narrated in terms, however figurative, of a myth of return. In the second its resolution is postponed by the effects of Rinaldo's ambition. The reestablishment of hierarchical order and the stability of Carlo's court that occurs at the end of the second sequence of adventures is, moreover, problematic.

The irony that colored the aggression of Manfredonio and Erminion now reappears in Carlo's effort to rule with Gano at his side. Despite Gano's part in Erminion's invasion, he anticipates that Gano will serve him well, as he did in earlier times, "pel tempo antico" (11. 5). Gano's reappearance at court always signals an end to its harmony and in this instance Rinaldo and Uliviero quarrel. Carlo, banishing Rinaldo, neither suspects the duplicity in Gano nor the dark side of things in general. His wish "not to doubt more" ("sanza più dubitar", 11.8) implies that he has renounced any obligation to be critical, to examine events in all their contingency. His complacency is challenged by what the occasion then demands of him, a historian's appreciation of the particular circum-stances that give an event its significance, a faculty that grounds judg-ment in careful analysis rather than the application of formulae. Pulci likens this restraint to the virtue of compassion.

When Astolfo is arrested, both Carlo and Gano voice *sententiae* that reflect timeless moral standards: without justice a city withers, after the sweet must come the bitter and so forth (11. 56, 61). To these abstractions Astolfo responds with a casuistic argument; he stresses his long service at court, his father's loyalty to the crown (11. 63, 67). His observations create for his crimes a historical context and show the inflexibility and hence the inadequacy of simple justice. He links the act of remembering, *ricordare*, with forgiveness, *avere pietà*, repeatedly invokes the example of Jesus, and couples Gano with Judas. In his apostrophe to Carlo, Pulci suggests that the Emperor's lack of mercy will cause God to judge him in a similiar fashion.

The conclusion to the episode exhibits once again the perspectivizing technique by which the poet offers his readers an impression of his subject as a complex whole that can only emerge through the process of reading his poem. Having elected to administer justice, that is, to ignore Astolfo's plea for mercy, Carlo is saved by an act of mercy. Orlando, concerned lest Rinaldo kill the emperor and "spoil the court" ("che guasta sarebbe la corte", 11. 119), tells Rinaldo of a dream he has had of the dead Carlo (11. 123), which so moves Rinaldo that he agrees to forgive the Emperor. Orlando then arranges Carlo's return from hiding as if from the dead—"Carlo seems dead from grief" ("per dolor [Carlo] non parea vivo,")—and the court celebrates his reappearance and ascent to the throne (11. 132). Orlando's merciful lie demonstrates that political order is not the result of the application of rule to case, as Carlo believes, but rather of the assent of those who submit to authority. It waits on acts which shape opinion and solicit agreement. His action recalls the Aristo-telian distinction between justice, which is inherently abstract and math-ematical, and equity, which depends on the interpretation of a particular situation and consequently involves participants as subjects.[28]

As an example of historiography, however, the episode is obscure. Pulci is obviously at pains to establish an image of empire that fulfills the expectation that such a state is not only stable but coextensive with time. But he has also committed himself to the proposition which defines a critical and disciplined assessment of particular events as a historiographic norm. Not only does he show Astolfo's casuistry in a positive light by contrasting it to Gano's harsh legalism, but he also presents Carlo's return as the consequence of a ruse exploiting a rhetorical fiction, the notion of a *vir bis*. As a result, he demystifies the idea of imperial renewal, imagined as the return of the "dead" emperor, and implies the immutable fact of death in human life. The action comments—at a level more abstract than that addressed by Morgante wishing to imitate Orpheus (2. 38)—on the limited extent to which Christians can expect to enjoy a stability in time. Here Pulci seems to raise the possibility of renascence (in imagery that specifically recalls the return of the mythical Arthur) in part in order to characterize it as a fiction.

In contrast, the action describing Ricciardetto's arrest and rescue, which precipitates Rinaldo's exile of Carlo, reemphasizes what the entire first sequence of adventures (i–i') has implied: that historical events are unique and unrepeatable. At Carlo's restoration, Gano is once more banished from Carlo's court but, correctly reckoning that Carlo still trusts him "in the old way" ("al antico modo", 12. 4), immediately persuades the Emperor to ask him back. That Carlo goes on trusting Gano indicates his willingness to believe in the possibility of an absolutely recoverable past, an infinitely repeatable present. When Orlando observes that Carlo cannot live without Gano for even an hour (12. 13), the kind of continuity the traitor symbolizes to Carlo is more than ever evident. That he invariably acts in conjunction with a hostile fortune comments on its deceptiveness. As instances of peripetia, the results of Gano's activity testify to the real nature of time as changeful. The traitor's ironic function is to signal stability and to signify its converse.

The action imitates that of the previous episode but with inversion. Orlando does not intervene to save Carlo from Rinaldo's anger, Carlo is forced into exile, and Rinaldo is crowned amidst feasting. The celebration is marred by Orlando's absence, which he intends to make permanent (12. 37). In fact he does return later to help Carlo against another infidel invasion (vi'), but his departure here, and the sadness it provokes in Rinaldo, obliquely comments on the nature of Rinaldo's rule. It does not constitute a legal succession. The queens he proposes to take— Carlo's wife Gallerana, or his own mother Beatrice—suggests that he usurps a father's place and commits an act of political incest.

The conflict just described in these two episodes—between a lord, characterized as feeble or inept, and his young powerful vassals—is typical in narratives of the matter of France and the matter of Britain. Both Arthur and Charlemagne suffer periodic attacks of one or another form of incompetence. The popular cycle relating the exploits of Renaud de Montaubon, later the Rinaldo of the Italian narratives, particularly focuses on the nature and circumstances of this struggle. In the *Morgante* Pulci makes of Rinaldo's coronation, comprehensible yet also reprehensible, an event about which questions may be raised that are specifically applicable to the debate for and against republicanism among fifteenth-century historians in Florence. That the Emperor's rule is threatened by his own incompetence, upheld by his principal vassal who is later a defender of the church, usurped by his most troublesome vassal who incarnates reason, and finally restored by a fatal turn of events (Rinaldo is summoned to help Orlando in Pagania, action that begins the adventure of Chiariella, vii) is a logically inconsistent and confusing sequence of events. Nevertheless, it would have been comprehensible to Pulci's readers, both as a humanist critique of the idea of a God-willed universal empire and a refutation of that critique, authorized by custom and indicative of a mistrust of notions of government that appeared to give greater scope to the forces making for change. The ambivalence of the poem at this point recalls Salutati's self-contradiction late in the previous century. While defending the ideal of republicanism and the *vita activa* in his letters, he also wrote *De tiranno*, a vindication of Caesar's dictatorship: "For so many misfortunes, so much injustice will as a rule follow upon a change in the order of state that it is better to endure anything whatever rather than court the danger involved in change."[29]

The last phase of the conclusion to Merediana's adventure, which appears later in the narrative as an episode in the adventure of the Chiariella (vii), provides the final comment on these adventures and aptly illustrates the conditions under which Pulci will envisage the survival of the political entities, empires and monarchies, whose histories, however romanticized, he relates. Abandoned by Uliviero who has gone again to fight in Pagania, Merediana instructs Morgante to tell Uliviero where she is, so he may return to her in her own country, "for she remains unhappy and wretched" ("che rimanea scontenta e meschinella", 18. 111). But in fact she fades from the narrative and is heard of no more. Restored to her country and her throne, yet hurt by a discourteous love and anticipating an illegitimate succession, she exemplifies the problematic state of the virtue of temperance in temporality. The characters who are models of chivalry have been unable to guarantee the stability of Carlo's court; the codes by which they govern themselves have not functioned well or consistently. These characters have been subject to erotic desire and perhaps an even more compelling desire for changelessness, for a kind of immortality. Their codes provide for a continuity of chivalric life that is constantly violated, that endures in a state of having been violated.

The theory of history established by the action of the first sequence of adventures is essentially Boethian and generally implies the eternity of empire transcending instances of loss and death while at the same time also suffering them. This emphasis on the eternity of empire that comprehends both a triumph over change and the pathos of experiencing it does not render the *Morgante* anachronistic but, on the contrary, all the more a product of Florentine fifteenth-century culture. While some humanist historians writing early in the century, such as Bruni and Salutati, saw Florence in its origins and periods of self-defense against the Visconti as heir to the Roman republic's *libertas*, other historians, such as Villani, Dati, Salutati (who, as we have seen, reverses himself), and later Acciaiuoli, Landino and Verino, celebrated the city's connection with the traditions of the empire, centralized rule, and a hierarchical society. In Lorenzo's Florence, the case for such an imperial connection was bound to be polemical. The Medici obviously had little interest in libertarian theories of government. Dependent on them for his livelihood, Pulci would have been prepared to subscribe to an imperialistic vision of the Florentine past and perhaps also future, as the octaves beginning the *Morgante* imply. In the interest of making this vision compelling, he evolves in part 1 of his poem a historical allegory in which the reader can perceive generally significant examples of moral and political behavior. Conceptually, such a narrative resembles humanist histories in which the past is valued chiefly as a repository of exempla to inspire and admonish the reader and to construct social and political paradigms. Yet he also includes in his poem, and increasingly as it progresses, certain passages in which the qualities of what will become the posthumanist historiography of Guicciardini and Machiavelli are already evident. He becomes absorbed in analyzing events that demonstrate the ambiguity of fortune, the definitive importance of circumstance, the role of fiction(s) in determining reality, the irony of desire.

# 3

## TYPICAL ADVENTURES

THE paradox that time both maintains and destroys life is doubtless ancient. In Ovid's *Metamorphoses*, Pulci would have encountered an extended meditation on it and perhaps specifically noted the odd ambiguity in Pythagoras's description of the effects of time, where the philosopher asserts that time devours everything and that nothing is lost.[1] Both propositions are, in any case, vital to Pulci's vision of history. The action in the first twenty-three cantos of the poem mediates these disparate experiences of time in stories that illustrate a heroic command of temperance. The virtue is brilliantly exemplified in Merediana, who survives and is generative although she is abandoned and violated. In her oxymoronic union of human creativity and its limitation in death, she dramatizes the link between history and the technique of perspectivizing that has become the focus of the poet's interpretation of the events in his narrative. As her name indicates, she is a sundial, a figure in whom temporality or the passage of time is understood in spatial terms. Metaphorically she reveals that human beings apprehend what they call time only by way of local and particular phenomena, that time is an abstraction based on an experience of the contingent.

The adventures in Part 1, all of which describe the restoration of a monarch to his or her throne, exhibit certain repetitive features which may suggest their derivation from a single source: the hero confronts a situation in which a rightful king, queen, or princess associated with light is threatened; he rescues the sovereign; and he restores him or her to the throne. Love, if it plays a part, is subordinate to the main action. The lover, who is not a heroic character, functions in a negative or ironic capacity. This plot, which appears in the *Morgante* only by inference, resembles a myth of light, a myth that must also be, inevitably, a myth of return and therefore of time. In physical or scientific allegory, a comprehensive version of such a myth would describe diurnal, mensual, and annual time. The light-giving sovereign may be represented as a sun—he sets off day from night; as a moon—she measures each sequence of twenty-eight days; and as summer or the green half of the year—he (or she) establishes the succession of seasons. Allegorizations of the Ceres myth in such popular mythographies as Boccaccio's *Genealogie deorum gentilium* almost achieve such comprehensiveness; there Proserpina figures both the moon who returns from death and the spring moisture which revives her mother the earth; although she is never the sun, she is closely associated with it because she both reflects its light and arrives with longer days.

It is this mythic mediation of time that the successive realizations of the typical plot of the *Morgante* most appear to represent. Their parallels to the plots of particular myths need not be pressed too closely. What is important is the extent to which Pulci reinterprets elements of mythic plots to suit his purpose. Reduced to a simple form, Pulci's typical plot features a hero whose task is priestlike: he presides over the rebirth of heavenly lights and in a certain sense can be said to bring them back. Insofar as the plot can be seen to convey a moral experience—as it does in its various versions in the *Morgante*—the hero's experience resembles that of the novice in philosophical or religious study, struggling to develop the light within himself.[2]

Renaissance treatments of myths describing the return of light occur in literature of different kinds and, in the absence of specific references to any particular myth or myths, it is impossible to establish verifiable sources for the *Orlando* or for Pulci's own additions to the *Morgante*. Pulci alludes to the myth of Proserpina in the adventure of Florinetta (b), and the moralizing comments of its heroine suggest that he has in mind some popular allegorization, perhaps something like Berchorius's. In this case, he merely makes explicit what the plot of the poem has already expressed. Since the adventure is itself a close retelling of an earlier one, Uliva's (a), and evidently the poet's invention, the reader can regard it as proof that Pulci was sensitive to the mythological dimension of the *Orlando* (much less obvious than that of the *Morgante*), and that he enjoyed constructing allegories on the basis of it. What does seem worth examining is the status of such myths in relation to theories of time and temporality as they are described in representative early Renaissance mythographies and in works as authoritative to Renaissance readers as those of Vergil, Ovid, and Statius. These reveal that the notion of a return from darkness or death, in effect an eternal return, is treated with ambiguity. They therefore provide the historian with a rich set of allusions by which to refer to temporality as exhibiting both change and continuity.

Ambiguity with regard to the possibility of a second life on earth is a feature of the matter of Britain, where Arthur's death is sometimes presented as problematic. He may be healed by Morgan le Fay and the other ladies of the mysterious isle of Avalon, as the *Mort Artu* supposes; he may, on the other hand, have died a Christian, as Malory prefers to think.[3] While Pulci may not have known the *Mort Artu*, he probably was acquainted with the tradition of Arthur's doubtful end. He himself alludes to the possibility of Orlando's returning to live a second life, and also to the figure of Ogier, "il Danese," who waits at the edge of the world for the time when he will reenter it. From a Christian perspective, these possibilities must appear illusory; Morgan le Fay actually prefigures the Circe-like ladies who in later chivalric romances delay heroes in gardens of eternal spring. Her healing is thus ambiguous, in part expressing a fear of death, in part acknowledging death as a state mortals must accept. Pulci never hints that Carlo will return in his own person but we know the possibility was entertained figuratively in contemporary prophecies concerning the arrival in Italy of a second Charles. The image of a once and future king, though it had to be ruled out of serious consideration on doctrinal grounds, obviously appealed to historians and writers of political propaganda.

For readers of Latin literature the figure of a returned king is chiefly represented in Hippolytus or Virbius, who is variously described. Vergil's treatment of the figure in the *Aeneid* is as doubtful as it might be were he a Christian poet. Hippolytus appears as the father of Virbius, a warrior who fights with Turnus and also, a few lines later, as Virbius himself, renamed after his revival from the dead by Aesclepius at Diana's command.[4] This inconsistency seems intentional but what Vergil wishes it to signify is puzzling unless one assumes that he has committed himself to rewriting the myth as an account of generation: Hippolytus is only born again in his son. Servius, in his gloss to the passage, denies the truth of both possibilities and specifically states that Hippolytus was chaste and always lived alone. Virbius is, in his opinion, a name describing Diana's divine power, *numen*.[5] He does not mention Hippolytus when he explains that the grove sacred to Trivia (Diana) at Aricia is a place of sacrifice.[6]

On the other hand, the scholiast on Statius's third eclogue in *Silvae*, celebrating the completion of a temple to Hercules near this grove during the August dog-days, makes a crucial identification between Hippolytus and the fugitive priest-kings who preside over the altars of Diana at Aricia, although it is not present or implied in the text he is glossing. He declares that the returned Hippolytus is renamed Virbius *and* that he is the *rex Nemorensis*, the runaway who, sheltering in the grove, becomes its priest-king. The origin of this identification is not evident in the commentary; the scholiast merely states that Diana hid Hippolytus in the grove and, perhaps assuming that the runaway must also be in hiding, identifies Hippolytus as the king of the grove.[7] In any case, his representation of each of these kings as a single reborn hero protected by Diana perfectly illustrates the paradox of the once and future king.

In general, mythographers tend to be skeptical about, if not actually to discredit, the return of Hippolytus and other similar figures. The second Vatican mythographer, who describes the myth of Hippolytus as one of return, also notes that Vergil denies it. According to him Vergil believed that the hero "could not have escaped the condition of death."[8] The mythographer may be thinking of Servius rather than Vergil (or of Vergil's comment on Theseus) but the force of the objection he refers to is obvious: for human beings death must be final. And in fact Servius reaffirms this notion in his gloss on the *Aeneid* 6, where he casts doubt on Anchises' description of the underworld as a stage in an endlessly repetitive cycle of life for all except the few honored in Elysium. While Landino was later to link the passage reporting the return of souls to a second life with the doctrine of Pythagoras (cf. Ovid's rendition of Pythagorean doctrine in *Metamorphoses* 15)[9], Servius interprets Anchises' lines so that they seem to establish an eschatology. He interprets all aspects of Vergil's underworld as purgatorial and denies that it is eternal. Overlooking the implied meaning of these passages, he states that even the days in Elysium will come to an end, that Vergil's "the cycle of time completed" (perfecto tempori orbe, 6.345), means "the appointed time being over" ("finito legitimo tempore"). He later glosses Vergil's "They rolled the wheel [of time] for a thousand years," ("mille rotam volvere per annos," 6.348) as "they brought up to an end the required time through the flight of years" ("exegerunt statutum tempus per annorum volubilitatem"), and implies that time is fulfilled and history complete.[10] Vergil himself may be thought to give support to the view that time is irreversible when he writes that Theseus, whom Hercules descends to the underworld to rescue, is actually confined there forever.[11]

Ovid's account of metempsychosis in *Metamorphoses* 15 is, as I have suggested, similarly ambivalent. Pythagoras asserts that nothing dies, that all change is only apparent, and that the world is constantly self-recreating. But he also mentions the four ages of history, a testimony to a temporality that is irreversible. He stresses, moreover, that human experience is marked by a progressive deterioration. The individual hero suffers the decline of his faculties. And for Helen, the repetition of an event is ironic: her rape, first by Theseus and Pirithoos and then by Paris, is evidence of eroding time, *tempus edax rerum* (232–34). Ovid suggests a difference between real physical time which, embracing immense periods, is cyclical and the brief interval of a human life which is not. Helen's experience is typically human. The very theoretical nature of Pythagoras's analysis of physical time as cyclical makes his picture of human life comparatively realistic as well as pathetic.

The restorations of female in contrast to male figures in the *Morgante* recall the myth of Ceres and Proserpina. The connection between such restorations and the myth, explicit in canto 22 when Filisetta identifies herself as "Proserpina," is established by a common imagery. Like Proserpina, both Forisena and Merediana are associated with the sun and the moon; Uliva and Florinetta suggest vegetation. Both Ovidian versions of the myth emphasize its reference to time and state that Ceres gave agriculture its "laws" ("leges"), a record of the proper time to carry out agricultural tasks (5. 343). In the *Metamorphoses*, Ceres' legislation orders what the myth explains: the seasons of the year. Before Proserpina's rape, the world enjoys a perpetual spring (5. 390). This is ruined by Pluto who, moved by *eros*, seizes Proserpina gathering flowers with girlish eagerness ("puellari studio") and takes her underground. Ceres lights torches at Mount Aetna and searches over sea and land. Finding Proserpina's girdle in Sicily, she curses its soil and blights its seeds (5. 481). Jupiter tells Ceres that the fates have decreed that Proserpina can return to earth if she has eaten nothing in the underworld. But the simple girl ("simplex") has plucked a pomegranate and eaten seven of its seeds while wandering ("errat") in Pluto's garden. Her wilfulness, implied here, recalls her earlier enthusiasm for gathering flowers and emphasizes a connection between death and love as desire or *eros*. Jupiter consequently decides that Proserpina must spend half the year each above and below the ground, alternately loving and dying. Restored to earth, she reappears in the world as the sun from behind a cloud: "her face was changed immediately, both in its general character and its smile, just as the sun, having been covered by watery clouds, emerges victorious from them" ("vertitur extemplo facies et mentis et oris . . . ut sol, qui tectus aquosis / nubibus ante fuit, victis e nubibus exit", 5. 568–71). Ovid's image combines naturalistic detail with a suggestion of the conventional gesture of the bride unveiling herself before her husband. In the figure of Proserpina are united allusions to forms of return as well as to human sexuality. She is the light that brings on the summer and its crops; she is therefore the rebirth of the spring's greenery. She evokes both male and female, the sun and his bride the earth, and indicates a recreative harmony in a vision of opposites.

In the *Fasti*, Ovid follows a version of the myth celebrating the Eleusinian mysteries, where the theme of time and change is treated not in the context of the seasons but of mortality.[12] The goddess, having lost her daughter to Pluto, attempts to make immortal Triptolemus, a boy at Eleusis who is her foster child. She casts him in a fire to burn out the "burden of humanity" ("onus humanum", 4. 554). But she is thwarted in her efforts by the child's mother who cannot understand the strange manner in which the goddess confers her favors. Ceres decrees that Triptolemus will be mortal but also that he will be the first to cultivate the land. The conjunction of these two features of his existence distinguishes human from natural or vegetable time. Ceres honors Triptolemus but also underscores the very limitedness of his life that she had intended but was unable to overcome.

This version also poses what might be thought a third alternative—a state in which life and death are not clearly differentiated—and reveals that this state is not open to mortals. Before Ceres reaches Eleusis and the house of Triptolemus, she finds and eats a poppy to kill her hunger. She then administers the drug to the boy to bring on his sleep so that she can begin the purgative process which she believes will lead to his immortality. For Ceres, the drug has functioned merely as a sign of the famine of winter; she is the fasting earth and represents symbolically the condition of human beings in winter. She appears to starve, seems to die, and then returns to life. But for Triptolemus, the drug is not allowed to work; for unlike Ceres (or Adonis) he cannot participate in eternal recreation, either as a god of seasons or as seasonable vegetation. His fate is to be the object of a divine love that holds out the always vain hope of an earthly immortality in order to teach the discipline of temperance through an acceptance of temporality.

Servius had identified the myth as an allegory of seasons and his interpretation is followed by the Vatican mythographers for whom Proserpina signifies both the moon and its moisture.[13] This brings Ceres or the joys of harvest. As the moon, Proserpina divides time into months and years by growing and waning for six months each. As moisture she is drawn to earth by Pluto where she is sought with torches by Ceres, to whom hot days are sacred. She is also the grain which ripens in the earth for six months during the winter. As a goddess she is one of the three aspects of Diana, the others being Luna and Diana herself.

Boccaccio, drawing on Ovid's two accounts, follows the Vatican mythographers who read the myth as physical allegory.[14] But he also implies its relationship to the evolution of agriculture and to temperance. Ceres is first the earth, moon, and fruits of the earth.[15] After Proserpina is born from Ceres' union with Jupiter, *she* is the moon and also the grain which does not grow unless Ceres, now specifically the earth, is warmed by the sun, Jupiter. As grain, Proserpina vanishes when she is sown in the autumn, a time when the land is overcultivated, that is, at the end of its period of sustaining growth yet still too wet for seeds to germinate.[16] At this time Ceres, who is now embodied in farmers, breaks the tools of cultivation and sets the fields on fire to dry them out. These actions are signified in the goddess's destruction of Sicily and seem expressive of the laws of agriculture that Boccaccio, following Ovid, later states the goddess gave to the island.[17]

Boccaccio presents Jupiter's decision to divide the year in half as a sequel to the moment in which creation is threatened with an anomalous temporality, where darkness and light are indistinguishable and without fixed limits. Following the *Fasti* (but adding to the events it describes), Boccaccio relates that after Proserpina's rape Jupiter tells Ceres to eat a poppy and sleep: he will then restore Proserpina to her provided the girl has eaten nothing in the underworld. Jupiter can, of course, only fulfill his promise in part. With Proserpina's return he wakes Ceres, but his decision implies she will sleep again. Boccaccio interprets this event as a representation of the cessation of agricultural labor in winter and its resumption in spring: "By this repose is signified the cessation of cultivation so that the earth may recover its aridity."[18] The image expresses periodicity in relation to the possibilities of a perpetual winter and so complements the obvious significance of the myth. While Proserpina's loss indicates a finite summer, Ceres' awakening represents a finite winter and thus a control over a primitive terror of autumn as the death of the world. By establishing the restorative purpose of a fallow period, moreover, Boccaccio endows the myth with moral content. By veiling laws governing agricultural labor and setting limits to work and play, it refers to a self-cultivation ordered by temporality.

In general, mythographers allegorized myths describing the return of seasons so that their treatment of the passage of time was perceived to bear on the question of human hopes for immortality in one form or another. This association is developed in the adventures in the second major sequence of Part 1 (vi–vi'), which draw on several myths of return and further perspectivize not only the problem of moral behavior but also the problem of political stability.[19] The relationships depicted in this portion of the narrative fall into two distinct groups: those concerned with Chiariella, whom Orlando must save from the Sultan, and those concerned with Antea, whom Rinaldo must honor but not love. The chivalric loyalties of each are tested in relation to their ladies. In each case, the hero plays some portion of a part in a recognizable myth of return. The loosely repetitive action of the narrative gives it the dialectical form and thematic integrity I have described in Chapter 1.

### *The Preservation of Political Order: The Adventure of Chiariella*

Travelling into Pagania, Orlando encounters Chiariella, daughter of the Governor of Persia; she is beseiged by the Sultan of Babylon, who is assisted by a giant Marcovaldo, also enamored of the Princess. Orlando overcomes Marcovaldo in a battle, but when the Governor learns that Orlando is a Christian, he throws him in a dungeon. The Governor and the Sultan then join forces and agree to kill Orlando, whereupon the Sultan withdraws to Babylon. Chiariella falls in love with "the Christian," and they send to Rinaldo for help. On his way to rescue Orlando, Rinaldo delivers Marsilio's kingdom from the ravages of a wild horse. He falls in love with Luciana, Marsilio's daughter, who gives him a four-sided tent depicting all of creation and promises him twenty thousand men when he needs them. Rinaldo rescues Orlando, the Governor dies, and the Sultan sends his daughter Antea to plead his right to the Governor's throne. Rinaldo, now with Orlando and Chiariella, falls in love with Antea and, in a battle with her, forfeits Uliviero and his brother Ricciardetto as hostages. He pursues Antea to Babylon on foot (his horse is stolen after his battle with her) and at the Sultan's command he fights a wild man of the mountain, "il Veglio," in the understanding that this will earn him the freedom of Uliviero and Ricciardetto. Rinaldo converts the Old Man to his side. Antea meanwhile has left to besiege Montalbano. On the way she imprisons Gano. After some delay, Orlando leaves Chiariella as ruler in the father's place. He rescues the Princess Uliva from giants, and Morgante, having met the half-giant Margutte, rescues Princess Florinetta from giants. Morgante joins Orlando and Rinaldo to do battle with the Sultan. The Sultan is killed by the Old Man and Orlando is crowned in his place. Malagigi orders the paladins to rescue Gano, and Antea returns to Babylon which she finds desolate. (Adventures vii, viii, a, and b)

To give meaning to these adventures Pulci frequently relies on a range of mythological associations without necessarily identifying the action in them with any one myth. The reader has initially to ask whether the adventure resembles a myth of return and then how, if at all, such a resemblance gives it significance. In general, these adventures do not appear to be adequately motivated unless they are understood as versions of myth. Psychological factors do not in themselves provide intelligible explanations for the events that occur. At the same time, the allegory generated by these mythological associations is inconsistent rather than sustained. The tendency of the narrative to break off and then resume, or to change its mythological references and adopt a new imagery with different associations, gives it the episodic quality and layered texture of an interrupted dream-sequence where images will reappear and, because a single image may refer to more than one waking experience, often reveal multiple and even ambivalent or contradictory meanings.

The principal plot line of the adventure of Chiariella recalls that of

Merediana but as a complicated variation. The lady is again associated with light, since she shines more brightly than the morning star (12. 40). Yet because it is not only she but also Orlando who experiences a period of darkness—Orlando terms his prison an "inferno" (15. 69)—the story of her rescue must include an account of her male double who is to be restored to light as well. In fact, the plot in this portion of the narrative imitates a conflated version of two myths of return; the restoration of a lady of light is made to be contingent upon her hero's return from the underworld, a return made possible by the intervention of a brother hero.

In its most elementary form, the myth in which a hero rescues a brother hero from death tells the story of the Gemini; a more complex version, in which fraternal functions are doubled and the action motivated initially by the disappearance of a lady of light (in this case, Proserpina), is the myth of Hercules, Theseus, and Pirithoos. Because in this adventure it is Rinaldo, already termed a Hercules, who rescues Orlando, one can begin by asking whether this myth explains Rinaldo's part in Orlando's rescue.

Pulci has identified Rinaldo as Hercules to illustrate his rationality. Here, however, he concentrates on Rinaldo's possession of another of the mythical hero's characteristics: a love of fame.[20] While Rinaldo retains his rational character (when, in other words, he is not in love), he achieves a Herculean task: he rescues a brother from the prison of death; when, however, he falls in love with Antea, who is fame, he loses (temporarily) two of his real brothers to the enemy, the Sultan, who imprisons and threatens to kill them. The nature of this loss is important because it stands in ironic relation to his initial success. By loving fame, symbolized as the lady Antea, the Sultan's daughter and therefore his own beloved enemy, Rinaldo puts the lives of his brothers in jeopardy. That is, having rescued one brother he loses two. This irony is present in most interpretations of the myth of Hercules and Theseus.

Hyginus's version of Hercules' descent is the most complete and optimistic. Unlike other versions, he portrays Hercules saving both Theseus and Pirithoos; he also portrays this myth's retributive sequel, the Gemini's punishment of the heroes for their rape of Helen. As Theseus and Pirithoos have stolen her, so the Gemini steal their women.[21] Many later mythographers link the fate of Hercules, Theseus, and Pirithoos to that of the Gemini. The first Vatican mythographer, for example, while he does not explicitly associate Hercules with the twins, describes their descent in similar terms. In both accounts of descent and return, death claims one of the pair. Like the Gemini, only one of whom can live at a time, the friends Theseus and Pirithoos must in this version be parted by death. Hercules saves only Theseus and not even entirely:

the Athenian king leaves a part of his buttock glued to his seat in Pluto's hall.[22] (Implying further doubt about the possibility of return, the second Vatican mythographer notes that Vergil does not admit that *either* Theseus or Pirithoos returns to life.[23]) Like the first Vatican mythographer, Boccaccio divides the friends. Hercules rescues Theseus, but Pirithoos is eaten by Cerberus. His story of Castor and Pollux repeats the same separation of a pair or double; both pairs of brothers are subject to death, that is, descend to the "inferno," but only one of each pair returns to life.[24]

Of these two myths of return, that of the rescuer Hercules seems the more complicated way of mediating the experience of death. Castor and Pollux are obviously representatives of time in nature and like Proserpina exemplify eternal return. In contrast, Hercules represents a divine ability to return from death and, moreover, to bring another with him, while Theseus, who sometimes returns, sometimes not, and sometimes in part but almost always without his friend, Pirithoos, illustrates mortality. His various fate appears to indicate the uncertainty that is provoked by the concept of eternal return when the subject of the myth in question does not clearly refer to the regular motions of heavenly bodies or time-markers. It is as if the redactors of the Hercules myth, uneasy at its implications, incorporated in their versions of the descent the negative element in the Castor and Pollux myth in order to account for what they knew to be the human experience of time. In his several manifestations, Theseus can be said to share Hercules' ability to return from the underworld as an expression of a (mortal) hope in the possibility of an earthly immortality, but also to suffer the fate of Pirithoos in recognition of the fact that this hope is futile.

Pulci begins his account of Rinaldo's rescue of Orlando by establishing the quality that enables his hero to succeed in returning his brother to life; he follows it with a sequel which recounts a contrasting loss. Rinaldo's temperance before his rescue of Orlando is conveyed by his control of a wild horse that plagues Marsilio's kingdom; his intemperance after his rescue by his refusal to fight the Sultan's daughter Antea. The first establishes that his reason controls erotic passion, the second that his reason cannot control his love of worship.

Rinaldo's conquest of the wild horse is bound up with his love for Luciana, Marsilio's daughter. Like previous ladies of the narrative, she is a sun creature; like the sun, she dazzles Rinaldo with her splendor: "che più che'l sol m'abbaglia di splendore" (13. 49); and Rinaldo, looking at her, rises like an eagle to the sun (14. 41). He shows, however, that he reins in his love for her by taming the horse, "which was completely uncontrollable . . . it seemed a devil in a desert" ("ch'era sfrenato . . . / e pareva un demòn là in un deserto", 13. 51), but once bridled, became a "lamb of humility" ("un vil pecorella") and his gift to her (13. 55–57, 68). In return for this favor, she promises him twenty thousand men whenever he needs them. The allegory to this point is straightforward; it makes use of the tropes common to illustrations of temperance as the control of passion: the wild horse who must be bridled.[25]

In the next episode, however, Luciana's significance is developed through mythological associations. She is no longer merely a figure who causes her lover to burn with passion; she becomes more directly identified as a sun and signifies his enlightenment. She celebrates her lover's conquest of the horse by giving him a shining tent depicting all of creation in its four elements (14. 44). This structure itself is like the sun in its brilliance (14. 86, 89), and recalls Ovid's description of the house of the sun in the *Metamorphoses,* on whose doors Mulciber has carved the seas, earth, and sky (2. 5–7), that is, all creation and its constitutive elements.

It becomes an appropriate attribute of Luciana, if she is considered to be the goddess that Ovid in the *Metamorphoses* identifies as "a daughter of the sun" ("sata Sole", 14. 10), that is, a Circe. Most commonly characterized by Renaissance mythographers as a temptress who lures men to bestial behavior, Circe is also capable of being a teacher who, if dominated by a hero like Ulysses, instructs men in wisdom and practical affairs. Boccaccio, for example, writes that Circe, before allowing Ulysses to leave, "taught him many things."[26] Mythographers knew, of course, that Circe taught Ulysses the way to the underworld; this was knowledge she might be assumed to possess because, as a relative of the sun, she would travel there each night. On this knowledge depended Ulysses' return to Ithaca and civilization, that is, to his former life and by implication to himself. If Luciana is a Circe, her tent, depicting all creation or what the sun sees, can similarly be seen as an image of what she knows and offers to Rinaldo, the self-knowledge and self-control he has already shown he possesses by bridling the wild horse. It is because Rinaldo has what the tent signifies that he is able to rescue Orlando from the "inferno." By these allusions to the Ulysses and Circe story, Rinaldo's Herculean nature is augmented to include the second hero's cunning and restraint—qualities more specifically intellectual than rational.

Rinaldo's relationship to Antea—that, unlike his relationship to Luciana, is debilitating—is developed by reference to yet a third myth. Antea seeks fame and she also embodies it. A paragon of masculine virtue—"she was manly in her speech . . ./ with a noble and lordly bearing" ("nelle promesse sue sempre virile . . ./ con un atto magnalmo e signorile", 15. 103)—she loves Rinaldo before she sees him (15. 98). When she meets him she repeatedly praises his "fama" (15. 13, 14, 15). Her power to inspire love resembles fame's power to elicit great deeds:

"She had a certain sweetness of manner that would make a hundred Narcissuses fall in love with her" ("Avea certi atti dolci . . ./ da fare innamorar cento Narcisi . . .", 15. 102; See also 16. 21). And when Rinaldo asks her who she is, she answers that she delights that he is spoken of throughout the world: "You are spoken of throughout the world and this pleases me" ("Di te si favella / per tutto l'universo, e ciò m'è a grado") and implies she is Echo (16. 15).

These references, especially remarkable because they are Pulci's additions to his source, suggest the nature of the power Antea will have over Rinaldo. Echo was widely allegorized as fame and Narcissus as the lover who rejects her for pleasure.[27] For Rinaldo to love Antea is therefore for him to pursue fame as a means of winning her. Here, however, Pulci inverts the obvious significance of the myth and shows that the love Antea inspires is essentially idolatrous. Because of it, Rinaldo allows her to carry off his brothers, and Orlando twice accuses him of faithlessness (16. 48, 74).

That Antea as fame should have prevailed to separate chivalric 'brothers' recalls the debate, continuous throughout the Renaissance, on the merits of seeking worldly glory.[28] Pulci's sources for Antea as fame are undetermined, but it is likely that he knew both Boccaccio's and Petrarch's accounts of the goddess. Petrarch's Fama in the *Trionfi*, a "bella donna" who advances like a star from the East, is especially reminiscent of Pulci's Antea.[29] In both accounts, fame is finally superseded and controlled by a greater force. Petrarch's fame yields to time, which swallows all wordly renown; Pulci's Antea is controlled by Providence, which shapes each person's life more decisively than he can himself.

Rinaldo's moral education takes the form of a humiliation common to knights who have been intemperate; he must travel and fight without a horse. In the context of a story about fame, the figure of the horse acquires the extra significance of a Pegasus, who is frequently allegorized as the "desire for fame."[30] Since it is this desire that has marred Rinaldo's fellowship a shepherd must steal Baiardo as the opening move in Rinaldo's effort to recover his virtue. But in itself this is insufficient instruction. Having walked to Babylon where the Sultan holds his prisoners, Rinaldo learns that Antea refuses a battle on foot (17. 3) and that to free his brothers the Sultan demands he fight the "Old Man" ("Il Veglio"), who the Sultan has dreamed will kill him and of whom he is therefore fearful. By this plan, the Sultan intends to thwart his destiny. Rinaldo, however, neither kills nor is killed but instead forces the Old Man to the ground and converts him to his side.

The conquest is symbolic. In effect, Rinaldo releases the force of destiny incarnate in the Old Man, brings it into play on the side of chivalry, and by extension allows Providence her role in writing history.

As prophesied, the Old Man finally kills the Sultan in a battle between the paladins and the infidel, and Ricciardetto and Uliviero are consequently released. The event suggests not only that a knight should function as part of a fellowship and so limit his desire to acquire fame, but also that this enterprise is itself limited by a superior form of control that here is termed destiny. Pulci attributes the Sultan's death to not a human but a divine will, one which, moreover, is beyond human appeal. "The [Sultan's] spear broke, as heaven wished . . ./ that which is destined cannot be altered" ("L'aste si ruppe, come il Ciel voleva . . ./ ché quel che è destinato tòr non puossi", 18. 66) The ambiguity surrounding the precise cause of the Sultan's death is important; the Old Man kills the Sultan, but only because heaven has wished the Sultan's spear to break. Thus destiny (or Providence), working though human agents and exploiting what appear to be accidents of pure chance, is seen to determine historical events, albeit in mysterious ways. The entire episode describing Rinaldo's relation to Antea implicitly constructs a moral hierarchy: a paladin's love of fame is subservient to his obligations to a fellowship and the chivalric enterprise is, as a whole, subject to divine will. When Antea confronts this will, as she does in canto 24, she too becomes insignificant.

The episode also contributes to a reassessment of the virtue of temperance in Rinaldo by exposing its negative elements or excesses. By revealing within his hero a new kind of illicit love, one that thrives not on ease and pleasure but on hardship and pain, Pulci demonstrates that chivalric discipline which is restricted to a mere denial of appetite (the bridled horse) does not in itself conduce to chivalric behavior. He thus offers a critique of his hero's reasonableness, previously established in action that referred to such figures as Hercules, Perseus, and Ulysses. This effectively places it in a new perspective and calls into question the significance of previous episodes (especially in iii) where Rinaldo's reason was presented as sufficient guarantee that events in which he had a hand would conform to divine will. Pulci here begins to reformulate the relationships he established in early cantos between reason, right action, and the course of a Providentially ordered history.

Orlando's relations to Chiariella provide Pulci with the basis for a second allegory of temperance, argued in this case in relation to what one might call a new manifestation of the titanic pride he overcame earlier. The allegory alludes to the various myths concerning Proserpina. Orlando is like Theseus in needing to be rescued from an underworld where he went to seek a lady of light confined against her will, but unlike Theseus (and like the fully divine Ceres) in finally accomplishing the mission he undertook initially, that is, to return this lady her freedom. His success, signified in Chiariella's coronation, has analogues later in the poem in his return of Uliva to her father, and in Morgante's return of Florinetta to hers, episodes which more obviously imitate the Proserpina myth. All these achievements are preceded by Orlando's education. Specifically Christian allegorizations (like Berchorius's) usually interpret the Proserpina myth as a lesson in continence and picture the goddess as the moral self led astray. Pulci, in contrast, presents the error as the hero's, who only through self-discipline can find the light again. His adaptation of the moralizing elements of the myth takes place through another set of associations developed from similar mythic material. Orlando's eventual triumph over the error in which he finds himself recalls the self-knowledge and self-control mythographers attribute to the hero Ulysses when he leaves the goddess Circe. In this portion of the narrative, Pulci exploits differently elements of the same myth he referred to in the adventure of the wild horse.

Chiariella is to Orlando as Circe was to Ulysses, a sun-lady whose effects are ambivalent; she can imprison but she can also set free. When in prison, Orlando sees her helpful role—sending for Rinaldo—in mythical terms; she plays the part of a divinity who can return him from the underworld:[31]

> Tu se' colei che l'ulivo e la palma
> m'arrechi e che mi cavi dello inferno,
> e la tempesta mia converti in calma. . . .
>
> (15. 69)

You are she who hands me olive and the palm and saves me from the underworld, who converts my tempest to a calm.

But he finds that restoring her to her throne entails a confrontation with her sinister aspect: her ability to delay his return to chivalric action. Her charms keep him "within the city" ("insin fuor delle mura"); "every day they give themselves over to dalliance" ("ogni dì se ne vanno a sollazzo", 15.89). He acknowledges his own intemperance indirectly when he comments on the manner in which Chiariella is crowned, that is, in haste, and only after Rinaldo and Orlando learn that the Sultan has taken Antea's prisoners to Babylon. Orlando blames Rinaldo but his remarks also reflect his own fault: "Now we need a plan right away; this is no time to play the lover" ("Qui si bisogno sùbito riparo, / e tempo non è più d'essere amante", 16. 93). Obviously, to restore Chiariella to her proper place in the world is also to renounce her as a lover. The mythical analogue to this action is Ulysses' renunciation of Circe (and Calypso) where the hero's return to his homeland depends upon his dissociation, as a mortal, from his immortal helper.[32] Chiariella's characterization as one who can deliver another from an "inferno," and the effect of Orlando's dalliance with her—to delay her coronation and his (eventual) return to Carlo—establish that Pulci was aware of the moral significance traditionally given to the myth his story imitates. Orlando cannot dally with Chiariella for obvious reasons; in so doing he would violate social, political, and moral decorum. But the most subtle and powerful arguments against this match are to be discovered in the episode's mythical dimension, which engages a level of the allegory that can best be termed anagogical. Orlando's experience of intemperance imitates Rinaldo's in a grander key. The latter is seduced by the immortality fame confers, the former with the more mysterious possibilities conveyed by the hope of union with a creature whose attributes and mythical associations suggest she is divine. His flirtation with Chiariella masks an attempt to efface the absolute differences at this mythical level, and so to conflate the two orders of creation, mortal and immortal, that myths of return generally seem most interested in distinguishing.

Orlando's attempts further to understand the nature of his spiritual enlightenment are represented in his rescue of the Princess Uliva. The giants imprisoning the lady are remarkable because in the course of the episode they appear to multiply. Of an original five woodland giants, Uliva's captors, the paladins kill two; at King Falcone's city (in a digressionary episode), however, Orlando encounters two or more who claim that they live by the sea and that they, with their woodland brothers, compose a gang of eight. The giants of the shore regularly demand a sexual tribute of young girls from King Falcone, but Orlando forces them to discontinue this practice. His action against successive sets of giants draw attention to his difficulty with the sin of pride, while Uliva's name identifies her as a representation of Chiariella: "tu se' colei che l'*ulivo* . . . m'arrechi e che mi cavi dello inferno." In effect, this episode restates by way of mythical references that have a common allegorical interpretation what the Chiariella episode has already made clear. In his relations with both ladies, Orlando's acts of renouncing or controlling desire are the necessary prelude to the establishment of various kinds of order— political, social, moral, and anagogical. These acts depend on his having made appropriate distinctions between characters and what they signify. The gift of King Gostanzo, Uliva's grateful father—an army to defeat the Sultan and rescue his prisoners (18. 3)—confirms the constructive effects of Orlando's perfected virtue.[33]

Orlando's education is fully realized in Pulci's comprehensive treatment of temperance in the story of Morgante's restoration of Florinetta. This requires the invention of another character, the half-giant Margutte, whose relation to Morgante corresponds to Morgante's relation to Orlando. The giant has always appeared as an exponent of the hero's pride, which is early linked to his physical strength. Orlando's conversion of Morgante (ii) has signaled his control of that element in his nature and serves later to guarantee that his *virtù* will be deployed correctly. Margutte appears on the scene when the figurative dimension of the action describing Orlando's lessons in temperance demands another image: one that represents a pride linked to a heroic strength which is not physical but rather intellectual.

Margutte represents the appetitive wit, free from moral or spiritual constraints. This is evident in his credo: "I don't believe more in black than in blue but in fish . . . but above all I have faith in good wine" ("io non credo più al nero ch'a l'azzuro / ma nel caponne. . . . / ma sopra tutto nel buon vino ho fede", 18. 115). He dismisses religious faith as "dream" ("sogno", 18. 116), and declares that "faith is experienced like a tickle" ("La fede è fatta come fa il solletico", 18. 117), and he appears to wish to defend himself only by professing an inability to be treacherous: "I never betrayed anyone" ("tradimento ignun non feci mai", 18. 142). But since Margutte's character is, by his own admission, deceitful, no statement he makes, including this one, can be regarded as true. There is a particular appropriateness to his incarnating the Cretan liar paradox, for, as a figure of wit, he must naturally exploit all its resources. Despite Margutte's rejection of the name of traitor, Morgante is undeceived and admonishes him against treachery, a warning that becomes prophetic:[34]

> Di tradimento guàrdati, perch'io
> vo' che tu creda in questo mio battaglio
> da poi che tu non credi in Cielo a Dio. . . .
>
> (18. 144)

Watch out for treachery, for I want you to believe in this clapper of mine since you don't believe in God in heaven.

Morgante meets Margutte just before he begins his rescue of Princess Florinetta, that is, at the point at which he must renounce any desire he might have to possess her, a desire she has already experienced as a prisoner of the giants and, in her account of her capture, expresses by her representation of herself as a Proserpina (19. 2, 10, 12). There she implies that if her rape was not caused by her own unreasonable wishes, it was at least a morally logical consequence of them, a view she states directly later when she is safe again with her father:

> così va chi se stesso pur trastulla;
> ed è ragion s'alfin mal gliene coglie,
> chi vuol cavarsi tutte le sue voglie.
>
> (19. 111)

so it happens to one who seeks only his pleasure; it's right that whoever wants all his desires encounters evil at last.

Pulci emphasizes the connections between desire and intelligence when he describes the way Morgante finally separates himself from Margutte. This involves a distinction between Margutte's appetitive wit and a reason that is available even to Morgante, who heretofore has been chiefly noted for his strength, goodwill, and innocent faith. That Margutte's wit is finally *only* desire and has no relation to reason is conveyed in his appearance. He wears a yellow hat resembling a cock's comb crowned with sharp spurs. His attributes parody those of Mercury, the god who functions as rational intelligence in the Circe myth. To Morgante he proves to be a guide whose example the giant must ignore. When Morgante achieves his quest, having conquered the temptation Margutte poses, Florinetta describes the giant as "fraternal" and "courteous" ("come fratel," "come gentil") in clear contrast to the licentious behavior Margutte has exhibited (19. 113).

Morgante's anger at his companion's rudeness (19. 101) seeks a form of redress that specifically establishes his own rationality. He elects the weapon characteristic of the moralist: satire. Ironically but fittingly his choice is dictated by what Margutte himself desires: that their conflict be resolved in laughter (19. 144). Morgante steals Margutte's hat while he sleeps and places it on the head of a monkey who lurks nearby. When Margutte wakes and sees the strange creature, he dies laughing, killed by the perception of his own simian character. The action suggests the nature of the moral reform Morgante (and by extension Orlando) experiences by Margutte's death: a wit dominated by appetite is destroyed by the efforts of a counter-wit, rationally controlled, that by representing its errors to itself in the mirror of art makes them repulsive and derisory.

Pulci's critical treatment of Margutte's appetitive wit exploits an association of intelligence with the idea of return that is specifically characteristic of the Circe myth. Ulysses' ambivalent relations to Circe—a goddess of enlightenment but only if the immortality that remaining with her implies (an immortality explicitly offered by her counterpart, Calypso) be renounced—really articulate the condition of human intellect, particularly as it was defined in Platonic terms. Its greatest and most constant task is the acknowledgment of its own limitations. It is obviously crucial to the development of Orlando's chivalric character and to the integrity of the role he will play at Roncisvalle that he be capable of renouncing aspirations to a personal and individual salvation and sanctity. As a crusader, a martyr in a Holy War, he must accept that his destiny is a matter of Providential dispensation. By establishing so dramatically Orlando's humanity, the adventure of Chiariella anticipates events that receive their full representation in Part 2. It serves to link the material in both parts of the poem which, although they remain disconnected in a formal sense, share nevertheless a developed and coherent characterization of their principal hero.

The adventure of Florinetta is the most triumphant in Part 1 because the least implicated in loss and death. But it is also the most self-consciously rhetorical; its overt reference to its mythical parallel distinguishes it from earlier accounts of return and restoration which preserve their mimetic illusion. That Pulci ties Florinetta's adventure so explicitly to myth creates a new tension within the narrative—a tension produced as the significance of the adventure comes to be perceived as fundamentally different from the significance of the poem as history. In Part 1 generally, the differences between myth and history have been harmonized in patterns organized in relation to the concept of process: the paladins participate in history because (or insofar as) they have the perfected moral characters that appear in allegorized myth. But, in this adventure, action which is characterized as mythic and allegorical begins to be set off from political activity, to which it previously had such a direct relevance.

The terms of this tension are evident in the bipartite ending to the adventure of Chiariella. The first part of this ending, preserving the strongly mythical mode of Florinetta's adventure, culminates action which bears on the perfection of Orlando's character: Morgante, embodying the self-renewing force in nature—"He purifies everything" ("Ogni cosa rimonda", 19. 176)—destroys Babylon and thus permits Orlando to crown himself Sultan. A festival mood triumphs over the ruined city, and Orlando is celebrated as hero and savior. The second part, resuming the thread of the narrative as history, addresses political relations which obtain between France and Pagania: after Orlando and Rinaldo have been asked by a shepherd to leave Babylon and rescue Gano, Antea, the Sultan's daughter, is restored to his throne. Her return to Babylon is marked by an awareness of the devastating losses inflicted by Morgante on that city (21. 96). Despite her people's welcome, an uneasiness pervades the occasion: "[A]nd the city *seems* restored" (my italics) ("e la citta parea risucitata", 21. 97). This action reperspectivizes the moment of the paladins' victory and makes clear its tragic results. It thus provides a realistic conclusion to an episode that is now seen primarily as the story of a military conquest.

### Providential Evil: The Rehabilitation of Gano

Antea has imprisoned Gano but Malagigi demands his release. Gano is then captured by a witch, Creonta, and a shepherd persuades the paladins to rescue him. On their way to him, guided by the pilot Greco, Morgante dies of the bite of a tiny crab. In Mezza, they kill the Emperor who seeks a vendetta against Christians. In the process, the Old Man is killed by a servant of the Emperor's chief officer—the servant turns out to be Aldighieri, Rinaldo's brother. The paladins crown the innkeeper, Chiarone, governor of Mezza. Malagigi oversees the death of Creonta and the liberation of Gano. Orlando assists Astolfo in killing the evil king Chiaristante and crowns him in his place. (Chiaristante has confessed that he has taken the throne from Greco.) Rinaldo supports the claims of Chiaristante's queen, Filiberta, against Astolfo and Greco. Rinaldo and Orlando fight; their quarrel is interrupted when they hear that Carlo has been attacked by the infidel king, Calavrion. They begin their return to Paris. On the way, Aldighieri kills Diliante, who has been informed by Gano that Aldighieri is a Chiaramonte, his enemy. In France, Gano arranges to murder Aldighieri; Gano persuades Arpalista, an officer of Calavrion, captured by Rinaldo, to intercede for him with Carlo. Carlo pardons Gano, but Calavrion kills Arpalista and returns to Pagania. Rinaldo, meanwhile, has left for Pagania; he rescues Filisetta's kingdom from a demon, Fuligatto. Carlo sends Gano to find Rinaldo. (Adventures viii, c, d, vii', ix.)

Nowhere in these adventures does Pulci make use of a plot of a myth of return *except in ironic or parodic terms*. This change in mood is accompanied by expressions of skepticism and disbelief in the kind of history that earlier adventures illustrated. The vision of history the *Morgante* has thus far entertained is in its principal points Boethian, dedicated to maintaining a complicity between fortune and Providence. Moreover, the paladins argue that events follow a course not only determined by God's will but also rationally demonstrable as just. In comparison to the paladins' early vision of history, however, the last episodes in Part 1 contribute new elements that markedly change its character. Specifically by inverting in irony or parody the terms of what has been his typical plot—a version of a myth of return—Pulci challenges his earlier historiographical model. His strategy has two consequences. Providence is no longer perceived to act in rationally comprehensible ways and, as a result, human agency, in large measure dependent upon the operation of reason, is no longer treated as important or even very interesting. In the early cantos of the poem, the paladins can be said to have made things happen and to have comprehended the justice in events. But in the last cantos of Part 1, they are no longer capable of bringing about much that is of value; indeed, the notion of what is valuable itself changes.

Pulci's claim that a Providential order is maintained through these complicated events—a claim he expresses by showing the paladins inspired, guided, and fed by angels—is significantly weakened by the portrayal of a capricious fortune who operates as mere chance and no longer as an index or judge of human folly. Readers mindful of the picture of the operations of fortune in the first sequence of adventures, notably in the story of Erminion, will notice this revision, strikingly manifest in the episode describing Morgante's death. This occurs as the paladins set out to rescue Gano, their first test on their return to Carlo's court (vi'). The giant is bitten by a "little crab" ("granchiolino") and when the wound festers, he dies. "Look where fortune leads that person! . . . Our life is uncertain and full of misfortune" ("Guarda dove Fortuna costui mena! . . . O vita nostra debole e fallace!", 20. 51, 56), Pulci observes. These exclamations on the power of fortune are not a warning to sinners (cf. Erminion's remarks in i'), but reflections on the devastating interventions of chance on the plans and programs of persons of virtue. Morgante's death is obviously symbolic of the paladins' loss of the capacity to shape events, but the manner of it also indicates they will be unable rationally to judge events in the future. Morgante's death takes place in the context of action that will testify to the power of God to determine history by miraculous interventions. As fortune is depicted as progressively more like chance, its function in a Providential history must be increasingly to augment the need for faith.

The adventure of Gano (c), fittingly introduced by Morgante's death, cannot be understood in rational terms. Why Malagigi insists that Antea release Gano, why Gano hangs the thief who stole Rinaldo's horse, why the paladins are persuaded by an eloquent but ignorant shepherd to rescue Gano from the witch Creonta's dungeon is never made clear by the action alone. There is no suggestion that Gano is different from what he was, no obvious reason for a Chiaramonte, Malagigi, to want him at large. To the paladins attempting entry, Creonta's castle is horrifying. It is guarded by lions, her offspring; she herself is like a dragon and is accompanied by creatures like the Furies (21. 26). It is simply ironic that the paladins undertake to deliver Gano from so desirable a sequestration and to return him to the world of the poem.

Inside Creonta's castle, however, the conditions of the conflict change and make clear the significance of Gano's rescue. The witch is impervious to physical attack and appears to be immortal. On the other hand, she frees Gano from his dungeon immediately. But neither the paladins nor Gano can leave the castle. Creonta possesses a force inimical to both their interests and must signify the existence of a level of conflict which transcends that which the poem has described to this point. Malagigi, who by magic perceives the situation from afar, discovers the solution to this apparent enigma. His actions reveal that Creonta has attributes of both Meleager and Proteus. He informs the paladins that her life depends on the preservation of a small wax figurine which, if consumed in fire, will bring her own life to an end. If this figure is threatened, she is capable of assuming any shape she likes, and the person who intends to kill her must have the courage to hold her through these changes (21. 69). Instructed by Malagigi, the paladins persevere, Creonta is killed, and her palace, now recognized as an illusion, vanishes. Its destruction clears the air and discloses what before had been obscured: the world outside. Creonta has instituted a mode of entrapment which has had as its primary purpose a permanent separation of the paladins from their chivalric enterprise.

The figure of Meleager does not receive comment in the most popular mythographies but Ovid's *Metamorphoses* makes it clear that he is associated with the precise operations of the Fates who, invoked at his birth, devise the magical brand that is coterminous with his life. Boccaccio identifies the Fates as Providence; the connection between the two is obvious and might well have occurred to Pulci.[35] In any case, Creonta's death, by repeating Meleager's, asserts a shaping power within history, whether fatal or Providential, that supersedes her own ability to control her victims through fear of change. In association with the figure of Meleager, Creonta's Protean character bears particularly on Pulci's understanding of the relationship between the changes of time and fortune, the fear they engender, and an heroic ability to sustain a belief in history as Providential, however fearful these changes appear. Ovid describes the sea god as the antithesis of those heroes, the strongest and the bravest, who, having taken a "form," remain true to it; "there are those [heroes], the very strongest, who, having once assumed a form, remain in this state" ("sunt, o fortissime, quorum / forma semel mota est et in hoc renovamine mansit", 8. 728, 729). That is, they exemplify the virtue of constancy by contrast to Proteus who changes. Boccaccio interprets the changes of Proteus as "the passions" ("le passioni") which the hero in search of counsel or wisdom must control and so retain a constant mind.[36]

In resisting the terrifying transformations of Creonta, the paladins obviously ally themselves with the strongest heroes and demonstrate that they are unaffected by the fear of changes they must experience in the course of history that is (nevertheless) divinely ordered. In a sense, their confrontation with her provides them with a means of eliciting this truth. Their superiority to her is revealed by the nature of her own vulnerability. Her Protean side is controlled and limited by what her similarity to Meleager means she must accept: her subjection to the decrees of the Fates.

The witch's complex of attributes is difficult to assemble into a single figure with a coherent function unless she is seen in relation to Pulci's concern with history. She must be understood in relation to the part she plays in an adventure which ends with the freedom of the paladins and Gano—on an equal footing. The context in which both freedoms are desirable is, of course, that of Providential history. By preventing both the good and evil French from leaving her castle, she thwarts the terrible but necessary conflict between the just and the unjust, the loyal and the treacherous. To the paladins particularly, she has proffered an inverted form of chivalry that comes into being when there are no more battles to be won. Creonta is fully defined by her capacity to delay and detain. Like Circe, whose diabolical aspects she incorporates, she rules a locus which, although in time, is eternal. Her palace represents a life of everlasting inactivity, attractive, as the imagery of the episode implies, precisely because the fear of change she induces is so difficult to overcome.

Gano's presence among the paladins, his reincorporation into the chivalric world from which Antea as fame and Creonta as an anti-Providence have momentarily excluded him, inaugurate the conditions for chivalric action in the rest of Part 1. The paladins' defeat of Creonta exposes them to a Gano whose *modus operandi* is different from what it was. Earlier a symbol of discord and linked to temporality, specifically to the effects of time, Gano now becomes a figure whose activities have a profounder meaning in the larger context of Providential history. His objective—to destroy Carlo's court and the chivalry it sustains—is to be reassessed *sub specie aeternitatis.* In this second perspective, the status of a particular court is of less significance than the struggle witnessing the salvation of the faithful.

Gano's rescue is an instance of an *ironic* use of a myth of return. Imprisoned in an earthly yet eternal prison, Gano plays the part that was previously Orlando's. His release does not, however, depend on a salutary acknowledgment of his own humanity but is rather arranged by Providence for reasons that have no immediate relation to the traitor's viciousness. This adventure is followed by another in which the action again imitates a myth of return but this time in a *parodic* mode.

Depicting the restoration of a queen with no legitimate right to her throne, the adventure of Filiberta (d) engages on terms quite different than heretofore the question of justice. The subject follows logically from the significance of Gano's sanctioned return to the fellowship of the paladins. If Providence can no longer be defined by reason, as it clearly cannot if Malagigi arranges for the release of Gano, then justice need no longer relate to truth and right, *ragione.* The images of political stability this adventure creates only testify to the relative moral weakness of Carlo's paladins. Their justice becomes expedience.

The adventure opens by describing the nature of the fortune who controls events in this new atmosphere. When Astolfo, in a fit of anger, leaves the paladins who are returning to France, Pulci accuses fortune, to whom he gives the character of chance:

> sanza pietà, sanza ragione alcuna:
> questa persegue i buon, perché gli ha a sdegno,
> insin che v'è delle barbe solo una;
> a fa de' matti savi e i savi matti,
> e chi prestar vorrebbe, ch'egli accatti.

(21. 82)

without respect, without any reason, fortune persecutes the good (because she scorns them) until there is not one left; and she makes madmen wise, and wise men mad, and he who would lend a borrower.

No longer counterpointing human error as she has done, fortune now operates despite moral logic and creates disturbing enigmas. Her sophistry will make problematic even the simplest events and transform the meaning of history as the poem has presented it. She will effectively alter the use to which Pulci will put the image of perspective. He will continue to relate his story in narrative units that reflect upon each other, but he will no longer have them construct the satisfying totalities represented in such adventures as Merediana's. Instead he will arrange episodes so that they form thematically self-cancelling pairs producing no third term or coherent whole. When, for example, Astolfo meets a group of hermits who have recently been robbed, he insists that they hang the thieves (whom he has caught); they argue for clemency in accordance with God's will. Astolfo defies them, hangs the thieves, and continues on his way escorted by angels (21. 93). Previous episodes lead one to expect that an action of this sort will illustrate the relationship between justice and mercy, but no such interpretation is possible. In fact, the episode reflects ironically upon that in which Astolfo himself has pleaded for mercy (i').

The action concerning the restoration of Filiberta is confused and incomprehensible when it is compared to similar action earlier in the poem. In the first episode Astolfo deposes Filiberta's husband, the tyrant Chiaristante, and Orlando intervenes to crown Astolfo in Chiaristante's place. These actions appear defensible and recall similar episodes earlier in the poem. Chiaristante has institutionalized rape and usurped the throne from Greco, the pilot of "good counsel" ("buon dottrina"), who, having directed the paladins to Creonta's castle, is currently of their company. But in relation to previous restorations the paladins' actions are unjust, since Chiaristante's crown belongs to Greco. Pulci exploits this inconsistency in his depiction of the "just scorn" ("giusto sdegno") of the people of Chiaristante's kingdom. They mutilate the dead body of their king—"Now see what force a just scorn has" ("Or vedi quanta forza ha il giusto sdegno!", 21. 147)—but later they will also reject Astolfo who delivered them from this tyrant. Not, however, because his rule is unjust, but simply because they are, in Pulci's words, "mad" ("pazzo", 21. 149). Pulci jeopardizes the concept of a "just scorn," which might indeed have had in Astolfo a not illegitimate traget, by confusing its source with the "madness" of the people. This evokes a new kind of despair in the poet, who declares that one must be resigned to such reversals and avoid public life. "So it is that it is often necessary to give up and to become indifferent to affairs of great moment" ("Tant'è che spesso è util disperarsi / e fassi per isdegno di gran cose", 21. 150). The process of perspectivizing has here led to the consideration of a point situated outside the frame of action of the poem. Pulci has spoken in a voice distinct from that of the narrator; moreover, to the problem of political stability he has advocated an answer in no way appropriate to chivalry. It conveys the pessimism of one who has reflected on the Pazzi conspiracy and anticipates his interest in the values associated with the conceptual mode of pastoral: retirement, privacy, contemplation.

The sequel to this episode continues to subvert the notion of justice the poem has earlier established. It shows that what is unpredictable is not fortune or the people but the paladins themselves. Astolfo is not, in fact, dethroned by Chiaristante's former subjects in favor of Greco, but by Rinaldo who crowns Chiaristante's wife, Filiberta. Rinaldo's motivation is obscure. A group of pilgrims, urging Filiberta to apply to Rinaldo to restore her to her husband's throne, declare that he is in the habit of righting wrongs (21. 157, 158), but this claim is soon falsified. Rinaldo accepts Filiberta's case without noticing what is plain to the reader: Filiberta resembles the other great ladies of the poem only by parodic inversion. The justice of Rinaldo's enterprise is never overtly at issue. Greco, explaining that he has not wanted to give fortune a chance "to delight in his complaint" ("la Fortuna ingiuriosa e rea / non avessi di me questo diletto"), proffers his claim to the throne belatedly (21. 168). Rinaldo praises Greco's magnanimity but he declines to reward it. That Filiberta regrets her past sins might seem to make her eligible for chivalric help, but her contrition has no sequel and is therefore unconvincing. Orlando and Astolfo accuse Rinaldo of uxoriousness (22. 8), but neither of them supports Greco. The throne will not therefore be occupied by a legitimate claimant. This situation, unique in the poem, further throws out of focus all earlier visions of political stability based on chivalric values. It is resolved not by the paladins but by fortune, who intervenes with an unrelated event: an attack upon Carlo by the infidel king Calavrion, avenging his uncle the Old Man. Expediency dictates a compromise. Filiberta is crowned but she will be succeeded by Greco (22. 34). Neither Orlando nor Rinaldo prevail in the way they have on previous occasions. Their brilliant *virtù* has undergone an alteration in kind; it is now devoted merely to pragmatic ends. Henceforth chivalric action will be decisive only when coupled with divine or magical forces.

In this adventure Pulci depicts a kind of causality he may not yet have altogether understood. It is clear that the notion of a Providential history that is also rationally comprehensible is discredited and that, if events are to continue to be understood as divinely ordered, the operations of Providence must be mysterious. To portray action that is significant according to this vision of history, Pulci must develop a new set of terms, a language of faith, a repertory of miracles. To sustain such a vision, he must also create an atmosphere where doubt is not occasional but pervasive and countered not by knowledge but by religion.

Such a reconstruction of historiographic principles is displayed in Pulci's account of Calavrion's invasion (vi'). It portrays the paladins' return to defend a world they have not fully known before—a world where political judgments are freed from connections with a verifiable reality and become instead a function of the perspective taken on a situation that is never wholly determined or entirely known.

The episodes describing Calavrion's defeat logically build on the themes of the previous adventure and develop contrasting positions on the roles of belief and persuasion in moral action. Having depicted justice as expediency, Pulci now proceeds also to deny that the concept of truth has any objective value. By presenting two episodes in which powerful illusions function first positively, as a beneficial falsehood, and then negatively, as a ruinous truth, he implies that human existence is sufficiently complex to require a casuistic understanding of the truth and the ways in which it is to be embraced.

On their way to Carlo, the paladins collect an infidel army to help defeat Calavrion. Previous episodes have led the reader to expect that such armies are acquired in recognition of the paladins' *virtù*. In this instance, however, the paladins' force comes from their use of deceit. The army belongs to king Diliante, like Calavrion a relative of the Old Man and therefore a person who should support a vendetta against the Chiaramonte. To conceal the role of his brother Aldighieri (20. 92–105), Rinaldo tells Diliante that the Old Man was killed by a giant. Diliante states that he regrets the case has been so misunderstood (22. 55, 56). But after Rinaldo kills a lion that molests Diliante's kingdom, the king gratefully acknowledges that Calavrion must be wrong to seek revenge against the French and offers Rinaldo his army (22. 65). In effect, Rinaldo tricks Diliante into supporting the very cause he should be seeking to hinder.

The advantage of such tactics to the party who employs them is obvious. In this instance, however, Pulci paradoxically claims that the duped also benefit. The positive effect of Diliante's illusion is clear after it is dispelled. Gano tells the truth to Diliante, who arranges to fight Orlando despite the risk of being killed because then, at least, he will be rid of his anger (22. 98). Diliante's temerity results in his death and this gives Pulci an opportunity to comment again on the matter of truth and falsehood. He redefines "ignorance" so that it no longer signifies a lack of knowledge of the truth, or a belief in what is objectively a lie, but rather intemperance. "Ignorance" acquires a moral not an epistemological reference.

> Ecco che tu se' morto Diliante,
> ch'era pur buono a Rinaldo credessi
> che morto avesse il tuo Veglio il gigante,
> e Ganellon discacciato l'avessi:
> tu fusti, come giovane, ignorante
> e furïoso; or lo piangi tu stessi;
> aspetta luogo e tempo alla vendetta,
> ché non si fe'mai nulla in fretta.
>
> (22. 108)

So now you are dead, Diliante; it would have been better for you to have believed Rinaldo, [who told you] that a giant had killed your Old Man, and to have driven Gano away. You were, like a young man, ignorant and passionate; now weep over it. One has to wait for a time and place for revenge, for nothing is accomplished in haste.

The octave actually conflates two arguments: one defending what might be termed a beneficial illusion, the other urging moderation. Pulci suggests that the beneficial illusion will protect the temperate man. That the truth can be socially divisive is, of course, a convention of the literature of courtly love, one that has already been illustrated in the Vegurto episode (i'). Here the context in which the convention is to have relevance is political. The octave implies that in theory the concept of a beneficial illusion can be invoked to justify, explain, or support a spectrum of deceit not only in private but also in public life.

Checking the possibility of an uncritical endorsement of such tactics, Pulci immediately offers a countercase: the example of another monarch, Carlo, who suffers from illusions about the character of his court. The Emperor's belief in the virtue of Gano has already been characterized as a form of intemperance. This has not been manifested in his haste or temerity but in an excessive regard for the status quo, an habitual dilatoriness. Astolfo, who has remained with Carlo, attributes Calavrion's invasion not to the infidel's wish for revenge, but rather to the tacit encouragement Carlo's state of delusion would give to anyone contemplating an attack on France. By fostering Gano and dismissing Orlando, Astolfo claims that Carlo has caused Calavrion's invasion: "for if the count (Orlando) had been here, these infidel would not have crossed the mountain (borders)" ("che se ci fussi stato il nostro conte / questi pagan non passavano il monte", 22. 119). Carlo's blindness has, moreover, encouraged the Maganzesi to complicate the defense of Paris by laying siege to Montalbano. Gano has no knowledge of the siege but, by the political calculus Pulci currently employs, his innocence hardly matters. In the context of his past behavior and in light of his professed intentions, all instances of his innocence, however verifiable as fact, acquire the character of illusion, and Carlo, in trusting Gano, assumes the role of his dupe.

Thus far these episodes have developed contrasting perspectives on the *effects* of illusion regarded as a distortion or suppression of the truth. Two final episodes each present a different kind of rhetorical performance as the *origin* of illusion. In the first, Orlando manages to persuade Calavrion to abandon his vendetta. Gano has killed Aldighieri in an opening skirmish at the siege of Montalbano, and Calavrion, who does not know that his uncle has just been avenged, grieves because he regards Aldighieri as a virtuous knight (22. 147). But it is Orlando's funeral oration that moves him to adopt the Chiaramonte's part against Gano. Fooled by Orlando's eloquence into doing what he would hate if he knew the truth, Pulci's Calavrion is nevertheless not a fool. Actually he resembles a wise man listening to reason: "[H]e changed all his opinions just as a wise man does when he listens to reason" ("ogni suo proposito mutòe, / come fa il savio udendo la ragione", 22. 152). In the second and complementary episode, this case is matched, like that of Diliante, with a countercase. While Orlando's oration has made a positive use of deceit, Gano's lying story to Arpalista, in the following episode, has a negative purpose and effect. Gano presents himself to Arpalista, an infidel whom Rinaldo has sent to pay homage to Carlo, as an honest man of plain speech, banished from court for being too outspoken: "I speak the truth too much" ("ho in somma della bocca / un poco troppo il vero", 22. 199). Gano claims he is further abused in being the victim of a malicious fiction which has unfortunately led to Aldighieri's death (22. 206). Arpalista agrees to tell Carlo and Orlando Gano's story; and, so honeyed his tongue (22. 209), he persuades them to forgive Gano. In contrast, Calavrion mocks Arpalista's "holy word"

("santa parola"), remains unconvinced, and finally kills him. Both Calavrion and Arpalista have been taken in by effective rhetoric but, while
Arpalista has been misled, Calavrion has been persuaded to good opinions.

None of these four episodes generates a rule about the uses and
abuses of illusion. Together they create a moral atmosphere that is new
to the poem. The uncertainty that now characterizes all aspects of chivalric action affects more than the future of Carlo's court. The play of
perspectives on the nature of truth calls into question the judgment of
individual paladins; events in France and Pagania are no longer easily
interpreted. It is not surprising, therefore, that part 1 ends by invoking
spiritual aid. The adventure of Filisetta (ix) is directed to the salvation of
souls—an angel tells Rinaldo to clear the way to Christ's tomb so that
pilgrims molested by Fuligatto, a wild man of the desert, can visit there
without fear. Only incidentally is this quest to involve the deliverance of
a besieged Princess Filisetta, whose city Fuligatto terrorizes.

The terms of the adventure are more characteristic of accounts of the
search for the Holy Grail than for worship. Rinaldo sets out alone and on
foot. His first action has a Christian not a chivalric context. Gano has
pursued Rinaldo in order to ask his forgiveness, which Rinaldo, advised
by the pilgrims he is supposed to be saving, agrees to give. The act has
doctrinal rather than psychological validity and answers the pilgrims'
appeal for humility (22. 240). The restoration of Filisetta's city is, moreover, formally incomplete. Although Rinaldo converts Fuligatto, he does
not return to Filisetta's city, which is apparently forgotten. Rinaldo's
encounter with Fuligatto is also untypical. He finds he does not have to
fight the fiend who falls in love with his reputation (23. 12, 13). They join
forces and proceed together through the desert to defeat bestial and
diabolical creatures (23. 45). But their quest is endless and without an
announced purpose. Nor is it an expression of their will, determination,
or skill. They are sheltered by hermits, fed by angels, and, it is implied,
inspired by God.

The first twenty-three cantos of the *Morgante*, far from comprising an
inchoate and plotless narrative, are organized as a series of modifications
of a few basic plots, which imitate well-known myths of return. With the
exception of the episode describing Erminion's invasion, where the story
follows a plot of the *de casibus* type and illustrates the disastrous consequences of pride, Part 1 retells the adventures of a hero who must
enter a locus of darkness and bring forth a figure of light. Ideally, such
an adventure would be exemplified by Ceres' rescue of her daughter and
explain the daily, monthly, or annual return of the sun or the moon to
the heavens, a return that is naturally complete and total. But the
adventures Pulci narrates tell an essentially different story. While they

invite comparison with a wholly successful myth of return, they are designed to show that human temporal experience is characterized by irrecoverable loss; it does not include an experience of renascence except in Boethian terms, that is, as generation.

The conflict between a human desire for immortality and the fact of death implied in these qualified returns gives Pulci's vision of history in Part 1 its psychological interest and its moral significance. The constraints imposed by the paladins' obligation to maintain political stability require them to be both reasonable and faithful. Initially, their achievements confirm their virtue. But as the narrative progresses, the terms by which chivalric behavior is judged—temperance, reason, honesty as a love of truth, frankness as a rejection of deceit—become qualified as they are seen to apply to ever more complicated relationships. The forces of evil, incarnate in Gano and intimately bound up with the passage of time, become difficult to explain other than paradoxically, and Pulci comes to stress the importance of faith to the virtual exclusion of reason. The last cantos of Part 1 illustrate the tragic implications of a Boethian truth: if history exemplifies divine justice, it does so in ways that cannot be understood. The fear of an incomprehensible God that Boethius admits to in his dialogue with Philosophia, underscoring the fact that his epistemological distress has not a philosophical but rather a religious cure, provides the actual if latent motivation for Rinaldo's last quest.

Yet the suggestion that historical events can be accepted as just only through a belief in God as just (actually a position close to Boethius's), can also be seen to provide the basis for (if not the content of) a second and essentially historicist vision of history. As men and God were seen to work less together to control events, and as fortune became less obviously Providential and more obviously capricious, historians became concerned to explain events without regard to morals or metaphysics, to speculate on questions of cause and effect in political, social, and indeed economic terms. The effects of the divorce between religious belief and historical investigation, comparable to the effects of the Ockhamist split between theology and philosophy a century earlier, were both liberating and frightening. Perhaps the most striking of these is inscribed in Machiavelli's *Principe,* where actions that are not virtuous—although they may reflect *virtù*—are encouraged for the sake of political stability and without fear of divine retribution. In the half-century that followed the composition of the *Morgante,* Italian historiography was transformed by its capacity to become self-critical, to incorporate in its discussion of events an explanation of its own methods of analysis and evaluation. It shifted from a mode that can be characterized as epideictic, dedicated (like epic) to the praise or defense of a particular person, state, or nation, to a mode that is demonstrably analytical, that is, prepared to examine the premises upon which any position from which the past is judged can be taken and maintained.

The examination Pulci undertakes in Part 1 of the *Morgante*—of the effect of human *virtù* and virtue on the course of events supposedly exemplifying divine justice—evidences an early effort to understand the premises of the new posthumanist historiography. This comes about through his exploitation of a technique I have termed perspectivism: the constitution of a subject by repeated representations, each registering a different aspect of it. The technique lends itself to the consideration of nonexclusive distinctions and, by a kind of dialectic, creates its subject as a richly complex whole. Pulci's repetitions are not dedicated merely to offering another point of view; they are rather engaged in a self-reflexive process in which the subject is observed at progressively more critical levels.

# 4

## POETRY AND HISTORY

When Pulci resumed writing the *Morgante* in 1481 he was no longer in the position of a *rifacitore*, a reteller of a story already told. For the second half of his poem he had no source comparable to the *Orlando* but instead several narratives concerning the disaster at Roncisvalle and the life of Carlo. Nor were these narratives stylistically or generically consistent. His principal source, the *Spagna in rima*, was, like the *Orlando*, a narrative poem, but, unlike the *Orlando*, it was concerned with a single event reputed by the poet and his contemporaries actually to have taken place. Pulci also drew on work of a directly historical character, particularly the humanist Donato Acciaiuoli's life of Charlemagne in prose, the *Vita Caroli Magni*. Both the nature and the variety of Pulci's sources placed him in a role he had not had to fill in Part 1. The obviously historical basis of the story in Part 2 opened to question, in a way not previously experienced, Pulci's claim to be Carlo's best historian. By introducing to the narrative the problem of the verifiability of reported facts, a problem complicated by the multiplicity of the sources from which these facts were drawn, Pulci was forced to defend as true certain events and correspondingly to discard as false certain others. That is, he had to contribute to the matter he was narrating not only the interpretative embellishments that would make it memorable and comprehensible, but also the judicious discrimination that would convincingly establish it as a factual rather than a fantastic fiction.

This task was one for which Pulci trained himself. What kind of talent he brought to it is evident in Part 1. A brilliant allegorist, he there interpreted the matter of the *Orlando* by exploiting allusions to such mythical heroes as Hercules and Ulysses and to the political associations these figures had come to acquire for Renaissance readers. Moreover, he showed himself to be a comic poet whose linguistic resources permitted him to sketch characters and brief scenes of conflict with a keen sense of what was required to present the eccentric, the hyperbolic, and the ridiculous in the context of a matter inherently serious. There is no indication that Pulci *began* the *Morgante* aware of the historiographic dimension he would eventually give his poem. He perceived himself as Carlo's best historian, but he envisaged his labor as the epic poet's— praising, and not as the historian's—weighing and judging, developing a case for his subject. His treatment of the *Orlando* material in Part 1 certainly reveals that he was capable of being challenged by the possibilities of writing history, specifically of conveying the relationship between change and continuity in the successive dramas of the paladins' departures from and returns to Carlo's court. But what he did not confront there was the most fundamental of the historian's problems, that is, the problem of authority. In Part 2, this problem is the focus of Pulci's attention.

The consequences of this conceptual shift become most sharply evident in Pulci's depiction of Carlo. An obvious change in the character of the Emperor, as the poem progresses from a reliance on the *Orlando* to an adaptation of several works on Roncisvalle, makes Pulci's obligation to honor Lucrezia's order—to write a history in praise of Carlo—the more problematic. In the *Orlando* Carlo is portrayed as a weak Emperor, old and addle-headed. His glory is truly in his paladins who provide the force within chivalric society that guarantees its stability. And in Part 1, after the opening octaves, Pulci does not refer to the Emperor's greatness. The material in his source is simply not conducive to praising Carlo, and Pulci confines himself to illustrating the chivalric virtues of the Emperor's paladins. He defers a consideration of the discrepancy between what the matter he narrates can be reasonably seen to establish and the judgment he has undertaken to render.

In writing the Roncisvalle story for Part 2, on the other hand, Pulci encountered a Carlo less petty, more grandly foolish, and finally more heroic. In the *Spagna in rima*, the Emperor's belief in the trustworthiness of Gano (in Part 1 an expression of the Emperor's fear of change) assumes a tragic character. It provides the rationale for Gano's embassy to Marsilio and thus for the betrayal of Orlando, and a focus both for Carlo's self-reproach and for Orlando's saintly forgiveness. After Orlando's death at Roncisvalle, the *Spagna*'s Emperor becomes a forceful hero— equal to Dante's assessment of him—by triumphing over his former enemies. Other sources that Pulci investigates for the last canto of the poem, notably Acciaiuoli's *Vita Caroli Magni*, present a Carlo even more compatible with Lucrezia's order. But, ironically, this material does not render Pulci's task easier. The divergence in these various portraits of the Emperor demands some kind of resolution. In the poem's last canto, Pulci has to consider Carlo's failings.

Other impediments to praising Carlo become factors in the composition of the poem. As long as his source is the *Orlando*, Pulci can exploit the resources of allegory to assert that the events of history are Providential; he can avoid considering the full pathos inherent in the Boethian paradox, that is, that *sub specie aeternitatis* what is evil to mortals is nevertheless good to God. In contrast, when his source is the corpus of narratives on the story of Roncisvalle in which events are described without reference to mythical figures, he cannot escape presenting this contradiction. Carlo's ineptitude, his overriding affection for Gano, his moments of vacillation, his pride, and his stupidity are the subject of considerable portions of the narrative, while Gano's plotting, Marsilio's treachery, the cunning of the Spanish ambassador Falserone are all vividly portrayed and invite logical criticism.[1] True, the entire story of Orlando's martyrdom is also understood at a typological level as a repetition of the Passion, an interpretation additionally supported by the references to Gano as Judas that rapidly multiply in cantos 25 and on, and by apocalyptic imagery marking the end of Marsilio's kingdom in 25 and 27.[2] But these images do not make any less cogent rational objections to seeing Carlo as a hero.

Pulci's changing representation of Carlo entails a further shift in the perspective he takes on the propriety of the vendetta. The narrative in Part 1 establishes the Boethian principle that the vendetta is prohibited to Christians; salvation may require persecution and the success of evil doers may be God's way of sending them to perdition. Yet this extreme position, implicit in the paladins' rescue of Gano, is undermined in Part 2 when Carlo avenges Orlando's death. Pulci has to gloss these events as part of a divine vendetta, even as he continues to condemn other instances of revenge (those of Antea and Gano) undertaken independent of Providential direction.

This ambivalence has thematic consequences. It gives the poet greater freedom to investigate the mentality of an avenger, to determine whether it is susceptible to rational analysis, and to suggest ways in which a wronged person can be made to renounce revenge. His treatment of the effect on Gano of the slap in the face he receives from Uliviero, and of Antea's decision to return home, gives the narrative a psychological interest it has lacked previously. At the same time, his portrait of Carlo cannot help but become more vexed. How can the Emperor be unable to recognize Gano's treachery, so obvious to everyone else? By what calculus can Carlo be blameworthy and in paradise? Pulci can only allude to the fact that Jesus was also betrayed; he never actually answers the question (28. 15–18).

Its stylistic and thematic complexities aside, the plot of Part 2 is straightforward. The narrative no longer exhibits a dialectical pattern of

stories as it did in Part 1. It does not entertain a moral allegory based on
the interpretation of mythical analogues but rather adopts an imagery
based on Biblical typology. Its principal characters, Orlando and
Rinaldo, continue to invite comparison with each other, but the terms of
their relationship have altered and they represent essentially different
attitudes toward life and history. Orlando triumphs by suffering in a
manner appropriate to a Christian martyr; Rinaldo triumphs because of
his strength and his intellect, and in a manner characteristic of the hero
of ancient epic. Orlando verges on being half-divine. He bears enchanted armor; he has a special destiny; he communicates easily with
angels; he is offered a second life but refuses it; and he is returned to
earth once after death. Rinaldo is more clearly human. Subject to varied
and conflicted desires, he dreams of new worlds on earth; he rejoices in
his own accomplishments; and he is preeminently a social creature.
Orlando's saintly heroism is obviously more suited to the Christian
vision of history as a drama in which God is instrumental and human
beings bear witness to their faith. Rinaldo's idiosyncratic adventurism
suggests someone for whom the possibility of choice is vital and the
experience of a degree of success essential to his existence.

The differences between the heroes do not relate to the ideals developed in Part 1, but to a larger concept of heroism which portrays
purely human agents determining the course of events in history, in
fact, to a heroism that derives from a quality similar to the classical hero's
*virtus*. Despite his depiction of chivalric martyrdom, Pulci neither relin-
quishes the hope that a purely heroic (that is, a human) *virtù*, motivated
by a secular or philosophical love of knowledge, is worth commending,
nor does he bring himself to term it illusory. His portrait of Rinaldo on
the way to Roncisvalle is at once an image of Christian devotion to duty
and of a humanistic commitment to knowledge for its own sake. This—
as a matter of intellectual style—forcefully marks Part 2 as a work of the
fifteenth century.

The unifying element in Part 2 is the narrative voice of the poet. Heard
at brief intervals in Part 1, it comes to dominate Part 2. The thematic
complexity, the display of conflicting attitudes, and the frequent allusions to ideas and theories of philosophy and theology are finally seen to
be circumscribed by Pulci's own imagination. They reflect his desire to
accomplish the task he undertook in a consistent and comprehensible
fashion. What was at stake for him is illustrated by the development
within the narrative of the figure of the poet according to different
conventions of historical narrative. He first appears as a singer of epic
poetry and then, more problematically, as a writer of modern history.[3]

The terms in which Pulci initially conceived of his task as Carlo's historian originate in the conventions of oral presentation that in this period governed the productions of the *cantimbanchi,* the itinerant singers of the stories of Charlemagne, the British King Arthur, and their knights. The poems of the *cantimbanchi* are divided into cantos which contain the material appropriate to a single day's recitation. Each canto typically begins with an invocation to a deity who can be counted on to inspire the poet and concludes with a farewell to the audience and a promise of further recitation. Pulci observes these conventions throughout the *Morgante,* although apart from his initial cantos none can be imagined as fitting into the few hours allotted to a single performance.[4] His first invocation is especially remarkable for the way in which it recalls the function of the Muse in oral as contrasted to literary epic. In the opening stanzas of the *Morgante* Pulci relates that he listens to a divinity who tells him the story he must relate. His Muse, an angel of God who is the Word—"era Iddio il Verbo e'l Verbo Lui"—is obviously Christian:

> mandami solo un degli angel tui,
> che m'accompagni e rechimi a memoria
> una famosa, antica e degna istoria.
>
> (1. 1)

Send me one of your angels who will accompany me and recall to me a famous, old, and worthy story [history].

He implies that the authority in the poem is not the poet's, whose memory is human and therefore fallible, but that of the angel whose memory is perfect.[5]

Pulci's appeal for angelic information is more than merely formulaic. It actually conveys the nature of his authorial situation at the outset of the poem. Transcribing and elaborating a single written source whose veracity he totally accepted—not because he could not in point of fact have questioned it by comparing it with other accounts of the same subject but because he chose not to—he resembles not Vergil, the poet of literary epic, but Homer, the poet of oral epic. He almost certainly knew no Homer, even in Latin translation, but his conception of the Muse as the bearer of *il Verbo di Dio* resembles Homer's in the conditions of authorship it implies.

The *Iliad* begins with this request: "Sing, goddess, the anger of Peleus's son Achilleus," and the *Odyssey* with one similar: "Tell me, Muse, of the man of many ways."[6] What it means to be thus divinely informed is clarified in yet another invocation, prefacing the catalogue of ships in the *Iliad,* Book 2:

Tell me now you Muses who have your homes on Olympos
For you, who are goddesses, are there and you know all things
and we have heard only the rumour of it and know nothing.

(484–86)

Homer's distinction between the Muses, the provenience of historical truth, and mortals, who unaided hear only rumor, invites his listeners to accept as beyond dispute his catalogue and by extension the information in his poem. It constitutes a form of judgment on mere "rumour."[7]

Such is not the position of the later and literary poet, Vergil. His Muse imitates Homer's but, because it provides a text to be read and interpreted rather than words to be repeated, it is also less authoritative. While the *Iliad* opens with a command that the forthcoming story be sung by the goddess, the *Aeneid* is sung by the poet: "I sing of arms and the man" ("Arma virumque cano").[8] And when Vergil imitates Homer in his catalogue of heroes, he calls on the Muses for inspiration, not for the poem itself: "you, o Calliope, I beg, inspire the singer . . . and roll out with me the lengthy scrolls of the war" ("vos o Calliope precor *adspirate canenti* . . . et *mecum* ingentis oras *evolvite* belli", 9. 525–8; my italics). In this instance the Muses work with the poet in unrolling the war's record, which is imagined as a literary text rather than as spoken words. Most important, by singing himself the poet implicitly retains for himself a critical function and remains the judge of the poem's content and style. His is the burden of invention, of the discovery rather than the recovery of the past.

Pulci's self-characterization as one who hears rather than reads what he narrates describes his initial intention in writing his poem and, to judge by a comparison of poem and source, his compositional practice in the first twelve or so cantos. Retrospectively, the archaism of his invocation and its (uncanny) correspondence to the actual facts of the poem's composition distinguish Pulci in the early stages of his work from the more typical poet who represents what he has seen, whether in fact or with his mind's eye, that is, through the recreative effort of reading—an act that would oblige him to decide between various authorities and to project from their accounts his *own* vision of history. For the poet whose work is entirely determined by oral tradition or by an earlier work regarded as so authoritative as not to admit substantial emendation, the words he sings are, in a sense, what he hears. For the poet whose work is composed from or under the influence of various literary texts, on the other hand, it is his vision of or insight into the nature of his subject that is finally authoritative.[9] For him the Word does not exist prior to his work but only as its words have meaning. He may invoke the Muses, as Vergil does, but he will see himself as the singer of his poem.

As long as Pulci listens to the *Orlando,* he does not experience poetic composition as a problematic process involving the evaluation of various kinds of evidence. His conception of his work alters when he is confronted with a multiplicity of sources (that is, after canto 22) and hence the obligation to imagine a representation of their contents that is necessarily his own. In Part 2, Pulci begins to describe the writing of the poem in complicated and sometimes contradictory ways. Pointing to the fact that his sources are no longer authoritative, he ends by pleading for the indulgence of an audience whose acceptance of his poem he can no longer regard as certain. And as he becomes more concerned with questions of authority, he also becomes concerned with an image—one of major importance in Part 2—depicting a transgression of limits: Rinaldo's excursion beyond the pillars of Hercules. The hero's act of crossing from known to unknown, proposed, deferred and at last achieved, suggests a conflict in which the idea of self-authorized enterprise is tested against that of doctrinal or intellectual orthodoxy.

### The Poet's Achievement: Malagigi's Art

Rinaldo wanders through the world and settles in Egypt; Carlo continues to rely on Gano. Antea wishes to avenge her father, the Sultan, by waging war on the Old Man's son, Buiaforte. Gano encourages Antea, attempts to persuade Marsilio to join her against Buiaforte and the French. Bianciardino, the Spanish ambassador, dissuades Marsilio from war. Gano discredits Bianciardino; Marsilio promises to fight Carlo and recalls Bianciardino. The paladins denounce Gano; Uliviero strikes him at court. Antea lands with thirty thousand Babylonians and two giants; she refuses to give up her vendetta. Malagigi devises a little phantom, Marguttino, who lures Antea's giants into a forest where the paladins kill them. Antea's army is badly beaten. Marsilio sends a second ambassador, Falserone, to explain Bianciardino's departure. Falserone declares Marsilio had no intention of helping Antea; Orlando believes him. Antea shows Falserone a tent upon which her father's career is portrayed; she refuses to add the story of her vendetta to it and returns to Babylon. (Canto 24)

Two major images in Part 1 can be interpreted to illustrate the poet's claim to heavenly knowledge and to suggest a conception of poetry and of the way it affects its audience that, while attractive and in a sense conventional, the poet must later withdraw. Pulci's identification of his Muse as angelic does more than imply that his poem will relate the truth of the past; it also creates an impression of his poem as an artistic substitute for the reality it represents. The poet himself can then assume the character of a magician and represent his work as a conjuration of an artificial or magical reality that is wholly indistinguishable from reality itself. And in fact it is in the activities of Malagigi that Pulci at first represents the work of an infallible poet.

His achievement is presented theoretically in the image of Malagigi's horse, a creation of the magician's art which functions perfectly in real situations. The occasion of its fashioning falls in a digressionary episode in the story of Brunoro's punishment (iii), as Rinaldo is on his way to find Orlando in Pagania. The episode has no place in the plot; its only purpose is to disclose the nature of Malagigi's power. Malagigi, disguised as an old man, begs for and receives a ride on Rinaldo's horse, Baiardo, whom the magician manages easily despite that animal's notorious capriciousness. He then creates his own horse from air and rides off on it after having given Rinaldo a root that will take away hunger and thirst. In being a wholly satisfactory substitute for an actual horse, Malagigi's magical creature proves that his art cannot be discounted as trickery or illusion. The magician possesses total control of nature, even to its creation, and he is clairvoyant. He sees the danger the paladins will encounter and this prophetic gift is symbolized in the root that anticipates physical needs. Malagigi's attributes are properly those of the poet who claims to be infallible and insists that his productions are absolutely true, that is, altogether like the subject they represent. Pulci implicitly reinforces his claim to access to a recording angel when he shows the art of Malagigi bringing forth creations that are in no way falsifiable as fact.

Luciana's tent, a more conventional image of divine knowledge, conveys a similar confidence in the creation of an artistic representation that corresponds to its subject (see the adventure of Marsilio's horse, v). The terms of the correspondence differ, however, from those governing the creation of Malagigi's horse; in this case the representation is not a substitute for reality but an image of it. Luciana's tent, a work of art, is remarkable because it depicts all of creation as Luciana (a figure of the sun) knows it. An image in an allegory of temperance, it is not itself an accurate record of the creatures of the universe but rather a symbol of what an accurate record would be. Moreover, it conveys the possibility that such a record—complete, definitive, and therefore not subject to emendation—might be communicated. Representing a closed rather than an open system, it reflects the essentially medieval concept of knowledge as a totality, a kind of *summa scientifica*.

Pulci does not qualify the powers he assigns Malagigi, and by inference the artist or poet, until canto 22, where he alters his conception of the magician and invents new limits to his power. These limits are, I think, analogous to those by which he now perceives himself to be restricted. They are related to the increasing difficulty he experiences in presenting his subject so that it is logically consistent, that is, so that what he relates concerning Carlo substantiates the judgment of him (Dante's orthodoxy) he is committed to make. They are further associated with a view of language that is new to the poem: language is no longer a repository of signs whose meanings are made stable by reference to a transcendent (metaphysical) reality but rather of signs whose meanings are acquired by reference to actual (historical) situations.

During the story of Calavrion's attack on Carlo (i'), Malagigi withholds crucial information from the paladins. Up to this point he has been the character who has overseen their activities; now he refuses to disclose to them that Gano is responsible for Aldighieri's murder.

> Malagigi non volle gittar l'arte,
> però che ne facea gran conscïenza,
> e non si può far sempre in ogni parte:
> convien ch'a molte cose abbi avvertenzia,
> e veste consecrate, e certe carte
> essorcizzate con gran diligenzia
> pentacul, candarìe, sigilli e lumi
> e spade e sangue e pentole e profumi.
>
> Questo dich'io, ch'i so ch'alcun direbbe:
> "Quando costoro avevon Malagigi,
> d'ogni cosa avvisar gli doverrebbe:
> 'Così fa il tal, così Carlo in Parigi.'
> Dunque costui come un iddio sarebbe,
> se sapessi d'ognun sempre i vestigi:
> i negromanti rade volte fanno
> l'arte, e non dicon ciò che sempre sanno."
>
> (22. 102, 103)

Malagigi did not wish to perform magic; he had many scruples about this, [realizing] that it was not suitable for all occasions: all kinds of things had to be constrained with great care: sacred clothing, certain letters imbued with magical power, stars, instruments, symbols, lights, swords, blood, oils and scents.

I say this because I know that someone will say: when Malagigi was with these paladins he ought to have advised them about everything. "This one does this, Carlo does that in Paris." But then he would be like a god, since he would always know the signs [would have foreknowledge] of everything. Frequently magicians know what's what but often they do not tell what they know.

Although Malagigi's art remains magical, it is now restricted to those activities which are specifically designated as human and not divine. The distinction is made to apply to a concept previously explored only indirectly: the affective potential of the work of art and, most important, its capacity to present moral options. Here Pulci implies that art creates not a substitute reality or its symbolic image but rather its image framed in hypothetical terms designed to draw its audience into an exercise of the will. To give this will due scope, Pulci declares, the magician is sometimes silent—that is, he does not prescribe (as he did), but merely illustrates. What he portrays may propose or even conduce to a certain course of action, but whether this course will actually be adopted is a matter for his audience's determination. Were Malagigi to go on protecting the paladins by revealing Gano's true nature to them, he would be "like God"; he would not only know all things but he would be able to perform all things also. Gano's presence among the paladins is, it is implied, crucial to their spiritual well-being and tantamount to a constant trial of their moral perception. The doctrinal implications of this passage, involving the degree of knowledge necessary to a free choice, are explored in later passages by Astarotte, Malagigi's diabolical accomplice. What is important here is that Malagigi's art is shown as confronting the paladins with enigmas—persons and situations—that will challenge their capacity to choose and act well. Their testing follows and is a function of a restriction of Malagigi's art.

Informing this modification in Malagigi's power is, finally, an alteration in Pulci's perception of the poet's task. Malagigi's silence, his refusal to put his instruments into play, his conviction that magic is not for all times and places, are obvious correlatives of the inversion of rhetorical and moral values that Pulci portrays from this moment in canto 22 to the end of Part 1. In narrating the circumstances of Calavrion's defeat, Pulci depicts a kind of discourse new to the poem. In the constructive illusions and creative lies to which the paladins resort to gain beneficial ends, the notion that art is excellent insofar as it truthfully represents its subject is challenged. The concept of language itself alters as its relationship to a metaphysical truth is jeopardized. It becomes bound up with the concept of temporality and forces the poet to see his own poem implicated in the condition it describes.

Pulci's redefinition of artistic activity, undertaken in Part 2, also draws on an important critique of illusionism that he has included in Part 1. That art could *avoid* responsibility for educating its audience is a possibility the poem entertains in Florinetta's adventure (b) when Margutte, in addition to being intemperate, also plays the part of a exploitative *metteur-en-scène*. Pulci condemns Margutte's easy manipulation of ap-

pearances and distinguishes it from the activities of the morally responsible artist in his depiction of Morgante's chastisement of Margutte.

The nature of Margutte's power as an artist who is given only to
illusionistic displays is conveyed by the nature of his dependency on
Morgante. His weakness, relative to Morgante's strength, is registered in
the limitations of his profession. While the giant is a hunter, one who
appropriates elements in the outside world necessary to human life, the
half-giant is merely a "cook" (19. 57), one who makes palatable their
assimilation. The division of labor between these friends establishes a
metaphorical model of artistic creation. It mimes the processes of inventing matter and dressing it in an appealing manner. When Morgante
takes Margutte's food away from him, in effect starving him, he reminds
Margutte, as a representative of the skills of rhetoric, of the importance
of his own function of hunting and gathering, that is, of invention. The
image draws on the considerable corpus of Renaissance criticism on the
art and processes of imitation and makes specific use of the trope of
ingestion; in these treatises the poet is frequently likened to one who
assimilates experience in order to render it more palatable to his audience.[10] Here Margutte, the artist whose function is merely to make
palatable, is educated in his dependence on what Pulci implies is the
more fundamental operation: that of discovering a subject. Margutte is,
in short, a kind of parasite artist, his activities limited to the witty
manipulation of appearances. Morgante's own use of Margutte's particular skill of dressing is crude but effective and exemplifies, in a ribald
manner, the correct way to combine invention and rhetorical embellish-
ment in the creation of a morally acceptable art. Morgante, having found
the monkey as he has found various other animals in the forest, does not
in this instance kill him and hand him to Margutte for cooking, but
rather does his own dressing (crowning him in Margutte's cockscomb)
and so creates what is in effect a dramatic work of art: an image of his
friend that, like all effective satire, destroys the vice it represents. Apes
were notorious for being purely imitative, for creating a pseudoart
which, because limited to the precise repetition of a model, is essentially
illusionistic.

In canto 24, however, reassembling all the elements of his portrait of
the artist represented in earlier passages, Pulci presents the reader with
a new model of poetic activity. Morgante, the inventor of matter, and
Margutte, its embellisher, are replaced by Malagigi, the magician who
sees—although he does not necessarily relate—everything, and Marguttino, his phantom creature. Their association confers a new purpose
upon art and redefines the relationship of art to truth. Art will no longer
be judged in relation to the status of its source, to the quality of its
invention, but rather to its capacity to generate change, in short, to have

an effect. This shift will entail a reassessment of its illusionistic quality. The episode marks the poem's *theoretical* break with the norms of composition it first proposed (a break actually experienced in canto 22) and explicitly proposes a mode of representation predicated upon authorial intention rather than upon access to a truthful authority. Here Malagigi uses his art to illustrate to Antea the nature of choices made for and against revenge.

Because Antea is not a Christian, she is not obliged to obey what Christians regard as the decrees of Providence. But by undertaking to revenge her father's death, she rebels against what she must (unless she denies her father's own dreams in which he reported his death as fatal) regard as a supernatural order. Emphasizing this implied contradiction, Pulci shows Antea as unreasonable. She insists on the "rightness" ("ragione") of her vendetta and on its divine sanction: "[F]or this work is not mine alone but given [to me] from above" ("però che questa alfin non è mia opra / ma così dato . . . è disopra", 24. 71). But when Uliviero reminds her that her father's death was "by chance" ("per sorte") and that therefore the "fault" ("colpa") must belong to "the fates and to heaven" ("i fati e 'l Ciel", 24. 80), she reveals that, whatever the terms with which she justifies her invasion, she is moved chiefly by a desire to fight Orlando (24. 82). Her words reveal the intransigeance that so often characterizes intemperance in chivalric romance and that will reappear, strikingly, in Gano's refusal to halt plans for Roncisvalle. Both episodes show that the logic of an inflexible will is always the same. Having committed itself to a given course of action it cannot turn away from it; it must, or might as well, go on. In passages like this, the choice to return to a starting place acquires moral significance.

Antea's unwillingness to accept what the fates have decreed is symbolized by her possession of two giants. They are her pride and most effective weapon, and are confounded only by Malagigi's art. When Orlando asks Malagigi what he and the other paladins can do to defend themselves from these formidable adversaries, the magician promises to perform a trick that will drive them mad with laughter (24. 65, 86). He conjures up a second Margutte, Marguttino, who, playing Pan's flute, dances about the crazed giants and gradually lures them into a deep forest where they become trapped in bird lime. Pulci stresses that Marguttino, while himself a product of magic and therefore by implication not to be classified with ordinary phenomena, operates in real situations. The wood, the bird lime are "not false illusions but have an effect" ("non falsa illusion, ma con effetto", 24. 97). But Malagigi's magical art also has limits; he tells Orlando to kill the trapped giants for he can do no more with his "art" ("arte") (24. 100).

The episode recalls Pulci's earlier circumscription of Malagigi's powers but goes further in its definition of what precisely the magician can achieve. At issue is the nature of his creation. Pulci defends his own representation of Malagigi's Marguttino as truthful, although without the substance and power that belongs to creatures of nature. He, Pulci, has seen what he reported "with his mind's eye" ("con gli occhi della mente") and it is not artificial ("simulato o fitto"). At the same time, Malagigi's art is incapable of actually recreating reality. To the person who complains that Malagigi could have destroyed Antea's giants like wax, Pulci replies:

> nota che l'arte ha modo e tempo e loco
> ché, se la oppinïon qui fussi vera,
> sare' troppo felice un negromante,
> anzi signor dal Ponente al Lavante.
>
> Ma quello Iddio che impera a tutti i regi
> ha dato termine, ordine e misura,
> e non si può passar più là che i fregi,
> però che a ogni cosa egli ebbe cura;
> e fatture, aüruspi e sortilegi
> non posson far quel che non può natura,
> e le imagin più oltre son di ghiaccio,
> perché e' fe'la potenzia nel suo braccio.
>
> (24. 106, 107)

Look, art has a time and a place; if the view you expressed here were correct, a magician would be too powerful, a real lord from east to west.

But that Lord who rules all kingdoms has set bounds [to human power] which must not be breached; he takes care of everything and the magical arts cannot do more than nature can do; the figures it constructs beyond nature are made of ice for "he hath shewed strength with his arm" (Luke 1:51).

By insisting that art has its limits and by implication that the world is not wholly open to human determination, Pulci proposes a status for artistic creation that appears paradoxical. In being constrained by what is natural, art is a kind of nature. Like magic, it exploits nature, reordering its elements to suit a particular purpose, but, unlike a "too powerful" ("troppo felice") magic, it cannot refashion nature entirely. Art that attempts more than what can be termed natural is without substance and fantastic, since the artist's power is no more than natural and cannot logically produce more than natural things. This argument effectively develops Pulci's earlier notion of the illusionistic function of art as he sets it forth in the Margutte episode. There, a distinction was made between misrepresentation—Margutte's facile lies—and Morgante's satirical representation of Margutte as a monkey in a cockscomb. Pulci insisted that art must declare its artifice and appear not as reality but as a recognizable image of it. Here, in contrast, Pulci explores the illusionistic aspects of art in relation to its didactic function. The artificiality of art is important precisely because it permits decisions to be made about the reality that it represents.

To give this idea a more precise formulation Pulci further distinguishes Malagigi's art from the vision or art of saints. Enlightened by grace ("per grazia") saints do perceive "divine truth" (*"arcana dei"*) whereas Malagigi, proceeding by "natural skill" ("virtù natural", 24. 108), merely sees how to create images in which his audience will be presented in more vivid forms the choices that it routinely confronts in life.[11] Malagigi can tempt the giants but he cannot kill them. They might have refused to listen to Marguttino's pipe and so escaped his trap, "for free will is denied no one, since it is given by God" ("ch'a nessuno è negato / libero arbitrio, che da Dio c'è dato", 24. 111). It is important to our conception of Malagigi's art later in the poem—where it is manifest as the magician's control over the devil Astarotte who is summoned from hell to guide Rinaldo to Roncisvalle—that Pulci classifies it here as natural. He prepares us for Malagigi's most phenomenal expression of artistic power: the strategem by which he arranges Rinaldo's return to Roncisvalle, an art that shapes history. At the same time, Pulci goes on to set art apart from the experiments he identifies as pure magic—"a lovely game" ("un bel giuoco")—and unconcerned with truth. The artist must reject pure magic because it lacks any moral reference, as the poet does here after he acknowledges his former involvement with necromancy: "[T]hat was my Parnassus and my Muse" ("questo era il mio Parnasso e le mie Muse", 24. 113). In Pulci's case, this confession represents the results of an actual choice between the magic described by Cecco d'Ascoli's *Acerba* (24. 112) and his own *Morgante*. But it refers also to the kind of art he has described earlier in his poem and now rejects.[12]

Pulci demonstrates the instrumentality of Malagigi's art by showing that Antea, after Malagigi has arranged to have her giants destroyed, is free to follow a constructive course of action based on a choice between two ways of interpreting the past. She renounces her commitment to a vendetta, shown in its inception as a result of her pride, and elects to listen to her "noble heart" ("generosa core"), that is, to remember what was pleasing in her relations with the paladins and to act on that rather than on filial loyalty. The choice is put to her by Falserone, Marsilio's ambassador, who, in referring to the "shame" ("vergogna") of her father's history represented on her decorated tent, attempts to revive her pride. But on this occasion Antea perceives the figures on her tent in a different way: "[F]or she wished to remember what was pleasing to her" ("che si vuol ricordar di quel che piace . . .", 24. 177). Pulci implies that the historical evidence for either choice is the same. What is determinative is how this evidence is regarded. It is important that Antea's decision is based not on reason, *ragione*, but desire, *disio*, the will or disposition to achieve a certain end. The episode has the effect of dissociating still more definitively the writing of history from processes intended to recover the truth of the past, and of situating it among the emotive arts of rhetoric and poetry.

Antea's choice suggests, moreover, a historiographic style. Her decision to return to Babylon is tantamount to her acceptance of closure, of the fact that a sequence of events in time can be seen to be concluded by the common consent of all interested parties. She decides that her father's history is complete and that she will not add to scenes already represented on her tent. Her choice appears to reflect her acceptance of the idea of a Providential history and to recall similar decisions by Morgante, Erminion and others. Yet Antea's situation differs from theirs. In her tent Pulci has presented the Sultan's history not as a sacred discourse but as a visual image composed by human art. This implies that history is not the product of a process in which truth is transmitted from one age to the next, but rather of an artistic endeavor. The very fact that Antea's pictorial tent must have a *design* (and Pulci refers to Falserone's "desegno" in proposing to Antea the choices she has, 24. 176) suggests that human beings experience history as a work of art intended to engage the reader's emotions and affect his will.

In light of this re-presentation of Malagigi in the role of artist, Pulci's invocation to canto 24, revealing that he can no longer accept without question the terms on which he undertook to write the *Morgante*, can be understood as a statement of reconceived intention, a deliberate and critical reflection on his claims to authority in the first octaves of Part 1. In the later passage, he begins to evolve the basis for a distinction between the concepts of authority and authorship, for regarding the first as a kind of deception and the second as a form of subtle pleading whose effectiveness rests in the strategies used for presenting certain choices as better than others. Having admitted that he must represent a displeasing historical truth, Orlando's defeat at Roncisvalle, he imagines that this obligation is a kind of "captivity in Egypt" from which he asks the Lord to deliver him (1). As he enlarges on the conditions of this captivity, it becomes clear that he is describing his relationship to his sources.

e benché il ver malvolentier qui scriva
convien ch'io scriva pur come altri scrisse,
per non far come all'alta storia argiva:
Omer troppo essaltò gli error d'Ulisse,
e del figliuol famoso della diva
non so se il vero appunto anche si disse.

(2)

and although I write the truth here unwillingly I must write as others have written in order to avoid the mistakes of the story of Troy. Homer praised the wanderings of Ulysses excessively and I don't even know if the real truth was spoken of the famous son of the goddess.

Pulci's determination to stick to authoritative accounts of his story, however poorly his heroes may fare in them, is apparently based on his belief that the poets of ancient epic lied. Implicit in this complaint is the conviction that the nature of authority the poet must face up to in Part 2 is somehow qualitatively different from that which he had earlier envisaged. The angelic Muse he called on in canto 1 has been replaced by the "others" he must imitate; their words constitute a form of captivity. At the same time he condemns the products of the epic Muse, Homer's *Iliad* and *Odyssey,* and thereby hints that she is a kind of fraud, at least insofar as she represents herself as a bearer of the truth. Despite its conventionality, this criticism of the Muse hides, I think, the real regret just expressed in the notion of the captive poet. Pulci suggests that the poet of ancient epic, in claiming the Muse as his source, enjoyed an *actual* liberty, experienced as a liberty to lie, that he himself is denied. To the poet of Part 2, the epic Muse has become merely a screen for an authorial independence from which he, by having to relate what he supposed was the truth of history, is necessarily excluded. How much Pulci may have wished to be his own authority is suggested early in canto 24 when he asserts that his sources for his account of Carlo's tragedy give him a picture of all the events he relates in his mind—"for I see clearly with the eyes of my mind, as if in a mirror" ("ch'io veggo scorto/cogli occhi della mente in uno specchio", 4). Intended to forestall criticism, this admission actually draws attention to the subjective nature of his account, which originates not in authoritative words (whatever the source) but in what the poet himself sees. Because this vision needs verbalization, it is the poet as interpreter who becomes authoritative.

In the following cantos, Pulci's analysis of his own role as poet is conveyed by his complex representations of heroism. The burden of resolving his dilemma—whether or not to continue to present his history in an orthodox manner following his sources—is projected onto various figures (especially Rinaldo), who represent the use as well as the abuse of *virtù*, the dramatic equivalent of the poet's willingness to challenge authority. Because the action in this part of the poem is fundamentally tragic, heroism is generally liable to criticism. Those characters—Antea, Gano, Marsilio—who are exponents of obviously humanistic enterprises, who pursue fame and extol the benefits of adversity, are classified as the enemy. In contrast, Orlando assumes a Christlike character, Carlo is apostrophized as Job, and Rinaldo, although he possesses the *virtù* of the classical hero—in Part 2, specifically of Ulysses—is also faithful to his Christian mission.

The notion of Providential history is given dramatic expression not only by showing Christians who triumph through suffering but also by attributing the punishment of the guilty—Gano and Marsilio—directly to God. The miraculous scope and grandeur of the events of Carlo's triumph over the infidel demonstrate that the Emperor participates in a history that is divinely ordained. Since this history is, moreover, presented as a repetition of the story of the Passion, its true end is in paradox: God's love is shown in the sacrifice of the most saintly.

### The Poet's Dilemma: Astarotte's Instruction

Carlo decides to send Gano to arrange a treaty with Marsilio. Gano tells Marsilio that Orlando foregoes his claims to Spain and will come to Roncisvalle to get a gift from Marsilio which will serve as periodic tribute. Prodigies occur foretelling the end of a kingdom. Orlando agrees to obey Carlo's order to collect Marsilio's tribute. Malagigi performs magic to discover the whereabouts of Rinaldo; he then summons the devil Astarotte to fetch Rinaldo back to France. They fly over the Mediterranean together; Astarotte tells Rinaldo that it is now possible to voyage beyond the pillars of Hercules; Rinaldo declares that he will go to the Antipodes to convert the heathen after he has fulfilled Carlo's commands. Astarotte describes some additions to Luciana's tent depicting all creation. At Roncisvalle, Uliviero realizes that Gano and Marsilio have trapped him and Orlando. Orlando refuses to sound his horn. Rinaldo arrives; all the paladins fight. Uliviero is killed; Orlando is wounded and dies. On this day the sun does not set in order to allow Carlo to take revenge on Marsilio. Gano is imprisoned. Rinaldo organizes the burning of Saragossa. (Cantos 25, 26, 27)

The story of Gano's treachery is in deliberate contrast to that of Antea's conquest. While Antea is flexible and returns to Babylon, he continues to pursue his course of action even though (and perhaps because) he knows he is damned. These events are seen to confirm the idea of

Providential history by their figural relationship to the events of the Passion—in this case also the context for the poet's denunciation of *virtù* conceived in the humanistic manner, that is, as a purely human strength. Gano's treasonable acts are actually based on the assumption that the infidel Antea and Marsilio will respond to the values exemplified by the heroes of classical myth and history. He uses the arts of language to create situations in which his audience—Antea and Marsilio—imagine they can act forcefully to shape the course of events. To Marsilio, for example, he employs the tropes and figures associated with the rhetoric of Roman civic life. He encourages Marsilio to oppose Carlo, to understand that "fame is not acquired without obstacles" ("non s'aquista sanza ostacul fama", 25. 34) and that "honor, glory, and kingdom are won in battle" ("ché combattendo . . . onor s'acquista, gloria e regno", 25. 36), and to reflect on Scipio's words to his fellow citizens urging Rome to preserve Carthage in order that the empire continue to have an enemy to fight (25. 35). The fruits of this advice appear in Marsilio's determination to conquer France, a decision the king justifies on the eve of Roncisvalle by quoting "Caesar" on the valid reasons for breaking a treaty: "to save a kingdom or for revenge" ("per tener regno, o per vendetta", 25. 189).

Pulci's consequent treatment of heroism is predicated on its obvious attractiveness: in order to vitiate it, he fashions a context in which its deceptiveness is readily recognizable. He continues to insist on the principle of free will, but correlatively he asserts that what passes for *virtù* is often a kind of feckless ignorance or obstinate pride. His strategy is to demonstrate, in successive portraits, the ways in which an uncritical notion of *virtù* can, on the one hand, trivialize choice, and, on the other, fail to entertain it fully. Conversely, he shows that *virtù* is not incompatible with Christian obedience, and courage is not necessarily engaged in tempting fortune. His heroes, Rinaldo and Orlando, each succeed in modifying their commitment to heroic self-definition in the interest of their salvation. This sequence of portraits, of Marsilio, Gano, Rinaldo, and Orlando respectively, composes a brilliant argument against the kind of experience to which Pulci must have himself been enormously attracted.

Pulci depicts Marsilio's decision to conspire against Carlo as an expression of his willingness to overlook the function of the will in determining a course of action. Defending himself against Carlo's requirement that he convert to Christianity before any treaty is concluded, Marsilio relates to Gano a parable concerning the choice of religion a human soul makes before it enters life. Marsilio portrays the soul before birth as a winged creature hovering about this or that religion, the "first"—and by implication the truest—of gold, the "second" of silver, and so forth. The one it lights on it espouses. It therefore possesses "free will" ("libero arbitrio"). Its choice is, however, extraordinarily limited by ignorance, for, as Marsilio says, "very simple souls know little" ("l'anime . . . simplicette sanno poco", 25. 45).[13] The parable would appear to be intended to instruct Gano (and the reader) in the merits of tolerance and in the possibility that the differences in religions may be relative to time and place, that from a timeless perspective they might all be aspects of a single truth. As an expression of *Marsilio*'s faith, however, the parable acquires additional meaning: its purpose is obviously to excuse the need for choice. Marsilio does not actually argue for religious toleration but rather for indifference; he diminishes the scope of the will by terming uninformed its choice in the matter of religion.[14] This argument is fully answered by Astarotte in the next canto.

If in Marsilio Pulci represents the spiritual *accidia* characteristic of the infidel and epitomized in scripture by Pilate's perception of truth as a jest, he represents in Gano the sin of despair. Gano cannot repent; he loses hope (25. 48); and, finally, playing out the part of Judas in Pulci's terms, he reckons his existence to be worth that of "a fly in the south" ("una mosca in Puglia", 25. 69). In refusing to admit the possibility of forgiveness and thus neglecting really to entertain the choices open to him, Gano conforms to a type common in chivalric romance—the knight who, inspired by his own *virtù*, pursues his quests independent of his lord and refuses to return to court to honor that authority. His transgression is often literal: he ventures beyond a certain limit or boundary.

That both Gano and Marsilio appear to be so obviously ranked with exponents of classical humanism makes Pulci's emphasis throughout Part 2 on the mysteries of Providential history all the more striking. Here, the pride of the infidel and his ally are answered not by human strength or wit but by divine power, celebrated by the repetition of sacred history in this history of Carlo and his paladins. In addition to the Christological aspects of Orlando's martyrdom, the scene of Gano's treachery is marked by imagery of the Apocalypse: the sun vanishes; a dragon of fire appears; the water of the fountain boils red; the carob tree drops blood (25. 73). Marsilio's magicians naturally misinterpret these signs (25. 78) and so compound the king's error.

But one sign in the episode—a laurel struck with lightening and burned, an image of classical not Biblical origin—refers to an event alien to the matter Pulci narrates, Carlo's history, and marks yet another moment in Pulci's exploration of the possibilities of a self-authorized poem:

> O Febo, come hai tu que' be' crin d'oro
> così lasciato fulminare adesso?
> Dunque i suoi privilegi il lauro or perde,
> che per ogni stagion suol parer verde?
>
> (25. 74)

O Phebus, have you let that lovely golden crown turn brown? Now will the laurel that used to appear green in all seasons lose this distinction?

Marsilio's magicians determine that the laurel, used to crown emperors and poets, signifies an empire; which empire, they declare, depends on the context in which the symbol appears. Marsilio learns too late that the empire signified is his and not Carlo's. Yet the laurel is also the sign of Apollo's empire, or poetry, and its preeminent "distinction" is to remain green throughout the seasons, that is, to signify whatever can be regarded as eternal in poetry. Pulci fittingly entertains the image of a burnt laurel just as he begins to write his major addition to the poem—an addition, moreover, that substantially revises certainly one of the most important passages in the *Divina Commedia*. To account for this revision he even invents a source. The action seems to dramatize the significance of the image and suggests that the notion of poetry as eternal is to be replaced by a concept of its temporality and of the ephemeral nature of poetic meaning.[15] To Pulci, clearly, the evergreen laurel has its place in a world of literary experience where authorities remain authoritative, a world no longer his.

The logical brilliance of Pulci's story of Rinaldo's return to Roncisvalle testifies to the compensatory effect that the poet's discrediting the notion of an eternal poetry had on the course of the poem. Not, however, without some qualification. Both Rinaldo and Astarotte, who together incarnate the spirit of what might be termed self-authorization, also fulfill the requirements of orthodoxy. Rinaldo, whose activities in the East prior to Roncisvalle could not be characterized as chivalric—he spends his time exploring the unknown world—returns to help the Emperor. He pauses before the great pillars at Gibraltar, where, denying his wish to go beyond them, he prays for help in the battle to come. And Astarotte, while encouraging Rinaldo in his intellectual aspirations, voices orthodox opinions about free will and divine judgment. As a devil who helps the cause he hates and has defied, he symbolizes the Providential conversion of evil to good. Trapped (like Marguttino) by Malagigi's art, he is constrained to accept a role he would not choose.[16] His service to Christianity signals the acme of the magician's power to deploy and redirect maleficent forces so that they achieve beneficial ends. But, in the tension implicit in Astarotte's motives both to serve and to warn, expressed when he tells Malagigi to have confidence in him since no wise man (even one damned) will act against his interest, but also not to trust devils (25. 160, 166), is reflected Pulci's appreciation of the risks the poet takes when he writes the kind of episode that Pulci is in fact about to write. For Pulci's account of Rinaldo's journey back to France is in one respect a celebration of the merely human *virtù* of the hero and, by extension, of the self-authorized poet. It is, moreover, a episode that acquires its significance by its revisionary quality; Pulci actually alters a text of Dante in order to provide a basis for the continuation of his poem. No clearer challenge could be made to the authority on whom he is supposed to be resting his case.

The episode itself is intended to be recognized as sourceless, that is, as *fiction*. Pulci attributes his account to a certain Arnaldo. But what he then proceeds to say about his own method of composition makes it clear that Arnaldo is simply Pulci himself. He declares he needs to walk in a path both "right and straight" ("diritto"), and complains that, "when he wanders a step from the way" ("che come esco un passo della via"), he meets with carping critics. For this reason, he goes on to say with evident illogic, he elects a solitary life (25. 116) and a natural or rustic Muse:[17]

> La mia accademia un tempo o mia ginnasia
> è stata volentier ne' miei boschetti,
> e puossi ben veder l'Affrica e l'Asia:
> vengon le ninfe con lor canestretti,
> e portanmi o narciso o colocasia;
> e così fuggo mille urban dispetti;
> sì ch'io non torno a' vostri ariopaghi
> gente pur sempre di mal dicer vaghi.
>
> (25. 117)

My academy and school I have chosen to set up in my little woods, where one can easily perceive Africa and Asia and the nymphs with their little pipes who bring me narcissus and perfumed flowers. Thus I fly from a thousand city torments: never shall I return to your establishment, you people who desire only to denigrate others.

The sequence of thought in these octaves does not make sense unless construed as a paradox: by walking out of the way, that is, in the woods, Pulci walks in the way and listens to a better behaved Muse. He later repeats the substance of this claim when, again justifying Rinaldo's presence at Roncisvalle, he declares that no reader can fault Arnaldo who says such beautiful things. At the same time, this beauty consists in variety and movement (and suggests creativity), not in unity and consistency. Pulci does not actually say that in composing this "varied" portion of his poem he wanders, but the image of it as a flowery way ("la nostra istoria è sì fiorita e varia"), recalling the travels of the disobedient Proserpina, certainly suggests it (25. 168). His allusion to his "academy" far from a hostile society of *literati* further defines his concerns as specifically political, that is, with Ficino and their quarrels. Later in the poem he will again register his anger at the philosopher for his reaction to the sonnet "In principio era buio . . ." (see 28. 42). But at a profounder level, the paradox indicates the developing significance of the concept of authority for the poet. In his story of Rinaldo's return, he will attempt to translate this paradox dramatically.

Pulci conveys his notion of the artist's power of conception and expression in Malagigi's control over Astarotte, a control which results in Rinaldo's return to France and thus in Carlo's victory over the infidel. What the magician can perform is an extension of the devil's power, harnessed in the interest of achieving a certain end. Once achieved, Malagigi promises Astarotte he will burn the particular "little book" ("libretto") by which he controls him (25. 120). The limits of Astarotte's vision (and therefore of Malagigi's in this instance) both recall and modify the vision of Dante's damned. Like the damned, Astarotte can see the past, but, unlike them, he can also see the present; in contrast, again unlike them, he cannot see the future except as do "astrologers" and "learned human beings" ("astrolagi," and "persone dotte", 25. 135). Astarotte excuses the relative weakness of his sight by explaining that no creature possesses wings long enough to attain divine knowledge or perfect knowledge of the divinity: "He who made all alone knows all, / even his son does not know everything" ("Colui che tutto fe', sa il tutto solo, / e non sa ogni cosa il suo Figliuolo", 25. 136; see Mark 13:32). The passage revises Pulci's earlier claim that saints saw the *arcana dei* (24. 108) by implying that the poet, in being human, will have access neither to the Word nor to a mirror (his own powers of reflection and imagination) that is wholly clear.

This excursus into the nature of human vision is complemented by a discussion of free will. Malagigi has earlier asserted that his works, the songs of Marguttino and so forth, cannot compel his audience to a course of action. From Astarotte he now learns that God's knowledge, though total, also does not constitute a form of compulsion. Astarotte's argument, both familiar and orthodox, reconciles the doctrine of divine omniscience with that of free will. Here it is of interest only because it shows how tenaciously Pulci held to the conception of *libero arbitrio* and how fully he was prepared to link it with his poetics. Just as Malagigi has seen everything but can do no more than represent choices, so God, while omniscient, allows human beings to shape their destinies. And as Malagigi controls Astarotte for Rinaldo's and finally Carlo's benefit, so Providence dispenses evil for a larger good. The episode answers indirectly Marsilio's claim that human life is dictated by random choices. Through Astarotte, Pulci exposes a more complex and paradoxical reality. Human beings cannot know the full truth; nevertheless, they must accept the burden of choice.

Rinaldo's choice at the pillars of Hercules, the principal event in his journey back to France, illustrates Pulci's idea of the ways in which human beings experience independent thought yet are also controlled by authority and tradition. Before his return to France, Rinaldo exemplifies the directionless folly of a person whose intellect has yet to be directed toward moral ends. He resembles the "spiriti folletti" against whom Astarotte, about to set out to retrieve Rinaldo, warns Malagigi. To be useful, these spirits must be constrained in water or a mirror (25. 160), that is, dedicated to reflective purposes. As Astarotte tells the magician, Rinaldo has wandered through the Holy Land, travelled to India, seen the pillars of Hercules and, wishing to conquer the Atlantic, praised Ulysses for venturing into the "other world" ("altro mondo", 25. 130). Astarotte adds that Rinaldo does not intend to return to Christendom (25. 131). In effect, he has renounced the moral heroism of Hercules, his earlier model, and instead espoused the dangerous course of Dante's sinner, Ulysses. That Malagigi's charmed Astarotte induces Rinaldo to abandon these activities indicates the effectiveness of the magician's art—an art now recognized as both informed by extraordinary insight (Astarotte's diabolical heterodoxy) and constrained by human factors (Malagigi's purposeful though limited magic). What, precisely, is at stake in this conversion is made clear when Pulci describes Rinaldo's decision to forego the temptation to sail beyond the pillars of Hercules, that is, to reject Ulysses as a model. It is really a mark of Pulci's genius that this conversion does not proceed on the grounds set forth by Dante.

Readers of the *Inferno* have yet conclusively to determine if the sin for which Ulysses is damned includes the cause of his voyage beyond the pillars and consequent death, or if it is limited to his treachery at Troy.[18] Pulci's treatment of Rinaldo—a second and differently motivated Ulysses—would suggest that he considered Dante's voyaging hero not merely unenlightened by Christian faith but actually sinful. To him, I think, the significance of Ulysses' transgression was to be deduced from these lines in the *Inferno*:

> né dolcezza di figlio, né la pieta
> del vecchio padre, né'l debito amore

lo qual dovea Penelope far lieta,
vincer potero dentro a me l'ardore
ch'i' ebbi a divenir del mondo esperto
e de li vizi umani e del valore. . . .

(26. 94–99)

neither fondness for my son, nor reverence for my aged father, nor the due love which would have made Penelope glad, could conquer in me the longing that I had to gain experience of the world, and of human vice and worth.[19]

Implied in Ulysses' drowning is the view that intellectual life which divorces itself from human concerns is simply illicit. When Rinaldo, visiting the pillars of Hercules on his way to France under the direction of Malagigi's captive Astarotte, decides to proceed to help Orlando rather than to fulfill his earlier wish to explore unknown regions, he not only sets Christian warfare before the satisfactions due an individual intellect, he also accepts the moral strictures of the earlier poet (25. 245).[20] But while Pulci bases Rinaldo's conversion on what he understands to be the significance of Dante's Ulysses, he deliberately rejects the philosophical and intellectual position on which he perceives Dante's portrait of the hero rests. He alters what Dante's image of the "known world" implies—that it is defined in terms of limits—and in effect distinguishes moral knowledge from objective or scientific knowledge. In so doing he makes available to his hero a kind of experience that may indeed lead to a licit originality.[21]

To begin to establish a basis upon which one may achieve an independence of thought within an intellectual tradition or, to refer to the figures of the text, discover new worlds without losing touch with old ones, Astarotte must inform Rinaldo of the true dimensions of the globe. He tells him that the pillars of Hercules no longer ward adventurers away but rather beckon them onward:

E puossi andar giù nell'altro emisperio . . .
e laggiù son città, castella e imperio;
ma nol cognobbon quelle gente prime:
vedi che il sol di camminar s'affretta
dove io ti dico, ché laggiù s'aspetta;

e come un segno surge in orïente,
un altro cade con mirabile arte,
come si vede qua nell'occidente,
però che il ciel giustamente comparte.
Antipodi appellata è quella gente;
adora il sole e Iuppiter e Marte,

e piante ed animal, come voi, hanno
e spesso insieme gran battaglie fanno.

(25. 230, 31)


And one can go to the other hemisphere . . . and there below there are cities and castles and government, although we do not know these people. Look how the sun hurries on its journey to the place I have described, for there it is awaited;

and when a constellation rises in the east another falls with wonderful art, as one sees it here in the west, for the heavens are precisely divided. These people are called the Antipodes. They adore the sun, Jupiter and Mars; have plants and animals as you do and often make war.

The prospect of the Antipodes brings Astarotte, prompted by Rinaldo, to enlarge on the possibilities for salvation of the heathen. His treatment of the problem insists again on the primary importance of the will and relates its function to knowledge, specifically to Christian knowledge. He provides an answer to the question Marsilio dismissed earlier with such levity—what is the nature of the ignorance that damns?—with a seeming paradox: everyone is saved by the cross (25. 233) and Heaven loves simple piety, that is, obedience, fear of divinity, devotion and awe (25. 234). This statement, however, leads to a further point. Astarotte appears to situate Christianity in a temporal perspective which allows for salvation outside the church: the ceremonies of the Romans please God (25. 235); one day the whole world may be Christian (25. 232). What, then, saves or damns? Not the fact of being Christian, but "the mind is that which saves or damns you / if too much ignorance does not mislead you" ("la mente è quella che vi salva e danna / se la troppo ignoranzia non v'inganna", 25. 236). The ignorance to which Astarotte refers is not of the Word but rather the willed ignorance of the Word known and rejected:

però questa nel Ciel non truova scusa:
"*Noluit intelligere*" il salmista
dice d'alcun, tanto ignorante e folle
che, per bene operar, saper non volle.

(25., 237)


however this heaven does not excuse: the psalmist said of one who was so foolish and ignorant that he did not wish to know how to behave well—"Noluit intelligere."

According to Astarotte, the "Fathers" in limbo are redeemed (238). By contrast, the Jews and the Moslems are damned, because the former knew of Jesus through the prophets, the latter from scripture (25. 241–43).

The theological points in this exposition are remarkable, particularly the innovative claim that an ignorance of the Christian faith is not damning in itself. Astarotte contradicts Dante, though not, it must be noted, either Augustine or scripture, at least in any clear and uncontrovertible way.[22] It could be argued that the saint indicates God's favor to the Romans when he discusses the relative merits of their virtues, particularly their love of fame which, although itself a vice, controls other vices of a baser nature. For this reason, he states, God grants to them an empire.[23] And Luke, describing the early missionary activities of the apostles, notes that Peter refuses to limit knowledge of the Word to specific nations: "Of a truth I perceive that God is no respecter of persons. But in every nation he that feareth him, and worketh righteousness is accepted with him" (Acts 10:34–35). The apostle's remark is obviously directed at discouraging a conception of Christianity as nationally or tribally circumscribed. It could, however, be construed to imply salvation outside the Christian faith and in this way to anticipate support for what Astarotte actually maintains—that the will, not an accident of history, is spiritually decisive.

The context in which Astarotte's idea of salvation makes sense is supplied by his earlier statements concerning human in contrast to divine knowledge. There the devil reported that a certain ignorance is inherent in the human condition and he referred to the quality of his own—and by extension Malagigi's—insight into the nature of absolute truth. Yet this ignorance, as we learn here, is a kind of innocent ignorance. It does not damn because it is independent of any choice to reject the Word. That choice must depend on a knowledge that the Word exists; in the absence of that knowledge, the will continues to function to save or damn on other grounds. What these are Pulci leaves obscure, an omission doctrinally correct inasmuch as his view of knowledge stresses the absolute difference between divine and human kinds. In any case, it is, presumably, a particular form of this ignorance under which the Antipodes, like the "Fathers" in "limbo" (for Pulci a kind of redemption), blamelessly labor. On the other hand, because it is the mind exercising the will that saves or damns, Astarotte also implicitly asserts that human beings always have a workable sufficiency of moral knowledge.

The philosophical basis for Pulci's revision of Dante's view of salvation is represented in Astarotte's view of the world as fully navigable, that is, as a virtually limitless object—epistemologically if not morally speaking. In sailing west, Dante's Ulysses commits the error that Homer's hero specifically avoided when he declined the offers of Circe and Calypso to share in their immortality.[24] Dante's Ulysses seeks to follow the sun, metaphorically to live without the awareness and presumably the effects of the passage of time. His journey is significant as an image—highly traditional in content—of heroic pride. For Pulci, however, the image of the westward journey is de-moralized; the sun "hurries" to sink in the west not as a sign of human mortality but because it is expected by the Antipodes, a new world essentially like the old one. Its light is the natural light by which one sees the world objectively, not the metaphorical light that informs the intelligent being of its temporal condition.

The conceptual change this implies is more fully expressed in Astarotte's revision of Luciana's tent, the *symbol* of the hero's knowledge in Part 1. Rinaldo, flying over Spain, expresses a wish to see his old love Luciana. He tells Astarotte of her marvelous gift, the encyclopedic tent. But Astarotte decries Luciana's work because it omits many creatures. The devil describes a series of animals that typify the kind of results a scientific inquiry might produce. Avoiding Luciana's medieval classifications of creatures according to their relation to the four elements, Astarotte catalogues creatures only as representative of a species. In contrast to Luciana's tent, a fully comprehensible symbol of a knowledge of all things understood in moral terms, Astarotte's extension is a structure conceived as extensible. Astarotte ends his description of it by stating that he has not mentioned all the creatures that exist. In effect, he declares the extension open to further revision, that is, he anticipates its continued development.[25]

Astarotte's extension of Luciana's tent is a logical development in Pulci's revision of Dante's image of Ulysses and the significance of his westward journey. With regard to the earlier poet's perception that human knowledge needs to be linked to the needs of family and country, Pulci critically distinguishes a kind of experience that Dante does not account for: the experience of the world as an object. Yet in so doing, he avoids endorsing a pursuit of knowledge for its own sake, unconstrained by a moral purpose—exactly what he had condemned in the "spiriti folletti." Rinaldo responds to Astarotte's implied invitation to sail beyond Gibraltar by declaring that *after* he finds Orlando (and fights for Carlo) he will seek new lands where he will acquire knowledge and give scope to his *virtù*:

> Disse Rinaldo: "Orsù troviam Orlando.
> Poi, perché di' colaggiù [dice che laggiù] si fa guerra,
> io voglio andar que' paesi cercando
> e passar questo mar dove Ercul erra,
> ché vivere e morir vuolsi apparando. . . ."

(25. 245)

Then Rinaldo said "Let's find Orlando. Then, since you say that below they make war, I wish to voyage searching for those countries, and to sail beyond that sea where Hercules travelled, for it is desirable to live and die learning."

Rinaldo's resolution of his dilemma is based upon his attempt to harmonize the two orders of experience that Dante's Ulysses ought to have distinguished. Rinaldo is prepared to pursue the kind of learning whose fruits are inscribed on Astarotte's additions to Luciana's tent *and* to honor his obligations to Christian society at the same time. Pulci's revision of Dante therefore goes further than addressing questions concerning the nature of knowledge; he attempts to articulate a condition of knowing in which the pursuit of objective knowledge is incorporated into the demands of a Christian life. It is important that the information concerning westward travel and what it implies comes from Astarotte, a devil under the control of a Christian magician, for in itself the information is simply misleading, powerfully reminiscent of the words of Dante's Ulysses. Because a charmed Astarotte speaks them, however, they lose their power to mislead and, situated in a larger perspective created by Malagigi's intention to further the cause of Christendom, acquire a new significance.

In the course of harmonizing the claims of *virtù* with obedience to God, Pulci has identified a new kind of matter upon which his hero, and by extension the poet, must exercise his intelligence and his poetic skill. By representing the world of hero and poet as objectively open to experience which is cumulative and time-bound, that is, predicated on historicity, Pulci establishes not that human beings may become self-authorized but that they must be so of necessity. History therefore becomes for him the basis for authorial freedom as well as the source of inherited obligations. He was clearly concerned to define his own literary endeavors in terms recognizably orthodox, both poetically and theologically. His gradual discrimination of the practice of magic from the responsible illusionism allowed the arts, as they are represented in Malagigi's use of Marguttino, had served as the basis for his defense of himself against such critics as Ficino, a defense which was, moreover, preceded by his renunciation of the actual practice of magic, as it was described in treatises like that of Cecco d'Ascoli. But now his poetics also allows that another component of magic—its capacity not to create a second reality but rather to investigate the natural world in its temporal unfolding—have due consideration. His willingness to entertain the possibility that what Dante's Ulysses sought might have a place in a Christian world is based on his opinion that human knowledge may be based not only on the moral wisdom necessary to the well-being of society, but also on knowledge of physical reality, a knowledge that history teaches us is time-bound. Astarotte's extension, an image of the kind of knowledge Rinaldo will acquire beyond the pillars of Hercules, represents the rupture of a given frame of reference in which human knowledge is to be pursued and the superposition of a second frame. It figures, proleptically, the alteration in conception and structure registered in the development of the *Morgante* as a whole. But it also conveys an impression of how actual changes in natural philosophy might have affected intellectuals in the last decades of the fifteenth century. In other words, it is itself a sign of the historically contingent.

Pulci's most probable source for Astarotte's description of the Antipodes, and thus of the vision of history he derives from it, is the work of Paolo Toscanelli, who was patronized throughout much of his life by Cosimo, Piero, and finally Lorenzo de' Medici.[26] In Toscanelli is reflected the curious blend of science and magic that so frequently characterizes the pursuit of Renaissance natural philosophy: his astronomical discoveries were matched by his interest in astrology. His calculations of the paths of comets in 1433, 1439, 1456 (Halley's comet), 1457, and 1472 effectively destroyed the Aristotleian conception of the cosmos above the moon as perfectly regular in its motions. His measurements of the sun's meridian altitudes led to his revision of the tables, based on the Ptolemaic system, that established the chronology of the seasons. Yet he was also summoned by the Signoria to determine the auspicious moments for certain political events. His function in this regard was no different from Ficino's, who informed Lorenzo when he should beware of the influence of certain planets.

Toscanelli's major contribution to Renaissance science was in cartography. The astronomer composed a number of maps of the world in the 1470s when he became involved in a map-making enterprise in Pisa. Certainly by 1474 Toscanelli had made up what he referred to as a "sea chart" on which he indicated that a westward journey would bring the navigator to the same land of spices which Europeans knew, from journeys overland across Asia, to lie in the east. In 1487, Toscanelli wrote to Christopher Columbus a letter in which he conveyed this "sea chart"—he identified the chart as the one he had made four years earlier for Canon Fernão Martins in reply to an inquiry put to him by the canon's patron, the King of Portugal—as well as encouragement for the project Columbus had proposed.

Astarotte's words contradicting the opinion that the world is flat— "this idea is wrong" ("questa oppinione è vana")—and asserting that the sea is totally navigable because the earth is round encapsulate Toscanelli's position. They offer a clear challenge to Dante's vision of the place of knowledge in Christian history—a challenge Pulci meets by suggesting that to the moral requirements of the Christian the discoveries of science, however objective, are not necessarily inimical. The question of the existence of the Antipodes was particularly vexing in this regard. Christians were obliged to doubt the existence of the Antipodes because to admit it would be to contradict scripture. Since the people of the new world could not but be ignorant of Christianity, their presence on the other side of the globe could not be reconciled with St. Paul's assertion that the words of the Apostles "went into all the earth and . . . unto the end of the world" (Romans 10: 18). Pulci answers this question by presenting Rinaldo's willingness to search for knowledge in the Antipodes, a people as yet ignorant of Christianity but included among the totality of humankind who are to be saved by the cross (25. 233). In other words, Pulci historicizes the event St. Paul refers to by implying that salvation is a continuous venture coterminous with history itself.[27]

The choice Rinaldo confronts at the pillars of Hercules is, in its essentials, Pulci's own as he contemplates the task of writing Carlo's history. The limits both hero and author consider breaching have been established by Dante. Rinaldo is a figure created not only to reflect on Dante's Ulysses—he contemplates but does not actually commit the same mistake—but also to revise the concept of knowledge the Dantean episode conveys. Pulci's introduction of the content of contemporary natural philosophy into his narrative demonstrates that human knowledge, however objective and amoral (that is, of the "unpeopled world"), need not be illicit. Because it is undertaken, moreover, with the understanding that it is open to further revision, it cannot provide a basis for intellectual pride. If anything, the reverse is the case; it argues for a kind of humility, a constant awareness that the investigator is not alone in his researches but rather a member of a collectivity. In a sense, therefore, Pulci clears a theoretical space for himself—a new world—without actually violating the limits of the old Dantean world which restrict licit knowledge to that which can demonstrate its application to human needs. The extent to which Pulci both respects and revises Dante, in effect both honoring and reinterpreting the traditions he inherits from the older poet, is suggested by Rinaldo's echo of the pilgrim Dante's words as the poet is about to leave Vergil and to accept the guidance of Beatrice. Begging Astarotte to describe additions to Luciana's tent—in effect to break through the limits of the old moral knowledge to include knowledge of a purely objective character—Rinaldo exclaims: "For I feel again my old flame [love]" ("ch'io sento ancor della mia fiamma antica", 25. 310). On seeing a vision of Beatrice, Dante has said to Vergil: "I know the tokens of the ancient love" ("Conosco i segni de l'antica fiamma", *Purg.* 30. 48).[28] This is itself an echo of Dido's words to Anna on feeling love for Aeneas: "I recognize the traces of an old love" ("Agnosco veteris vestigia flammae", *Aen.* 4. 23). Thus, just as Dante departs from Vergil by quoting him, so Pulci now departs from Dante by quoting that very passage of Dante which signals his departure from Vergil. By borrowing the terms of his farewell to his mentor from his mentor, Pulci dismisses him with a compliment.

In narrating the story of Orlando at Roncisvalle, Pulci takes up these concerns again from a different point of view. Here his task—to retell the most traditional part of Carlo's history—presents him with a specific challenge: to fit an account of Orlando's death, which retains certain elements of the *chanson de geste*, particularly a celebration of heroism, with the idea of history as Providential. Both Gano and Marsilio, and to a lesser extent Antea, have been condemned for perceiving life as a conflict between human beings in which their *virtù*, rather than the will of God, is decisive. Pulci's portrait of Orlando as a martyr requires, therefore, the modification of certain elements of his character which might suggest an excessive enthusiasm for fame and world triumph. Both Pulci and the poet of the *Spagna* retain, it is true, some of the features of the Roland of the *Chanson*, identified as *preux* in contrast to Oliver who is *sage*. But Pulci subordinates these qualities to others (chiefly patience) required of the martyr. Thus Orlando, following the traditional story, refuses to sound his horn for fear of being a coward (26. 15). But his reluctance to seek help is not—as it is in the *Spagna*—a manifestation of pride but rather of humility. So much is clear when Turpin rallies the troops by asking that they die willingly for Christ and so commemorate the Passion, and when Orlando later declares that, by not sounding his horn, he waits to see "what fortune will do" ("quel che sa far Fortuna", 26. 33). This fortune, in presiding over events in a figural drama already identified as a "Passion," is clearly a figure of Providence, not chance. Orlando himself rejects the pursuit of fame, because it is a prize won in this world not the next: "[T]he soul has neither prize nor reward here" ("ma l'anima non ha qui premio o merto", 26. 38), and he decries the ancient Greeks and Romans who fight to leave in the world "a little boast" ("un piccol vanto", 26. 37). His anti-heroic posture is most conspicuous at his death, when he apostrophizes his dead comrades with the phrase Aeneas uses in a totally different setting: "o three- and four-times blessed" ("o ter quaterque beati", 27. 105; cf. *Aen.* 1. 94). For the Roman hero, the blessed are those who have died fighting for their homeland rather than having been drowned at sea. For Orlando they are simply those who are already in paradise.

Pulci further enhances Orlando's saintlike character when he describes Orlando's death as an exit from a labyrinthine earthly existence. Orlando prays to leave "our empty life, full of sin . . ." ("Il nostro viver vano . . . pien d'errori", 27. 124), but the angel Gabriel, urging him to consider his motives, asks him if he is "honestly" ("onestamente") weary of the world. Gabriel proposes to extend Orlando's life: "God will give you men again/and you will make the earth and sea shake" ("Iddio ti darà ben di nuovo gente,/e tremerrà di te la terra e'l mare", 27. 143). His invitation raises again the question of the hero's return, so important to the structure of the plot in Part 1, but in fact Orlando is being offered a miraculous cure, not a real second life. The angel has instructed him, moreover, to live his life as Job, suffering and obedient.

Even Carlo's right (or obligation) to revenge Orlando's death becomes attenuated by the more powerful right of Providence to its mysterious workings. The old Emperor assumes Orlando's saintly bearing, his capacity to endure the decrees of fate. When Carlo learns of the loss of the Holy Land, an event coincident with Orlando's death, he charges God with the task of revenge (27. 195). After his troops enter Saragossa, Pulci describes the suicide of the infidel as a "vendetta di Dio" (27. 258). And finally, when Marsilio is hung on the carob tree, thus fulfilling his role as a type of Judas, Carlo claims that divine justice has not slept. He describes his vision of history that, like Orlando's instructions to Morgante on the evil of seeking revenge in canto 1, postulates a Providential direction to human events (27. 271). Like Orlando, he sees Job as his model and calls on "Pazienza" rather than the more distinctively chivalric virtues that Orlando and Rinaldo have exemplified earlier. Carlo does, admittedly, promise revenge on the infidel but that act (27. 229) is framed by events which suggest God's control. Orlando is miraculously brought to life in order to hand Durindana to Carlo (27. 206) who, having accepted it and the obligations it entails, acquires the character of St. Peter defending Jesus in Gethsemane as well as of Christ the harrower of hell (27. 230). Implicit in these passages is a rejection of the value of *virtù* as a means to enhance individual status in favor of a kind of patient courage that undertakes to tolerate adversity for the sake of the general welfare.

How much Pulci believed in the story he was telling is another matter. The drama of betrayal and revenge played out in the mountain passes of the Pyrenees and later on the Spanish plain is punctuated by statements that cast doubt upon the truth of the subject represented. Much of the saintly heroism of these passages is understood to be merely formulaic. And even when Pulci narrates as if they were absolute truth the miraculous events he finds in his sources, and so lends credibility to a view of history as the scene of heavenly intervention, he manages to ridicule the works and authorities upon which he draws. These ironies effectively undermine the delicate balance achieved in the Antipodes episode. As the poet questions the idea of writing history, he compromises his obligation to respect tradition and orthodoxy.

Pulci begins an overt critique of his sources and the idea of authority by suggesting that he, the poet, is the first to record (and possibly even determine) the events he describes. He imagines he has—or might have—the power to decide the course of the narrative; he implies that he is a eyewitness to the battle of Roncisvalle; he states that he doubts he will not write tragedy (implying he can allow himself a choice); and he confesses that if help does not arrive, he will not be able to save Orlando (27. 1). (Earlier he has described his poem bringing its own subject into being—with his pen he moves the lances of Carlo's knights, 26. 49). To bring his own authorship into sharper focus, he declares that he is disappointed with the content of his poem and pretends to have been deceived: "And I thought that I would end my story of Carlo with a comedy" ("Ed io pur comedìa pensato avea / iscriver del mio Carlo finalmente . . .", 27. 2). That is, he deliberately underscores the least coherent aspect of his history: that Carlo is both responsible for Orlando's death and also a Christian hero. These assertions represent the poet in a curious double bind. He feels he must honor traditional judgment but he cannot help protesting its unreasonableness.

The complaint is Pulci's first statement to make explicit the historiographic problem that the poem presents him. It is not accidental that it is followed by two sets of contradictory instructions to the reader that together permit and forbid an interpretation of the poem as the deeply paradoxical work it must be if both the facts of Carlo's history and Dante's judgment are respected. On the one hand, Pulci asks his readers to understand the sense of his story as allegorical, "to imagine one thing for another" ("altro per altro immaginare") because the time has arrived to philosophize (27. 40). So, in effect, he attempts to preserve the integrity of Dante's essentially irrational judgment. On the other hand, he also asks his readers to "go straight to the literal sense" ("andate drieto al senso litterale") since he does not intend figurative meanings (27. 41). This injunction is ostensibly Pulci's response to critics whom he terms "Indian crickets" ("cicale indiane", 27. 41), but its deeper impetus derives from his unwillingness to abdicate any more responsibility for the logical, rational, and factual elements of his history. By defining the meaning of his poem in such different terms, he once again both honors and defies authority.

By implication, he again raises the question of the status of his narrative has history. If meaning is allegorical, then *any* set of events may serve to demonstrate the workings of Providence. If, on the other hand, meaning is literal, then only those sets of events in which the right triumphs qualify as evidence of Providence. In the former case reason gives way to faith; in the latter, reason is definitive. By opening up the possibility that the reader may be free to draw his own conclusions from the evidence the history offers, Pulci also frees himself from the Muse he has come to experience as onerous.

To emphasize the importance of the literal and its function in exercising the rational faculties, Pulci ridicules precisely that content of his poem which most tests the reader's faith: the account of the various miracles associated with Orlando's resistance at Roncisvalle and Carlo's subsequent punishing conquest of Marsilio and Spain. He first focuses on the numbers killed by Christian forces. He both insists on and at the same time disclaims any interest in the truth: he pretends reluctantly to report numbers which are at once doubtful and also unknowable except to one who has the sword of heaven (27. 76), numbers which could only be true if a miracle had occurred and the Archangel Michael had actually fought for the French. But, he continues, both the reliable Turpin and Ormanno accepted these numbers (27. 78). Moreover, he adds, these authors were followed by others and finally by the same (fictitious) Arnaldo who wrote of Rinaldo and the Antipodes episode with complete accuracy—"he wouldn't fib for anything/nothing" ("che non direbbe una bugia per nulla", 27. 80). The Boccaccian equivocation in this line suggests how deeply Pulci intends to undermine the premises upon which he represents his narrative as history.

These octaves on the historian's access to the truth in history conclude the process of self-examination in which Pulci has been engaged and have the effect of setting aside, in a dramatic gesture, the issue of authority. Henceforth, whatever he writes and whatever his source, he will no longer claim he writes the truth but merely ask to be believed. When, for example, he later debates the question of Michael's participation at Roncisvalle, he simply states that, whether or not this actually happened, the reader must accept his account of it: "Whether or not it's true, accept it without quarrelling" ("O vero o no, con pace si comporti." For the writer must follow his sources and what they say (27. 115). Pulci has, however, already signaled that he writes with an acute sense of the irony of his task. By identifying as a repetition his mention of the Archangel's presence at the battle of Roncisvalle, he implies that it is ridiculous; to repeat anything, he declares, is to sound like birds and beasts in May, that is, to do what the proverb "we are not in May" indicates is folly (27. 113).

Having adopted this position, Pulci can criticize, with further equivocation, writers who are careful researchers of fact as well as those who freely invent what they wish to relate. He concludes the case for his own excellence as a historian with a ludic defense of his poetry, which he contrasts to the careless writing of others.

Io me n'andrò con un mio carro a vela
e giugnerò le lepre e'leopardi;
ché in picciol temp la fama si cela
degli scrittor quando e'son pur bugiardi,
e rimangonsi al lume di candela
la sera al fuoco, annighitossi e tardi,
e gente sono prosuntüose quelle,
tanto che Marsia ne perdé la pelle.

(27. 175)

I proceed with my winged cart pulled by hares and leopards and in a short while the fame will vanish of those lying writers who, lazy and behind in their work, remain up in front of the fire by candlelight into the evening. These are presumptuous persons—Marsyas lost his skin for this.

This passage is apparently ironic: giving the historian a winged cart drawn by hares and leopards, an image suggesting pure fancy, Pulci assigns to the lying writers the midnight oil, the late and weary hours before the fire, images which suggest a scholarly respect for the truth. The point is that the poet has begun to regard these activities as interchangeable.

### Against Epic

Carlo orders the hanging of Marsilio. Pulci relates the history of Carlo according to three different historians. He describes his plans for a pastoral poem. (Canto 28)

The contradictions in this increasingly anomalous poem deepen in the last canto. Pulci began the *Morgante* as a poet who listened to an angelic Muse and intended to praise his subject as a "divine man." In the course of it, he showed his subject to be increasingly complex, illuminated by the shifting light of the passage of time, both as a concept (temporality) and a reality (the actual time spent reading and writing). He also altered his conception of himself. Originally perceiving himself as an epic poet, he used the methodological difficulties he encountered in writing history to question the basis upon which he or indeed any poet could write about the past. In the last canto of the poem, the tension between his obligation to listen to a source regarded as totally authoritative and a need to exercise his own judgment, a situation that requires him to distinguish between authority and authorship, is further developed but never really resolved. Pulci attempts to finesse the subject of the status of this history (and of epic composition in general) by considering the possibilities open to a poet who writes in a second and less exalted genre: pastoral. But finally these possibilities too he regards as ironic.

Pulci's concern with pastoral follows successive attempts all through the last canto to rewrite Carlo's history to justify Dante, but it is also clearly based on his perception that at some profound level he has failed irremediably in his task. Confronting in canto 28 the challenge of ending his poem, he attempts with deceptively forceful vigor once more to make coherent his portrait of the Emperor. But the effect of the epic gestures with which he begins his last apology—invoking Lucrezia, now translated into a star, and putting up more sails on his "epic boat"—is immediately nullified by his final assessment of Carlo. He returns to the line of reasoning implicit in the Boethian solution to the problem of evil and the apparent injustice in events. For by what other calculus than that which Boethius proposes could Carlo have been so duped by Gano and remain a "divine man"? Pulci dismisses Alcuin's history, although he will soon cite it as his source for the poem's most extensive account of Carlo's life, because Alcuin does not consider Gano at all—this is evidence of his "blind intellect" ("intelletto cieco", 28. 16). Later Pulci implies that Carlo simply had no good biographer, no Livy, Sallust, or Justinus. His own answer to the problem of Carlo's character is ambiguous. On a realistic level, he argues that Carlo is the victim of habit: "[O]ld ways count for a lot" ("molto può l'antica usanza", 28. 20), but the difficulty will be only solved by a leap of faith (28. 17). Otherwise, both poet and reader must remain in uncertainty. Pulci declares that the reader must be his own authority: "Now perhaps you, reader, can say how Carlo Mano could have believed him [Gano]" ("Or forse tu, lettor, dirai adesso / come e' gli abbi creduto Carlo Mano", 28.15). He cannot himself yet give an answer: "[C]h'io non fermo ancor la mia risposta", 28. 18).

On the condemnation of Gano, he is both more decisive and more interesting. He declares that Gano is a *natural* traitor" ("per natura traditore") and needs no authoritative definition. He directs the reader instead to contemporary events: "Remember Lampognano, reader, and don't look up any more old authors" ("Ricòrdati, lettor, del Lampognano / e non cercar d'altro antico aüttore", 28. 22). Here he implies a parallel between Gano's betrayal of Orlando and the murder of Galeazzo Maria Sforza by Andrea Lampognano and other young Milanese nobles on December 26, 1476. This instruction, unlike any other in the poem, establishes that there is no fundamental difference between making judgments about history on the one hand and contemporary events on the other; the historian is to be as much his own authority in the matter of the past as the citizen is in regard to the present he lives from day to day.

Pulci's inability to answer the question of the poem has an effect on his representation of Rinaldo, the hero of *ragione*, about whose appreciation of Christian duty Pulci is no longer certain. Stating that he draws his information from (the fictitious) Arnaldo, he relates that this author believes that, long after Roncisvalle, Rinaldo left Carlo and, because of what Astarotte told him, travelled beyond the pillars of Hercules. Moreover, Pulci speculates, it is said that an angel spoke to him so that he might convert those who adore the planets and other foolishness. One day he might return, rising miraculously again in the east like the sun: "Is this so marvellous? Who knows more, believes less" ("qual maraviglia? Chi più sa, men crede", 28. 34), an observation that opens to question all earlier speculation. For if "he who knows more believes less," then science and religion are inimical and the image of the intellectual Rinaldo waging wars of conversion beyond the pillars of Hercules and then returning to court is made ironic. Pulci implies that Rinaldo will *not* return to the Emperor, that is, that in contrast to his earlier dutiful course of action he will now simply exploit his *virtù*.

Passages immediately following these speculations on Rinaldo's problematic future explain obliquely why Pulci might have ironized the hero in whose ambivalent intellectual character he appears to have invested so much of himself. In these octaves, he permits himself his last anguished statement against the intervention of Ficino and his colleagues in his affairs. Defensively (and perhaps even at this date hoping to convince himself), he again endorses Dante:

> Io mi confido ancor molto qui a Dante
> che non sanza cagion nel Ciel sù misse
> Carlo ed Orlando. . . .
>
> (28. 40)

I still have great confidence in Dante who not without reason put Carlo and Orlando in heaven above. . . .

And he encourages Christian humility with regard to the secrets of heaven (28. 41). He declares himself unwilling to consider doctrine, to speak of faith with "those brothers" ("questi frati") who only accuse him. And he specifically refers to the "commotion" ("rumor") occasioned by his sonnet "In principio era buio" (28. 42). The significance to Pulci of the painful exchange concerning this work is now in part established (see the Introduction). Pulci's allusion to his quarrels with Ficinian orthodoxy here and his apparent willingness to capitulate to it suggest that he is no longer prepared to challenge authority and rationally to investigate and judge history. He appears to abdicate the role he has been in the process of inventing for himself, a role in whose oxymoronic union of follower and leader, son and father, he had endeavored to discover the basis for an acceptable poetics. To represent Rinaldo's *virtù* in terms that trivialize faith, and to decline himself to articulate his objections to Ficino because these objections regard matters of history on which faith not reason rules, are parallel responses to the challenge authority presents him. The first reveals his fearful fascination with the possibility of a free exercise of reason, the second his willingness to restrict rational inquiry by a superior obligation to believe.

How complicated is Pulci's response to what might be called his new servitude (and Rinaldo's new freedom) is manifest as he acts out in the last octaves of the poem, with a humor almost bitter, his part as Carlo's historian. As elements in a comprehensive strategy to show that the accomplishments of the Emperor outweigh the folly of his trust in Gano, Pulci retells Carlo's history two more times, and at each retelling he gives it more scope. But, at the same time, he mocks the authorities upon whom he draws and in effect nullifies his efforts. In the first retelling (28. 53–66), he begins with Carlo's deeds and concludes by alluding to the heroic exploits of Rinaldo and the Dane. Using accounts in the *Reali*, the *Aspramonte*, as well as two manuscripts in Lorenzo's library, Pulci attributes this second history of Carlo to a fictitious Lattanzio who, having mastered the details of Carlo's life as Turpin and Ormanno had written them down, sings the Emperor's history to Alcuin. Pulci dismisses Lattanzio's song even while repeating it. Lattanzio cannot say enough to describe all of Carlo's deeds, yet he says "so many things" ("tante cose") that he "stupifies" ("fece stupire") his audience and is forced to put aside his zither (28. 66).

Alcuin, whom Pulci has already discredited (28. 16), takes Lattanzio's place, and retells Carlo's history a second time (28. 68–128). He begins by apologizing for his poor skill and asks to be forgiven for resembling Filomena in telling of things beyond "human wit" ("uman ingegno", 28. 68). Alcuin's history is notable for its repetitiousness. Carlo enters Italy and saves the Papal court on three occasions: first from barbarians led by Desiderio, King of the Lombards; then from Arichi, Duke of Benevento; and finally from conspirators against Pope Leo III. Carlo, additionally, wages several wars against heretical Saxons, who stubbornly keep returning to their "former mistake" ("antico errore", 28. 85). And Alcuin's history itself contains the *Morgante*'s third account of Roncisvalle (28. 90, 91), already related by Lattanzio in octaves 37 to 61 and of course by Pulci himself in cantos 26 and 27. This history—of the so-called Alcuin—is Pulci's faithful digest of Donato Acciaiuoli's *Vita Caroli Magni*, a work that he knew the Medici regarded as true history. Considered out of the context Pulci gives it, it might well have served the purpose for which it seems to have been intended. In fact, because Alcuin has already been made a figure of fun, its intention is ironic and its effect is subversive; it jeopardizes, retrospectively, the epic intention of the poem. From the accounts of the ridiculous historians Pulci brings on stage to retell the story he has been unable to tell, to provide the answer he himself has confessed he is doubtful about, a new historiographic norm is constructed. The better historian Pulci aspired to be is effectively refashioned. He can no longer write history as if to reveal the truth of the past, single and irrefutable, but rather in the full awareness of his own historicity. These ironic portraits represent the culmination of Pulci's effort to obey Lucrezia's command, his final—empty—gesture as a court poet and, at the same time, a rational intellect. Having written himself into a state of paralysis on this score, he turns to contemplate pastoral. This reintroduces, in another key, the possibilities of a return of a "golden age," imagined at the outset of the poem in historical terms but now reconceived on altogether different lines.[29]

Pulci begins his concluding octaves by stating that he has brought his boat to port and reveals that he is not preparing for a second sea voyage (indicative of epic generally and an image of the *Morgante* throughout the poem) for fear of never returning to shore—"Now I don't want to try anymore to venture beyond Abila and Calpe [the pillars of Hercules], for my pilot doesn't sail there. . . ." ("non vo' più tentare ora Abila e Calpe / per che più oltre il mio nocchier non varca. . . .", 28. 130). This despite the fact that, were he to sail again in his epic boat, his lady Lucrezia, now a star in heaven, would guide him (131). One can assume that Pulci is here disclosing not only that his history of Carlo Mano is complete but also that he no longer projects completing (as he had earlier in the canto, 118) his historical poem on Ludovico, Charlemagne's son, the *Ciriffo Calvaneo*.

In the following octaves he continues to insist on a style which is not epic but pastoral:

> io non chieggo altra penna, altro stil d'oro
> a cantar d'Aganippe e d'Elicona:
> io me ne vo pe' boschi puro e soro
> con la mia zampognetta che pur suona. . . .
>
> (28. 138)

I don't seek another quill, another golden pen with which to sing of Aganippe and Helicon: I go among the woods, deep and dense, with my pipe sounding sweetly. . . .

And he further declares that he "will dwell among beech thickets and ploughmen, for they do not despise Pulci's muse" ("io mi starò tra faggi e tra bifulci / che non disprezzin le muse de' Pulci", 139); that he "will take his little boat" ("Io me n'andrò con la barchetta mia") where the water is shallow enough for small craft ("quanto l'acqua comporta un piccol legno"); and that his "plan" ("disegno") is merely to please by his "fancy" ("con la fantasia", 140.) This activity is clearly expected in the future and is described in images that have different associations than those appropriate to epic and history, which have characterized the poem he has just completed. He eschews the trappings of the high style, so prominent in the first cantos of the *Morgante,* in favor of the middle or low style and matter common to the pastoral poet. From this modest and limited literary production, "this very little flash of light" ("questa tanto piccola favilla", 141), he expects a melioration not only of his condition but also of that of the world at large: those who will read it will become inflamed with thoughts of Parnassus and will see at last the return of the golden age (28. 141–51).

Were one to search for a point of origin for Pulci's perception of himself as a poet of pastoral, it would doubtless be in the declaration he makes in canto 25, that is, that his academy is situated not in the city but in the woods (25. 117). There a self-defensive statement designed to excuse Pulci's independence of authority and his creativity, but without a correlative text in the poem itself (except insofar as Astarotte's return of Rinaldo can be considered Pulci's own invention), the poet's woodland poetics here gains in meaning. It suggests that the stylistic shift he signals there is fully accepted only at this point, where he reveals that he sees the task of celebrating Carlo Mano and thus bringing to Florence a model of chivalric excellence in pastoral rather than epic terms.

These statements may, of course—but do not necessarily—refer to that portion of the *Morgante* already written. If they do, they indicate the poet's retrospective revision of the poetics of that poem, his concern to represent what certainly began as an epic-romance as something quite different. If they do not, we must postulate his wish to write a second body of work that would stand in contrast to what he has just composed. Whatever the case, they serve to comment on the poet's initial commitment to Lucrezia: to compose a history in praise of Carlo Mano—an undertaking he has strenuously pursued until canto 28, when he questions and then abandons it.[30]

The age Pulci now wishes to bring back differs in some important respects from the Florence of Carlo's court that he celebrates at the outset of his poem. It is both hypothetical, providing the ideal *otium* of the country, and in a sense autobiographical. He imagines that by writing pastoral he will once again be in the company of Lorenzo and Poliziano, and that together the three will flourish in a new age of Saturn and under the youthful shoots of the laurel: "[C]ertain noble sprigs shoot from a young and precious laurel . . . certainly the golden age will be soon at hand" ("surge d'un fresco e prezïoso lauro / certe piante gentil . . . certo e' sarà presto il mondo d'auro", 28. 151). The image recalls the blasted laurel that heralded the destruction of Marsilio's kingdom and suggests that in Pulci's plans for a new poetry there is some reference to the political situation in Florence. If the image of the blasted laurel contains a covert warning to Lorenzo of the dangers of associating with a Marsilio (Ficino), that of the newly green laurel may have been intended as an encouragement to favor the right poets: Poliziano, with whom Pulci evidently never broke, and Pulci himself.

The nostalgic aspect of Pulci's pastoral is made clear when one takes note of the hopes he expresses in letters to Lorenzo in 1466 and 1467, before he had cause to imagine that he would not always be part of the Medici circle. In a letter dated March 1465 [1466], Pulci sends Lorenzo a pastoral *canzona* ostensibly on the subject of a "woodland nymph" but actually to complain of his patron's absence:

> Da poi che' Lauro, piu, lasso, non vidi . . .
> mi volsi ad me et dixi: "In che ti fidi,
> che se' da tte piu che da llui diviso?"

Since I, weary, have not seen my Laurel [Lorenzo] I have asked myself "In whom do you trust, you who are more separate from yourself than [you are] from him?"

The letter itself insists on the special privileges of Pulci's "pastoral" ("compagnuzze") or "private" ("domestiche") Muse—it is to be the means by which their absence is overcome: "I promise you, my dearest Lorenzo, returning to me with my pastoral Muse, I will make you one of us."[31] A year later he writes: "Some day I will be again with you in these woods and I will speak of you with my most domestic Muse."[32] This is not, I think, the Muse who is invoked to sing the *Morgante*, the recording angel, but rather the Muse of the sonnets, of the intimate poems in which Pulci did in fact address local, particular, and domestic matters. Two years later, in his *Giostra*, a poem celebrating Lorenzo's part in a tournament held in Florence, Pulci elucidates his patron's impresa, *le tens revient:* "[T]his can be understood to signify that time will return and the age renew itself" ("che può interpretarsi / tornare il tempo e'l secol rinnovarsi.")[33] Here Lorenzo becomes both the agent and the sign of temporal renewal, an identification given verbal expression in the puns so often made on his name: *lauro*, or the eternally green tree, and *l'auro*, or gold, certainly implied in the term *il mondo d'auro*. Considered in relation to the canzona "Da poi che' Lauro" and the *Giostra*, Pulci's renewed interest in pastoral verse seems designed to raise the question of the poet's own return and to situate it in a landscape made familiar by remembered associations. Against the failure of intention registered in the *Morgante*, this poetry, whatever it may be, appears as a kind of bulwark.

The truly formidable complexity of Pulci's motives in writing a Medicean pastoral is not, however, evident before the Vergilian echoes in these concluding octaves are understood. Pulci here appears in the guise of a poet who, by the power of his verse, can recreate a "blessed age" ("benigni secul") the reign of Saturn. He adopts the imagery and language of Vergil's *Eclogue 4* and presumably wants to capture some of the earlier poet's optimism. But, in fact, Pulci's Vergilian allusions in the *last* octave of the poem cast doubt on the very project they appear to extol:

> benigni secul, che già liete fêrsi:
> tornate a modular le nostre lire,
> ché la mia fantasia non può tenersi,
> come ruota che mossa ancor vuol ire.
> Chi negherebbe a Gallo già mai versi?
> *Pro re, paüca dixi* al mio desire.
> Or si qui fine al nostro ultimo canto
> con pace e gaudio e col saluto santo.

(28. 152)

Blessed age, that once was happy, return to tune our lyres, for my fancy cannot be restrained just as a wheel that rolls wishes to keep in motion. Who would deny Gallus verses? On my subject I have have said little to my liking. Now with peace, joy, and salvation we have come to the end of our last canto.

Pulci's reference here is obviously to Vergil's *Eclogue 10,* but it is unclear whether the poet identifies himself, the speaker of the proposed Medicean pastoral, with Vergil's pastoral poet, the speaker of the verses intended to console Gallus, or with Gallus himself, the martial character who grieves for the loss of his love, Lycoris. Pulci repeats the most important of the pastoral poet's opening words: "My Gallus, there are a few songs to be sung, but ones that Lycoris herself may read; who would deny Gallus these verses?" (pauca meo Gallo, sed quae legat ipsa Lycoris, / carmina sunt dicenda; neget quis carmina Gallo?", *Ec.* 10. 2–3), but in a context which suggests that he may also see himself as the Gallus to whom these verses are to be addressed: he cannot rein in his powers of invention and who would deny Gallus verses?[34] Three lines earlier he has asked the "blessed age" to return to *modulate*—a word he does not use elsewhere in the *Morgante*—the pastoral lyres of Florentines, repeating a line Gallus actually speaks later in the *Eclogue*, when he declares that he will play the Sicilian shepherd's pipe: "Let me tune the song-pipe of the Sicilian shepherd" ("Carmina pastoris Siculi modulabor avena", 51). It is possible, of course, that Pulci intends "Gallo" to refer to Lorenzo, for, like the historical Gallus, Lorenzo was both a statesman and a poet. Yet this identification, doubtful as it is, does not really alter the significance of Pulci's imitation. What is important is that Pulci has alluded to the figure in Vergil's *Eclogues* who most undermines what they celebrate: the recreation of a golden age.

The introduction of Vergil's Gallus to Pulci's pastoral world bears most directly on the representation of time in the octave. In Vergil's poem, the dialogue has a diachronic dimension: the pastoral poet proposes verses to assuage Gallus's grief; Gallus in effect declares they will be too late to do him any good. He sings of a counterproposal: his departure from the gentle pastoral world for the harsher realities of conflict, for war and the rigors of the hunt. Only in this ambience of dissonance will he play the shepherds' pipe, lamenting not what he has lost but what he never had: "That I had been one of you" ("atque utinam ex vobis unus vestrique fuissem", 35). Gallus is, in other words, one who declines the invitation to ease that pastoral offers. By including Gallus among his "shepherds," Pulci colors his proposal with the ambivalence that in Vergil's poem allows one to question, with Gallus, the enterprise of writing pastoral at the very moment it is being proposed.

Additionally, Pulci's Gallus diminishes the significance of the echo of *Eclogue 4* in the previous octave. Pulci's reference to the new shoots of laurel in the context of a return of the reign of Saturn alludes to Vergil's celebration of the baby boy who will reinstitute this world in Rome (6). In the *Eclogues*, the evident optimism of these lines is undercut at the conclusion of the sequence of eclogues by the temporal relations Vergil establishes between *Eclogues 4* and *10*. *Eclogue 4* takes place in a Sicilian milieu: "Sicilian Muses, let us sing something about greater things" ("Sicelides Musae, paulo majora canamus", 1), whereas *10* is situated in a period *before* that in which the pastoral muse Arethusa fled to Sicily.[35] The pastoral speaker in *10* pleads with an Arethusa whom he threatens with corruption of sea water if she refuses his request (4–6). That is, *10* stands in metaleptic relation to *4*, its subtle aporia providing the theoretical context for the hopeful projections of the earlier poem. By featuring the elegist Gallus as the figure who questions the performative function of pastoral poetry, the extent to which it can fulfill its promises and bring the new world it extols into actual being, Vergil in effect redefines the intention of the pastoral mode: it must provide the ground upon which questions concerning the relation of poetry and the poetic vision of ideal worlds to the realities of history may appropriately be asked. Gallus's departure from the pastoral world, antedating the moment in which its shepherds speak of a return to the earlier age of abundance, frames their assertions with an experience of privation and thus reveals it to be compensatory, a wish whose origins are in distress and disappointment. If Pulci were following the logic of his Vergilian model, his last octave would have to be read as a metaleptic contradiction, a request made on behalf of a Gallus who has already declined to accept what the request proposes to give. "Gallo" may represent either a facet of the poet's own consciousness which anticipates the futility of his task or his awareness of his patron's certain rejection of what he intends to offer. Such pessimism has its basis in the treatment Pulci thought he had received from Lorenzo earlier.

The *Morgante* itself, by its thoughtful exploration of its own historiographical method, offers the strongest evidence that Pulci understood Vergil's poems and wished to avail himself fully of their marvelous subtlety. Given what his imitation of Vergil's Gallus implies, it is hard to imagine that he expected to accomplish in pastoral what had eluded him in his epic history. The last octave of his poem really functions as a *correctio*, a prospect entertained in order that it be dismissed. It renders the two poems he has appeared to want to distinguish, the *Morgante* and the prospective pastoral, indistinguishable in their modality if not their content. We can see them as two perspectives on the same subject: both celebrate the Medici court, in the *Morgante* a mirror of the Emperor's, in the pastoral projection to be fulfilled in Arcadia; both draw their inspiration from the poet's connection to that family. Most important, both record—the first discursively and retrospectively, the second allusively and proleptically—their failure to bring about the restorations they had promised.

Of the various poets, philosophers, and historians who gathered at the Medici palace Pulci was perhaps the least likely to have composed a work in which the development of a historiographic method is recorded. That he did so is attributable to a variety of circumstances. Most decisive was his lack of sympathy for humanistic studies in general, and for such humanists as Scala and Ficino in particular. Probably derived from a recognition of his own limited knowledge of classical works and authors, Pulci's antihumanism served him well in unexpected and even paradoxical ways. His commitment to the popular forms of literary expression, his enthusiasm for colloquial speech, and his interest in the dramatic symbolism of chivalry effectively sequestered him from persons who, versed in Greek and Roman literature, would naturally have encouraged him to adopt classical models for his history. His relative ignorance of this literature was tantamount to a kind of critical innocence. While he doubtless had little opportunity to develop the detachment that formal study tends to inculcate, he also labored under no preconceptions; that is, he had no reason to uphold any particular notion of what literature, whether poetry or history, should be. True, he felt what was a comparatively powerful emotional obligation to praise the *virtù* of Carlo's court as a mirror of a contemporary French and Florentine chivalry. But he was exempt from the subtler forms of intellectual control that the actual disciplines of humanistic studies would have imposed upon him.

This intellectual freedom affected the entire composition of the poem; to it is owed the poet's changing conception of his task. The *Morgante* begins with a narration of action that is made comprehensible by reference to certain notions of destiny and cyclicity which, enshrined in the Florentines' consciousness of their past, have a particular meaning in a Florentine work about Charlemagne. In a larger sense, these notions are also typical of a humanistic conception of history and an element in what humanists considered its moralizing function. If the past was to be in any way instructive, as they believed it to be, it was only because valid comparisons between one age and another could be made. That is, human affairs had somehow to demonstrate a repetitiveness which would permit them to be analyzed on a comparable basis and, however obscure they might superficially appear, thus to reveal their causes and their effects. Pulci's interest in developing a perspectival narrative reflects his initial willingness to accept the validity of an essentially rational vision of history which is comprehensible in comparative terms, a vision he probably did not precisely identify as humanistic. To these features of his historiographic method, the epic modes of representating the past that Pulci adopted as part of the tradition of the *cantimbanchi* and, coincidentally, as logical for a poet who was actually transcribing and elaborating matter already well-represented, were naturally congenial. Because Pulci began by conceiving of his Muse as outside time and therefore immune to its effects, that is, because he did not expect that it would confound him with the terrible illogic of a judgment for which there was no evidence, he was able to interpret (in the first twenty-two cantos of his poem) the narrative of the *Orlando* as moral and political allegory.

The last five cantos of the poem are written in a different and fundamentally antihumanistic spirit. Consistent with the early part of the poem is an emphasis on the human will as capable of making decisions the effects of which are registered in historical events. In Part 2 of the poem we hear the voices of the characters who take part in the battle of Roncisvalle; they are the more articulate for being lifted from the allegorical matrix of the earlier cantos. But for all their clarity they do not function in a rational world. Their actions do not have identifiable causes nor can they, or we, predict what results these actions will have. The course of history is determined by the mysterious will and interventions of God. From demonstrating in Part 1 the reasonableness and the Providential direction of history, Pulci turns in Part 2 to describe a more radical vision of the past. He depicts a world where human beings are morally responsible, though for acts for which no consistent criteria are available, and where the importance of the local and contingent renders suspect expressions of faith in a Providential plan. Unlike Boethius and later Guicciardini, Pulci does not and perhaps cannot fully accept the concept of an inscrutable divinity. He not only regards with a skeptical mockery the suggestion that history is the scene of miracles and of heavenly intervention, but he also cannot agree to the Boethian proposition that the historical evidence available to him is so transformed, in the eyes of God, as to support judgments wholly irrational to human minds. His final doubt concerning Rinaldo's return to Christendom (a return which would signify the hero's continued obedience to traditional moral authority) informs his subsequent portrait of Carlo's historians. In attempting to do what he has been unable to do, that is, forge a reasonable link between Dante's Charlemagne and historical evidence, they are seen to be totally ineffectual. By his turn to pastoral he reveals that he is prepared to accept the idea that representations of the past have their origin in imagination ("fantasia") and a desire to please.

# AFTERWORD
# THE THREE 'ORLANDO' POETS

A corpus of poetic narrative as traditional as the matter of France was to poets in Renaissance Italy will obviously lend itself to a study of influences, and of sources and analogues. It is in fact difficult to think of three narrative poems more closely associated by bonds of convention, by common sources, by a shared content and imagery than Pulci's *Morgante*, the *Orlando Innamorato* of Boiardo (1494), and its sequel, the *Orlando Furioso* of Ariosto (1532). Published within a half-century and in city states made precarious by factionalism, and exposed to threats (and at last suffering the reality) of invasion from powerful nation states to the north, each of these poems bears in distinctive ways the burden of prescribing for its compatriot readers a civic identity.

They are nevertheless dissimilar works, a fact which must be at least in part attributed to the circumstances of their composition. For Boiardo and Ariosto, both Ferrarese poets patronized by the Estensi, the Emperor himself had practically no significance as a figure of civic pride nor could his paladins serve as a source for the *virtù* of their compatriots. Unlike Florence, Ferrara did not claim to have been rebuilt by Charlemagne or value a political connection with the house of Anjou and the French monarchy. In contrast to the Medici, the Estensi had been a political force in the Italian peninsula for centuries. They derived their power not from commerce and banking but from inherited titles and property. Like the *Morgante*, the Ferrarese epic-romances were intended as propaganda for their patrons, but the effects they sought were of grander scope than those Pulci's poem aspired to: the celebration of the history of their patrons' family from its beginnings in the legendary past of Troy and the Trojan conquest of Italy. The emphasis that falls in the *Morgante* on Carlo Mano and Orlando, epic heroes on whom the poem builds its concept of a chivalric society and a Providential history, is carried in the *Orlando Innamorato* and the *Orlando Furioso* by the pagan prince Ruggiero and his Christian lady-knight, Bradamante, together the putative founders of the Estensi. The court of Charlemagne provides the setting and the ethos for this union, which is thus endowed with all the virtues of chivalry.

The Ferrarese poets also differ from Pulci in their representation of *virtù*. In a sense both are more Boethian and less concerned to celebrate epic values than Pulci is, at least in the opening cantos of the *Morgante*. For them, there is no possibility that a purely human *virtù*, unassisted by mysterious forces, can be identified as an element in Providential history. They—and particularly Ariosto, who defends himself from accusations of blasphemy by showing that human and earthly vision is partial and limited—make the true meaning of history visible only *sub specie aeternitatis*. Absent from both later poems is the optimistic vision of *virtù* as a form of divine agency that appears in the opening octaves of the *Morgante;* in neither is there a figure who signifies what Morgante does, for to Boiardo and Ariosto an alliance between heroic strength and divine grace is no longer a feature of Providential history. Not until Rabelais' Gargantua and Pantagruel is this kind of causality again imaginable and then its basis is not in some idea of a renascence of chivalry but rather in the extraordinary amalgam of humanism and popular culture that Rabelais himself creates.

These are the significant differences that distinguish the Tuscan from the Lombard poems, differences that readily express the particular intentions of their poets, the nature of the political situations in which they found themselves, and their obligations to their patrons. Yet it is also possible to see in all three poems a common concern, that is, to define the role of the poet as a historian, one who tells a story about a subject that is represented as past, and thus to establish a historiographic style. To what extent, if at all, either of the later poets were directly affected by Pulci's work is unclear. What is certain is that all three poets recognized that, by writing narratives that claimed, however tenuously, a historical reference, they had undertaken to distinguish historical fact from (timeless) fiction, the truth of the past from the lies necessitated by the exigencies of the present, and finally the historian from every other kind of writer—poet, orator, rhetorician. It is equally the case that for none of these poets are these distinctions obvious or unqualified. In each of their poems the historian's role is inextricably merged with that of the apologist and the sophist.

For Boiardo the historian's task is defined and circumscribed by the rhetorical nature of *all* expression. His models are Ovid and Petrarch and from them he derives and reflects in his poem the pathos of the effort to represent a past, however private and individual, and indeed to interpret accounts of the past so that they yield a coherent and rationally analyzable picture of reality. For Ariosto the question of history as the truth of the past is moot. The question he addresses is rather one of purpose. He asks to know the means and the terms by which the past, as it is represented in various forms including that of local custom, shapes the present moment and creates expectations for the future. For both poets, the text possesses a self-reflexive dimension where these matters have a place; they include in their poems passages in which the acts of interpretation and expression are represented, and thus instruct their readers in the art of understanding history.

To move from Pulci's world of Pagania and Roncisvalle to Boiardo's of indeterminate and supernatural loci, a mysterious realm constituted as a series of projections of the subject, is to recognize in the later poem the relative insignificance of any of its references to history.[1] Even with the introduction in Book 2 of the hero Ruggiero, the *Orlando Innamorato* remains a poem largely determined by the poet's vision of the past as the scene of a pervasive interiority, the response of a single self in fortunate, unfortunate or sometimes freakish contact with a reality defined only as it is known to that self. Lacking more than a vague sense of fellowship and of Carlo's court as a political community, Boiardo's paladins inhabit a world of terror and almost morbid beauty, private, isolated, and fantastic. Controlled by a fortune embodied in the elusive Angelica, a figure who represents both the strength of human passion, whether love or hate, and the illusory possibility of attaining in this earthly life some sort of heavenly perfection, their *virtù* is chiefly pathetic. It cannot merely exploit chance and so triumph, for its aspirations are too high, nor can it control its longing to achieve worship by recognizing a Providence behind events. Pulci's belated recognition of the divorce between Providence and fortune, at least as these historical determinates might be discerned and defined by human beings, appears the slightest of heterodoxies beside Boiardo's much darker forms of doubt, even when these are disguised in the trappings of romance.

What Boiardo perceived his task to be is clear from many of the opening octaves of his cantos. In place of Pulci's heavenly muse, which was still charged, as I have argued, with the power to compel a certain kind of belief in the truth of the poem, Boiardo's inspiration is really his audience's love of pleasure. He asks for an opportunity to relate "cose dillettose e nove," ("things delightful and new") in order to entertain his listeners.[2] The impulse to narrate is here defined as the impulse to respond to desire. The poet's voice becomes eroticized and his image as narrator is characterized by his need to affect his listeners. His refusal to represent his poem in epic terms points up the subjectivity of his vision, a subjectivity shared by his characters.

Like Petrarch, whose poetic persona wandered through a landscape in whose configuration he perceived the shapes and forms of his own desire, Boiardo's heroes actually confront themselves in their surroundings. Particularly in the images of bodies of water that appear throughout the poem, the springs, fountains, lakes, and rivers, with their capacity to mirror the onlooker and to engulf him in that act of self-contemplation, the mental nature of all the action of the poem is expressed. It is action that resists discrimination by categories or analysis in terms of cause and effect. By establishing differences of character but then failing to show them in relationships of complementarity, it tends constantly to thwart the construction of the complex perspectival wholes by which Pulci made similar kinds of differences significant in the *Morgante*. Like Pulci's characters, Boiardo's Orlando is afflicted with "paccia" (though it is brought on by *eros*, not by a conflict with Gano or what that signifies), and his Ranaldo is driven by a wish to demonstrate his *virtù*. Yet these qualities, far from creating situations in which both characters are more vividly represented, reduce to a kind of meaninglessness as the efforts of the paladins end in ironic reversals. In Book 1, Boiardo opposes the disloyal and lovestruck Orlando, who seeks only to serve Angelica, to the dutiful Ranaldo, who hates Angelica and returns early in the narrative to fight for Carlo Magno. But Ranaldo ends up at the pagan court of Albracca defending Angelica's interests, while Orlando, having employed all his stength to remain in Albracca in Angelica's service, is banished to distant (and hellish) Orcagna. The opposition of the two heroes is more forcibly subverted by the fact that, despite their contradictory attitudes toward Angelica (and hence, necessarily, toward Carlo Magno), both knights achieve comparable goals. Orlando, for example, destroys Falerina's garden, an elaborate image of greed, while Ranaldo kills Trufaldino who tries to usurp Angelica's throne.

The nature of the difficulty the reader experiences when he tries to interpret the poem is partly revealed by a look at its structure and mode of narration. Here Boiardo's primary model is Ovid's *Metamorphoses*. Like the Latin poet, Boiardo tells his story in a series of loosely linked episodes whose endings are usually the beginnings of subsequent episodes. Moreover, many of his characters enter the narrative as the subjects of intercalated stories told by characters in the main story and then reappear there to challenge or confront their former historians. Boiardo's narrative therefore undermines not only the notion of the story as history, a narrative of past events that has a formal integrity; it also casts doubt on its own pastness or historicity. By breaking the narrative frame that isolates his story from those his characters tell, Boiardo implictly questions the possibility of that frame and by extension any such frame: can he or his characters in fact tell a story or is the detachment that act implies a deception? This question becomes more urgent when such an intercalated story is an excuse for an action clearly in the storyteller's interest.

Fiordelisa's story of Iroldo and Prasildo is a case in point. Familiar in its main events as Boccaccio's story of Madama Dianora (*Dec.* 10. 5), Boiardo's Prasildo wins Tisbina, who loves Iroldo, by accomplishing the impossible: retrieving a golden branch from the garden of Medusa. Prasildo achieves this by seeing Medusa as Perseus did, only in a mirror; but Boiardo prevents us from understanding this event as an allegory of foresight. His moral is rather that love conquers all. His interest in restricting the opportunity to allegorize conventionally, an interest dependent upon the assumption that the interpretation of such mythic images proceeds by consensus and with objectivity, manifests itself most clearly at the story's conclusion when Iroldo, having courteously renounced Tisbina, is *not* rewarded by Prasildo's answering act of generosity. Tisbina soon reconciles herself to the change, for, as Fiordelisa says, every woman is "pliable" ("molle", 1. 12. 89). In fact, Fiordelisa's story lets Ranaldo know of her own willingness to be reconciled to the loss of her lover Brandimarte and that she might respond to him as Tisbina did to Prasildo. When Prasildo and Iroldo later appear as characters in Boiardo's own narrative, the case for regarding narrative objectivity as illusory is complete. In other words, a story does not open a window upon a past from which its existence as a representation of that past may be assumed to be detached and without a rhetorical intention; it exists as a feature of the world of its teller, an element in his desire to affect some change or other in that world. Boiardo clearly intends his story to exemplify the norms of literary interpretation as a kind of reinterpretation, shaped and given direction by the nature of the interests of the interpreter. He shows an appreciation for the function of rhetoric comparable to that which Pulci acknowledges in the last cantos of Part 1 of the *Morgante,* where the stories the paladins tell are designed not to instruct their listeners in the truth but rather to achieve an effect. While Pulci regarded the narrator as only occasionally a self-interested rhetorician (at least until canto 28), Boiardo sees him exclusively in these terms.

But merely because Boiardo denies objectivity to representations of the past and sees them motivitated by the desire of the narrator does not mean that he does not have a purpose for his own poem that goes beyond a wish to entertain or, more reductively, to obtain a particular favor or result. In Book 3, he presents the reader with an allegory of interpretation that proposes for its object the reader's clarification. He imagines that his poem will offer the reader a means to understand not only the essentially fallacious aims of chivalric *virtù* and the irony of its efforts of achieve worship but also that it will reveal that any representation of the past, particularly one that establishes fame or reputation, is a phenomenon of a present moment and import. The allegory is contained in the digression concerning the *Fonte del riso* (or *del riviera*), the last and most suggestive of all Boiardo's images of water, in which Orlando, Ruggiero, and Gradasso are all immersed. Orlando sinks into the fountain where he has perceived a group of ladies singing and dancing; Ruggiero is led there by the lady who emerges from the laurel he attempts to cut; and Gradasso rushes after a horse who plunges into the water and thence to the palace at its crystal depths. Brandimarte is prevented from making a similar mistake by Fiordelisa, the clever narrator of the Prasildo story, who places on his head a crown of grasses and flowers. This enables Brandimarte to retrieve his fellow paladins as well, each of whom is released from the fountain when they crown themselves as Brandimarte has done (3. 7.6–35).

Why Fiordelisa's crown has the power to release the paladins from their watery prison, or indeed what it means that their desire has led them into a place of sequestration which induces total forgetfulness, is explained only by reference to the imagery of the episode. By descending into the water of forgetfulness the paladins experience the fate of Narcissus who disdains Echo or fame, but their fall is paradoxical in that they are led to it by impulses that appear to symbolize chivalric endeavor. Ruggiero's love of laurel in particular has an ironic effect; rather than making him famous, it makes him a forgetful Narcissus or, as Boccaccio allegorizes the myth in his *Genealogie*, a fading and forgotten flower. The effects of the herbal crown—to bring about a self-recognition and an awakened memory—are equally paradoxical. By association an image suggesting transience and impermanence, especially in the context of the Narcissus story, the crown imposes upon its wearers the burden of their own identity and history.

This is the only crown of this sort in the poem and indeed the most striking image of flowers the reader encounters. Elsewhere flowers are either an image of the poem itself or of the essence of chivalry, which is like a flower in its beauty and fragility and in the brevity of the lives of noble knights. In the opening octaves of Book 1, Boiardo claims that had memory not come to the rescue of Alexander and Caesar, their valor would have flourished ("fiorito") in vain (2. 22. 1). He then complains that fame, a nymph who sings of glory, has disappeared; no one in his own time seeks her. He bids her descend to him; and later, in the opening octaves of Book 3, he celebrates the spring that causes the court to flourish more than ever (1. 1–2). Later he composes and weaves together the ancient honor of his subject with diverse flowers (3. 3. 1); and in yet another canto he compares its variety to that of a rich garden that he has planted with love and battles (3. 5. 2). By identifying the agent of self-recognition—Fiordelisa's herbal crown—with his own poem and by opposing its kind of instruction to that which fame provides, Boiardo discriminates between the memorability he can confer and those cruder forms that overlook the nature of discourse about the past that he has so carefully established. For Boiardo, his poem is neither like a laurel, in index of eternal values, nor is it capable of representing a formal order. His poetic flowers are nothing if not various and, more important, transient. To make the function of his story an illustration of its temporal contingency and its origin an impulse to give pleasure with variety and beauty is in effect to separate it from epic and from any notion that the poet's production reveals the truth of the past. It is no accident that the crown is Fiordelisa's invention, since it is she who has earlier told a tale of desire in order to accomplish what she desires.

For Ariosto, the poet as historian is both a simpler and more complex figure. Ariosto never renounces the role of the epic poet, however much he subjects it (and himself) to ironic treatment. For the Ruggiero-Bradamante thread of his story, he modifies the epic poet's task so that it becomes not simply one of praising a past that is claimed as fully known and truthfully set forth, but one of creating from the records of the past versions of history that are designed to serve the particular purposes of a present moment. He therefore releases his characters from the miasmic interiority in which they exist in the *Innamorato* without allowing them to become the models of perpetual excellence that they are in the opening cantos of the *Morgante*.

For this portrait of the historian, the poet's own image is less important than those of two of his characters, Orlando and Bradamante, each of whom perform acts of historical interpretation that reveal two essentially different attitudes toward the past, which in turn have different effects. The first, Orlando's, induces a catastrophic despair which, only after a struggle, ends in philosophic resignation; the second, Bradamante's, results in an innovative creativity. It is absolutely essential to his depiction of these acts of interpretation that they take place in the context of action that imitates that of a myth of return, for, in the possibility of an earthly immortality that action of this kind invariably suggests, the hopes of the hero for a history so vital as to be a second life can be expressed and, as Ariosto would have it, shown to be illusory. In contrast, Ariosto demonstrates that the true use of history is to create a future, a future that, while linked to the past, is in no way its repetition.

The first of Ariosto's interpreters, Orlando, is a figure whose significance seems to be registered in different ways and levels throughout the poem. In his ironic role as Angelica's lover, he represents Ariosto's perception of the fate not only of chivalry but also of those poets of chivalric narratives who remain unaware of the kind of writing they are engaged in.

Pursuing Angelica, Orlando imitates the goddess Ceres in search of Proserpina; he sets out to look for her because he dreams he has lost her, an image of eternal (returning) vegetation—and therefore also a figure of what is most vividly experienced as eternal in time—to a fierce wintry force. The mythical terms of his visionary loss suggest her return and serve both to motivate and represent the futility of his quest: they indicate that he has failed fully to understand the nature of human temporality—an error emphasized by Ariosto's ironic treatment of the hero in his assumed role as powerful earth goddess. Unlike Ceres, he lacks divine power (12. 1–3), and consequently he must suffer the knowledge that Angelica will never return to him, that is, that human time is not cyclical and does not allow for a recovery of the past.

Orlando confronts a subtle manifestation of what human time means to the historian in the sheer particularity of a historical text which he cannot interpret other than literally. In effect, this confrontation ends his Ceres-like quest. The text is the history of Angelica's marriage to Medoro, which the infidel foot-soldier has recounted in letters on trees. Reading this history for the first time, Orlando attempts to interpret it as allegory, that is, to understand "Medoro" as "Orlando," to see himself figuratively represented as his lady's lover, and thus to continue to dream of recovering Angelica. But he soon finds that the literal meaning of Medoro's verse is incontrovertible, for it is corroborated by accounts and evidence from other quarters. Because he can no longer hope to possess Angelica, that is, to see in the circumstances of his earthly life the possibility of attaining what she, a Proserpina, signifies to him, he goes mad.

Orlando's failure to possess Angelica, to bring about her return, is therefore a revelation of the primacy of the literal which is at the same time a sign of the temporal. That the text resists the discovery of metaphorical meanings means that it cannot be made to signify that which is other than itself. What that other might be is less important than that it is other and therefore disconnected to the time and place of the composition of the text, to its particularity, its historicity. That Orlando is thwarted in reading Medoro's history as allegory means that he is held within a mode of verbal experience that is simply temporal. There is nothing about Medoro's history that can be made to suggest that for Orlando earthly experience will yield a knowledge—imagined as a possession—of Angelica and what she stands for. In other words, timeless knowledge hidden in history as allegory is an illusion. Orlando's madness is a measure of the intensity of his desire for such knowledge, of the frustration of his hope that he might have it.

As Ariosto continues to describe his understanding of the historiographic condition, it becomes clear that, however terrible Orlando's madness, it is in a sense closer to sanity than his former state of illusion. To rave at not having Angelica, to confront one's humanity, is a state of mind closer to the reality of life than to believe that one can attain her, to entertain the hope of having relations with divinity. (Medoro is exempt from the chivalric temptation to see Angelica in this way, since for him, a mere foot-soldier, divinity is securely in heaven as Diana or the moon; he does not perceive Angelica as other than a woman.) It is important that Orlando's wits are returned to him by Astolfo, the paladin who is privileged to witness the full extent of human loss and therefore a demystified vision of history—the lunar landscape in which the desiderata of the past are gathered, a testimony not only to human incompetence but to the ravaging effects of time. It is in this locus too that Astolfo hears the most profound (although comic) statement of the historian's inevitable connection to his own time and place: the confession of St. John who reveals that history, even his own of the Lord, is not the truth but a way of praise. As a logical extension of the Boethian position on the limits of earthly vision—even that of saints—this is not simple heterodoxy, nor need we attribute Ariosto's characterization of St. John as an epic poet to a wish to blaspheme. Had Ariosto read the *Morgante* (among other texts) and noted specifically Pulci's reference to Mark 13, he would have discovered precedents for his characterization of St. John.

It is also in keeping with the logic of this analysis of history that Orlando recovers his wits only after he is tied down, forced to the ground, an act that is symbolic of the hero's historicity and to be associated later with his vision that human life acquires a true meaning only *sub specie aeternitatis*. At Brandimarte's funeral Orlando demonstrates what it means to have gone mad at the loss of Angelica and then to have recovered his sanity: the discrimination of the world of human experience and history from that transcendent realm of absolute truth. He declares that in heaven is the paladin's "recompense" ("guadagno"), a word practically synonymous with those the poet uses to describe what the paladins lack when they pursue and lose Angelica: "ricompensa," "guiderdone," "merto," which mean "reward."[3]

This clarification of the nature of historical texts so nearly approaches a paradoxical point of despair that, were it not balanced by a contrasting vision of history as actually creative, it would touch off the kind of irony that no amount of comic action could mitigate. But, as it happens,

Ariosto writes a second allegory of interpretation in which he redeems from the condition of utter contingency a historical text and shows it open to a reinterpretation which is redemptive in its effect. The action is again described in terms of a mythical return. The interpreter is the lady knight Bradamante, and the text is the quasilegal custom of Tristram's castle, instituted by the example of that knight's behavior ages earlier. Literally this text establishes that in the future the castle may be entered only by the bravest knight and the most beautiful lady. Determined to enter the castle, Bradamante in her role as knight overcomes all other chivalric (and male) contenders and so observes and does not question the literal meaning of the custom. Having entered the castle, however, she discovers that she has been preceded there by the lady Ullania, who, because she is less beautiful than Bradamante (now revealed to be female), must therefore leave the castle. At this point Bradamante does not observe the custom of the castle but effectively reinterprets it so that it admits a new practice. She declares that because she entered the castle as a knight and not as a lady, her contest with Ullania is invalid; the question of who is most beautiful is therefore moot. Bradamante insists that Ullania remain indoors, an action that affects her as if she were a Proserpina. At the threat of wintery exposure (it is snowing outside) she had become grey and shrivelled but when she hears Bradamante's words she is restored to vigor (32. 65–108). Bradamante herself is described as a sun that appears from behind a cloud, in lines that are in fact a close translation of those describing the Ceres of the *Metamorphoses* after Jupiter's decision has restored Proserpina to her.[4] The parallel to Orlando is clear; where he has failed to imitate the goddess, she has succeeded.

Bradamante has based her reinterpretation of the text governing the entrance to the castle not on regarding it as metaphor but rather on reading it with a certain casuistry. That is, it has meaning for her not as a symbol or sign that points to another and possibly more universal meaning but only as it can be made to apply to a specific moment and a given set of circumstances. Bradamante sees that it has application to her insofar as she is male, not her case in fact but only *de facto,* and confronts a lady in distress. And she is moved to discover this meaning because she desires—quite independent of this history—to achieve a certain end. How profoundly Ariosto understood here the implications of his analysis of the process of interpretation is revealed by the fact that Bradamante leaves the castle without forcing its inhabitants to change its custom. She does not, in other words, attempt to rewrite history (unlike her counterpart, Marfisa, who does change the laws of Marganorre's city). She accepts its representation of the past; one could even say that she preserves it for the future. But, by her example, she demonstrates how careful its interpretation may be, how, without resorting to metaphor and instead by attending to the nature of the circumstances in which a text representing the past is to be understood, its reader can discover meanings that the historian could not have intended it to have.

Ullania's return to the land of the living is of course figurative. But it reminds the reader that from the beginning of the poem Bradamante has signified the future of the Estensi; to her is given the important vision of the generations of the family that imitates the vision of the future of Rome Aeneas sees in the underworld in the company of his father. More important, it is a future that she "knows" as Aeneas does not know his, for she is instructed in the identity of her descendents, who are depicted on her wedding tent woven by Cassandra, while the Trojan hero lifts upon his shoulders a shield whose figures he does not recognize (*Aen.* 8. 730). Bradamante's insight into the future is predicated upon her ability to interpret the past, not as a sign of things eternal but rather as the ground upon which present choices must be made.

There is no direct evidence that either Boiardo or Ariosto developed their conceptions of history and historiography from reading the *Morgante*. The fact remains that in this poem are registered the principal concerns of the posthumanist historiography that were to be fully explored by writers in the next century. That the Florence of the Medici, particularly of Lorenzo, should have been the locus of this activity is not surprising. More than any other city in the Italian peninsula it was the scene of a conflict of ideologies, of propaganda for empire designed in part to mask and in part to make acceptable the commercial and political operations of the persons who governed it. Pulci found his most important subject in the perceptible incongruities between a history that he was obliged to regard as true and the evidence that was proposed to support it.

# NOTES

## Introduction

1. For the relationship between a given interpretation of history and questions of political legality, see particularly Hayden White, "The Value of Narrativity in the Representation of Reality," *Critical Inquiry* 7, 1 (1980): 5–27.

2. For the principal events in Pulci's life, see G. Volpi, "Luigi Pulci: Studio Biografico," *Giornale storico della letteratura italiana* 22 (1893): 1–64; and Carlo Pellegrini, *Luigi Pulci: L'uomo e l'artista* (Pisa: Nistri, 1912).

3. For a study of the mythical histories of Florence see Donald Weinstein, "The Myth of Florence" in *Florentine Studies: Politics and Society in Renaissance Florence,* ed. Nicolai Rubinstein (Evanston, Ill.: Northwestern University Press, 1968), pp. 15–44.

4. For Bruni's historical work see Hans Baron, "A New View of Roman History and the Florentine Past" in *Crisis of the Early Italian Renaissance* (Princeton: Princeton University Press, 1955, rev. ed. 1966), esp. pp. 61–75; for its recent evaluation, see also David Quint, "Humanism and Modernity: A Reconsideration of Bruni's *Dialogues,*" *Renaissance Quarterly* 38, 3 (1985): 423–45; for Salutati, see "A Citizen's View and a Humanist's View of Florentine History and Culture: Cino Rinuccini and Salutati" in *Crisis,* esp. pp. 94–103.

5. For Bruni's account of the foundation of Florence by Sulla and his soldiers, see the *Historiarum Florentini populi liber,* ed. Emilio Santini, Rerum Italicarum Scriptores, Vol. 19, pt. 3 (Città di Castello: Lapi, 1914), 1:5, 6; for Bruni's denunciation of Roman emperors after Tiberius and his description of the decline of the empire see 1:14, 15; for an account of ancient Etruria see 1:7, 8; for Bruni's opinion of Charlemagne see Chapter 1, note 1 below.

6. For the concept of "civic humanism" that emerges from these debates, see Hans Baron, *Crisis;* especially "Florentine Humanism and the Volgare in the Quattrocento," pp. 332–53. The bibliography on this subject is vast. Among many useful studies see Jerrold Seigel, *Rhetoric and Philosophy in Renaissance Humanism: The Union of Eloquence and Wisdom, Petrarch to Valla* (Princeton: Princeton University Press, 1968); Nancy K. Struever, *The Languages of History in the Renaissance* (Princeton: Princeton University Press, 1970); and D. Wilcox, *The Development of Florentine Humanist Historiography in the Fifteenth Century* (Cambridge, Mass.: Harvard University Press, 1969).

7. Lauro Martines, *The Social World of the Florentine Humanists: 1390–1460* (Princeton: Princeton University Press, 1963), p. 278; for further discussion see pp. 271–303.

8. Nicolai Rubinstein, *The Government of Florence under the Medici* (Oxford: Oxford University Press, 1966), p. 49. This detailed history gives a full account of the political developments in Florence from 1434 to the death of Lorenzo. For a shorter version see his article "Florentine Constitutionalism and Medici Ascendancy in the Fifteenth Century," in *Florentine Studies,* pp. 442–62. See also John Hale, *Florence and the Medici: the Pattern of Control* (London: Thames and Hudson, 1977).

9. "Consilium de republica domi suae agitari," Rubinstein, *Government*, p. 128, note 2; quoting *Commentarii* (Rome, 1584), p. 89.

10. "quid in libera et populari republica possit privatus civis," Rubinstein, *Government*, p. 128, quoting Fabrioni, *Cosmi vita* (Nov. 3, 1463), ii, pp. 242–3, 245.

11. As Rubinstein observes, Cosimo "may have derived as much influence from his ability to bridge differences among the *uomini principali* as from any effective leadership of them." *Government*, p. 133.

12. Weinstein, "Myth," p. 21.

13.          Firmat, emit, fervens sternit nunc castra salute,
             Que mare, que terram, que totum possidet orbem
             Per quam regnantem fit felix Tuscia tota;
             Tamquam Roma sedet semper ductura triumphos. . . .

Quoted in Nicolai Rubinstein, "The Beginnings of Political Thought in Florence," *Journal of the Warburg and Courtauld Institutes* 5 (1942): 213, note 1.

14. "I Romani fecero decreto, come i loro antecessori avevano fatto e popolato prima la città di Firenze, così vi andassero a riedificare, e abitare delle migliori schiatte di Roma, grandi e popolani, e così fecero con quella oste dello Imperadore e de' Romani . . ." ("the Romans decreed that as their forebears had first made and populated the city of Florence, they would therefore rebuild it, and bring to it the best stock of Rome, both nobles and plebs, and thus they did with masses of the Emperor's men and of Romans. . . ."), Giovanni Villani, *Istorie Fiorentine* (Milan: Società tipografica de'classici italiani, 1802), 1, 3, 1, p. 142.

15. ". . . ordinarono il reggimento al modo di Roma, cioe per due consoli e per lo consiglio di cento senatori . . ." (". . . they governed it in the Roman manner, that is with two consuls and a council of a hundred senators . . ."), Villani, *Istorie*, 1, 3, 3, p. 149.

16. Weinstein, "Myth," p. 22.

17. Weinstein, "Myth," p. 34, 35.

18. The text of the manifesto in part: "Finalmente appare ben chiaro ciò che il serpente sta tentando con le sue blandizie. Ora si capisce bene il suo disegno. Il grande segreto ch'egli mascherava con una stupefante ipocrisia, per cui ammazzò il suocero, ingannò i fratelli, prese con raggiri Padova, Verona e Vicenza, le citta toscane e piemontesi, è svelato: egli vuole la corona d'Italia per coonestare definitivamente con lo splendore del titolo la sua tirannide. . . . Ma la l'esistenza nostra impediamo che gl'Italiani tutti cadano in servitù" ("Finally it is very clear what the snake is attempting to do with its blandishments. Now its plan is understood. The great secret it hides, with a stupefying hypocrisy, by which it has killed its father-in-law, fooled its brothers, taken by trickery Padua, Verona, and Vicenza, and the cities of Tuscany and the Piedmont, is revealed: It wants the crown of Italy definitely to justify its tyranny with the splendor of a title. . . . But our presence guarantees that all Italians will not fall into slavery"), Nino Valeri, *L'Italia nell'età dei principati dal 1343 al 1516* (Milan: Mondadori, 1949), pp. 258, 59.

19. Weinstein, "Myth," p. 35.

20. "Quod enim in solo patrio sumus, quod liberi vivimus, quod magistratus, leges, civitatem habemus, ea omnia Carolo accepta sunt referenda, ac eius memoria tam grata recordatione perpetua celebranda . . .", Donato Acciajolo, *Vita Caroli Magni* in *Scriptores Rerum Germanicarum*, 1, ed. J. B. Mencke (Leipzig, 1728), c. 827.

21. "Tanto mi piace ancora la virtù, che questo giù fra i mortali cura che per unito volere me gli fo amico; per questo mosso, e veduto che per carita del mio Firenze, il quale io già riposi in terra, eri morto, infino ad te discesi, per mostrarti la gloria s'aspecta da ciascuno che in vostra vita a questo intende", Matteo Palmieri, *Della vita civile*, ed. Felice Battaglia, Scrittori Politici Italiani, no. 14 (Bologna: Zanichelli, 1944), 4, p. 175.

22. See Alfonso Lazzari, *Ugolino e Michele Verino* (Turin: Clauen, 1897), pp. 153–189.

23. Richard C. Trexler, *Public Life in Renaissance Florence* (New York: Academic Press, 1980), p. 224.

24. In that regard the city seemed to be following a trend observable generally throughout Europe: "Large national entities both Italian and ultramontane pressed upon Florence with enormous resources. These neofeudal states were forthrightly aristocratic and authoritarian in both political and artistic cultures; to them Florence's determination to maintain its republican order seemed parochial, archaic, and self-destructive." Trexler, *Public Life*, p. 365.

25. For the activities of the Magi and Lorenzo's part in them, see André Rochon, *La jeunesse de Laurent de Medicis* (Paris: Les Belles Lettres, 1963), p. 44.

26. Trexler, *Public Life*, p. 424. For a study of the fresco of the Procession of the Magi (1459) in the chapel of the Medici palace depicting members of the Medici family, see Anna Padoa Rizzo, *Benozzo Gozzoli pittore fiorentino* (Florence: Edam, 1972). Years later, Botticelli was also to include portraits of Medici in his Adoration of the Magi (1475–78).

27. Rochon, *Jeunesse*, p. 73.

28.     Poi venne un giovanetto assai virile,
          Giovan di tempo e vecchio di sapere,
          E tiene ancora di boce puerile.
        Costui per più cagioni ha gran potere,
          Perciò che la sua casa molto puote,
          E questo chiaro si puote vedere,
        Figliuol di Piero e di Cosmo nipote;
          Però questi gentili il fan signore. . . .

"Degli armeggiatori quando e come" (a 1459 maggio), in *Ricordi di Firenze Dell'Anno 1459 di Autore anonimo*, ed. G. Volpi, Rerum italicarum scriptores, v. 27, pt. 1 (Città di Castello: Muratori, 1907), pp. 30–31.

29. For Pulci's poem see *Ciriffo Calvaneo di Luca Pulci, Gentil'huomo fiorentino. Con la Giostra del Magnifico Lorenzo de Medici* (Florence: Giunti, 1572), pp. 75–91.

30. For a brief account of Medici economic activity, see, among others, Hale: "It is difficult to think of a commodity that Medici enterprise did not handle, either with the general policy of spreading risks through diversity, or to satisfy the demands of special clients. . . . The sole personal link was Cosimo who, as the controlling partner in all of them [the foreign branches of his bank], was the directing influence in the organization as a whole. Professor de Roover has pointed out that 'in studying the organization of the Medici bank, one cannot fail to notice how closely it resembles that of a holding company.'" *Florence and the Medici*, pp. 33, 34.

31. "Quando altri popoli vedranno che hai governato la Toscana con giuste leggi, correranno tutti a te, figlio mio, a chiederti consiglio. Oh, con qual piacere guarderai questa città, quale impero di essa vedrai presto sorgere, quando i re vorranno piuttòsto obbedire ai tuoi ammonimenti che imporre ad altri la loro signoria. Abbattete i superbi, risparmiate i deboli, affinché l'Italia tutta si addatti al vostro dominio. Coltivate quelle arti per mezzo delle quali Firenze può onorevolmente governare gli italiani. Ora non posso ancora vedere i nuovi territori; ma mi rallegrero al sentire che l'impero toscano è cresciuto per la tua preveggenza" ("When other people see that you have governed Tuscany with just laws, they will all run to you, my son, to ask your advice. Oh, with what pleasure will you look at this city whose strength you will see increasing, when kings would rather heed your warnings that impose their rule on others. Strike down the proud, spare the weak, so that all Italy is under your control. Cultivate those arts by which Florence can honorably govern Italians. At the moment I cannot yet see new territories; but I rejoice to hear that

Tuscan rule has grown by your foresight"); quoted in Warman Welliver, *L'impero fiorentino* (Florence: La Nuova Italia, 1957), p. 42. The Vergilian echoes of this deathbed speech— "parcere subiectis e debellare superbos" *Aeneid* 6. 853—suggest that for Cosimo the example of Rome and Aeneas was to serve as a model for Florentine imperialism and Medici control.

32. Carl Gutkind, *Cosimo de' Medici, 1389–1464* (Oxford: Clarendon Press, 1938), p. 169.

33. See Alison Brown, "The Humanist Portrait of Cosimo de' Medici, *Pater Patriae*," *Journal of the Warburg and Courtauld Institutes* 24 (1961): 186–221.

34. Raffaello Ramat, "Introduzione," in Luigi Pulci, *Il Morgante* (Milan: Rizzoli, 1961), p. 11.

35. In that year Pulci composed a melancholy statement of the family's finances for the land registry office: "Trovianci come vedete con poche substanze sanza presta o buoi o bestiame a poderi sanza trafico o monte o denari o botteghe et con debito assai. Raccomandianci a voi." ("We are as you see [a family] of little substance: no livestock either cattle or other farm animals; no assets, either in the bank, in cash, or invested in trade; and we have quite a few debts. We recommend ourselves to you.") Volpi, "Pulci," p. 7.

36. Alison Brown, *Bartolomeo Scala, 1430–1497: Chancellor of Florence* (Princeton: Princeton University Press, 1979), p. 44. On Pulci's "antihumanism" in general see G. Vallese, "Il 'Morgante' e l'antihumanesimo del Pulci," *Italica* 30 (1953): 81–86, and Edoardo A. Lebano, "Luigi Pulci and Late Fifteenth-Century Humanism in Florence," *Renaissance Quarterly* 27, 4 (1974): 489–98. See also Salvatore Nigro, *Pulci e la cultura medicea* (Bari: Laterza, 1972).

37. "E' mi dispiace troppo che nel colmo della tua amicitia et benivolentia io sia così scacciato; avvisandoti che horomai sono tanto tuo, che questa ingiuria è fatta a tte. Pare ch'io sia un ribaldo in bando, in pena, in colpa: che ho io fatto pero? . . . Ma la mia buona fede *erga te* merita bene che tu mi m'ami. Amami adunque arditamente, che ancora ne sarai contento, et confesserai ch'io sia fedele. . . . Et ancora speravo per altra via tu mi facessi alcuno bene. Non posso più; mai pote' fare disegno che la fortuna non guasti in una hora quello ch'io ho condotto in molti anni. Io naqui come le lepre e altri animali più sventurati, per dovere esser preda agli altri e per dovere molto amarti e poco esser con teco. Quanto più ti disidero, più ti sono tolto. Non harà però forza il cielo ch'io non sia sempre teco in qualche modo: sempre ti vego, sempre parlo teco. Et così ancora afflitto delle mie povere et sventurate muse, ti farò parte d'una mia certa frottola. Et poi che sarò nella Mec, così in lingua moresca ti manderò qualche verso; poi che sarò nello 'nferno se potrò te ne manderò quassù per qualche spirito. Infine ti conchiugo, Lorenzo, che solo ch'io senta tu m'ami, sono più che contento, ne' boschi o dove io sia. Non m'a lasciato il cielo altro che te: non mi ti torre." Letter 2, *Morgante e lettere*, ed. Domenico De Robertis (Florence: Sansoni, 1962), pp. 938–39.

38. "Ma certo io non ho il torto a confidarmi in te solo, però ch'io sono tuo solo. . . . E se tu non m'aiuti, altra speranza non ho. Che debbo adunque fare? darmi al trecentomila diavoli?" Letter 4, *Morgante*, p. 943.

39. Ernest H. Wilkins, "On the Dates of Composition of the *Morgante* of Luigi Pulci," *PMLA* 66 (1951): 250.

40. Letter 15, *Morgante*, p. 960.

41. But Pulci's manner of dealing with Lorenzo was not unique. See Hale, *Florence and the Medici*, p. 62.

42. "Qualche infornata di pane pe' figliuoli di Lucha. . . . Vero è che il mio Bernardo è stato di latte, perché io gli dixi e scripsi della Marca 6 volte, quando era in sul conchiudere venissi arditamente a te, che gli daresti aiuto per qualche modo: è tanto timido et salvatico che non harà fatto nulla." Letter 21, *Morgante*, p. 971.

43. "Faresti bene alla tornata mia serbarmi quello mazzocchio, et cacciarmelo infino al naso, perché il mio padre l'exercitò 20 volte, et fu nel 39 Podestà di Colle di Valdesa, et nel 50 stracciato Capitano della montagna di Pistoja." Letter 22, *Morgante*, p. 973–74.

44. "Racomandomi a te, et spero m'aiuterai; et lungo tempo ho desiderato tu possa, per tua salute propria et de' tuoi cari servitori et antichi et del tuo padre, che a me pare esser di quelli. Aiutami poiché puoi, e i miei poveri nipoti per ch'io m'affatico, viveranno per te; perché sanza il tuo aiuto, Lorenzo, a parlare virilmente, sono ancora in più noia non credi." Letter 23, *Morgante*, pp. 976.

45. Volpi quotes Nannina's letter (actually in Pulci's hand): "Luigi de' Pulci molto divotamente insieme con gli altri questa mattina s'è comunicato et farà ancora 'buona riuscita.' " "Pulci," p. 34.

46. Sonnet 37 in *Sonetti di Matteo Franco e di Luigi Pulci* (Lucca?, 1759), p. 37.

47. For a discussion of Ficino, Lorenzo's *Altercazione*, and the contemporary cultural climate, see Rochon, *Jeunesse*, pp. 482–88; see also pp. 301, 302. For documentation of legal changes see Paolo Orvieto, *Pulci medievale* (Rome, Salerno, 1978), p. 237.

48. "Tu haria detto ch'io afrettai il partire per non trovarmi coll'academia. Lasciagli venire in qua, et sentirai ch'io te ne scardassi qualchuno. So mi capiteranno alle mani, et da lloro sapremo come andorno le muse; et se io non havessi havuto gran fretta ti contentavo costì; ma io ti farò più honore di qua, dove molti udiranno." Letter 32, *Morgante*, p. 986.

49. Orvieto, *Pulci*, p. 218–19.

50. "If my sonnet doesn't please you, don't speak of it" ("se non v'agrada/i mie sonetto, ne faren silenzio"). "Sempre la pulcia muor" is in the *Cronaca* of Benedetto Dei; Orvieto reprints it in its entirety. *Pulci*, p. 213.

51. Sonnet 145, *Sonetti*, p. 145.

52. Sonnet 5, quoted in Orvieto, *Pulci*, p. 226–27; for Sonnets 1–4, see pp. 224–26.

53. Volpi identifies this Marsilio as Ficino, but, given the enmity between Pulci and Ficino, this seems problematic. See Orvieto, *Pulci*, pp. 219–22.

54. "Io t'ò scripta questa colla mano che trema per la febre, perché stamani mi fu da' parenti recati sonetti dove erano coltellate, improverate et molte cose ch'io non sapevo ancora; di che hebbi tanta pena, ch'essendo dianzi in piazza mi ne prese le febbre. È venuto Cino a medicarmi, e dice quello gli ài detto. Io ti prego di questo, che mi dia tanto spatio venga a te, che se non havessi hora tremito sarei venuto, e che tu vogli udire uno tuo servitore prima che lo giudichi con ira e per detto di molti che m'ànno a lloro modo in preda. . . . Il bene vego non t'è raporto, ma Idio lo raporterà; e quando ti sarà passata l'ira, ancora cognoscerai t'amo forse più di quelli che mi t'accusono tutto dì. Fa' infine di me ciò che vuoi; verrò hora, e quando e dove mi dirai, a ogni pena, a ogni suplicio; e credo sarà buono io tolghi un bordone, e colla mia sventurata moglie ch'è qui stasera in questa buona festa, vadi peregrinando, poi che sono in odio a Dio, a te, al mondo." Letter 36, *Morgante*, pp. 991–92.

55. Orvieto, citing Marsilii Ficini, *Opera omnia* (Basle, 1576) 1, pp. 646–47, in *Pulci*, p. 235. See also Arnaldo della Torre, *Storia dell'Accademia Platonica di Firenze* (Florence: Carnesecchi, 1902), pp. 820–29.

56. "Gigi (Pulci) è animella delle vostre palle. Havete tolto a mostrare la magnificentia et humanita vostre in tenere a ghalla questa dispecto della generatione humana. . . . Fatta in furia, addi 24 di Gennaio, 1475" ("Gigi is a little animal of your mattress. You have shown your magnificence and humanity in dispensing with this annoyance to the human race . . . In haste. . . ."); quoted in Raymond Marcel, *Marsile Ficin* (Paris: Les Belles Lettres, 1958), p. 426.

57. Orvieto, *Pulci*, p. 235.

58. For Sanseverino see Volpi, "Pulci," pp. 20–23; Sanseverino wrote from Bologna the following note concerning Pulci to Lorenzo in Florence on April 4th, 1475: "Venendo lì Aloise Pulzi informato da mi di quanto lì è di nuovo, non me extendrò a dire altro, se non pregare V. Mia li presta fede quanto a mi proprio" ("Aloysius Pulzi is coming from here informed by me of news from these parts; I shall not say more except to ask you to trust

him as you would me"); quoted in "Nota Biografica," ed. Ramat, p. 1251.

59. Lorenzo de' Medici, *Lettere (1460–1474)*, ed. Riccardo Fubini (Florence: Giunti, 1977), 1, Letter 21, pp. 45, 46; see note 1.

60. Introduction to Letter 167, to Galeazzo Maria Sforza, dated July 3, 1474. Pulci's letter to Lorenzo is from La Cavallina, dated September 9, 1474; extracts appear in Sotheby's catalogue, dated March 14, 1967. *Lettere*, 1, pp. 530–31.

61. *Lettere (1474–1478)*, ed. Fubini (Florence: Giunti, 1977), 2, Letter 219, p. 175, note. 10. Lorenzo's letter to Guicciardini runs in part: "Io sono avisato dal Signor Ruberto non gli essere punto piaciuta la conclusione fatta costì per Luigi. Parmi ne resti molto male contento. . . . Io farò però dal canto mio quanto potrò col Signor Ruberto, che resti contento alla conclusione fatta costì, che invero me pare il meglo per lui; pure, io non li posso comandare, né fare di meno che non scriva a Luigi che facci quanto lui li ordinerà, che lo fo sotto le spalle vostre" ("I have been advised by Sir Robert that he was not pleased with the conclusion [of the business] made there by Luigi. He seemed to be very put out. . . . I shall do what I can with Sir Robert, so that he is satisfied with what is concluded there, for this seems to be the best for him; however, I cannot order him [about], nor do more than write Luigi that he do what he is ordered, for he is at your command"). Postcripta 219A, 2, pp. 182–83.

62. Letter 219A, 2, p. 285, note 1; the editor cites Pulci's letter, dated September 20, 1476: "Dal Signore ti rimandai in costà lettere. Ricordati delle pratiche antiche, da non lasciare però ancora per perdute, rispetto quanto vale sua Signoria et quanto t'ama" ("I sent you letters there by the Lord [Robert]. Remember the old ways, do not let them remain lost, considering how worthy your lordship and how much I am fond of you"). Letter 44, *Morgante*, p. 999.

63. "Io ho caro, in questo caso tanto, che egli è hora tuo tutto et tuo capitale, e tu solo puoi disporne a tuo modo, o qua o là, come vorrai" ("I am glad, very much in this instance, that he is now totally and fundamentally yours, and that you alone can direct him in your way, here or there, as you wish"). Letter 45, *Morgante*, p. 1000.

64. See especially Letter 243, to Tommaso Soderini and Luigi Guicciardini in Milan, dated February 17, 1477, 2, pp. 280–93, and Letter 244, to Andrea Petrini in Milan, of the same date, 2, pp. 294–98. Lorenzo's letter to Pulci in Milan, 255, is dated March 10, 1477, 2, pp. 324–26. On Soderini's interceptions, see 2, p. 324, note 2.

65. "Hola facta vedere a questi ambasciadori, et cotesti Illustrissimi Signori potranno intendere per questo et per molte altre cose che da quel dì in qua che il Signor Ruberto fu inimico di contesti Illustrissimi Signori, fu ancora mio" ("I indicated this to these ambassadors, and those noble lords can understand by this and many other things that, from that day forward that Sir Robert was an enemy of those noble Lords, he was also mine"). Letter 305, to Girolamo Morelli, July 15, 1478, *Lettere (1478–1479)*, ed. Nicolai Rubinstein, (Florence: Giunti, 1977), 3, p. 128; and Letter 306, to Girolamo Morelli, July 17, 1478, 3, p. 136, especially note 9.

66. "Perché, quantunque io ti venga poco inanzi, sappi che io sono sempre teco et più che mai tuo, e quello poco so et posso e lla roba e lla vita metterò a tua posta per te. Io t'ò veduto occupato e pieno di pensieri strani, et non ho saputo che offerirti; ma di tanto sia cierto, che io non ho dimenticato tanti benifici et dal tuo padre et da te, et so che tu non hai servito a ingrato, ch'io ho tutto scolpito nel cuore." Letter 46, *Morgante*, p. 1001.

67. Volpi, "Pulci," p. 24 and note 2; Letter 48, *Morgante*, pp. 1002, 3.

68. "Se io non vengo in sogno in Lombardia, o portato come le streghe dalla fantasima, io non arriverò più in cotesto paese; et non mi duole se non il mio et tuo messer Guasparre havervi tanto lontano. . . . Io ho ancora di qua amici e gratie, e qualcuno m'aiuterà." Letter 49, *Morgante*, p. 1004.

69. Castiglione, *Il Libro del cortegiano*, ed. Bruno Maier (Turin: Unione, 1964), 223–25.

70. "Di poi t'o a dire solo del s[ignor] R[oberto], lo quale lo trovato si bene edificato verso di te insieme co' figliuoli, che voi siete tutti o de' Medici o di Sanseverino." Letter 50, *Morgante*, p. 1005.

71. Quoted in della Torre, *Storia*, p. 825. For an account of this quarrel from Ficino's point of view, see Marcel, *Marsile Ficin*, pp. 420–33.

72. "Ricordati di me quando se' col Baccio, che altrimenti non credo te ne ricordi; ché da un pezzo in qua, o io ho havuto vaiuolo o morfea, o io sono cresciuto, che tu non mi ricognosci." Letter 45, *Morgante*, p. 999.

73. della Torre, *Storia*, p. 826.

74. For Pulci's treatment of the question of salvation outside the church and its relation to Ficino's teaching, see Chapter 4. For Ficino's interest in astrology and hermetic philosophy, see Wayne Shumaker, *The Occult Sciences in the Renaissance* (Berkeley and Los Angeles: University of California Press, 1972), pp. 120–34, 201–10, and D. P. Walker, *Spiritual and Demonic Magic from Ficino to Campanella* (London: The Warburg Institute, 1958), especially pp. 30–53.

75. In the drama of Carlo's duping by Gano, in which "Marsilio" assumes the leading role, Pulci condemns in poetic figures the treachery he thought he had suffered but could not establish openly. If Ficino had caused Pulci embarrassment in matters of morals and religion, only to endorse—at least in Pulci's view—the more sophisticated aberrations of his own religious beliefs, that Pulci felt betrayed is understandable. Lorenzo too is implicated in this drama; the poem's last canto is in large measure devoted to both accusing and defending the Emperor. Like Carlo, Lorenzo was duped (in Pulci's opinion) by an unscrupulous vassal (Ficino), but like Carlo, he was destined, by some divine calculus, to be found wise and good. Neither comparison remains unqualified, however; Pulci's defense of Carlo becomes one of the poem's ironies. For the connections between Ficino and Pulci's "Marsilio," see Orvieto, *Pulci*, pp. 244–83.

76. For a lengthy study of Pulci's religion in the context of contemporary attitudes towards free thought see Ernst Walser, *Lebens- und Glaubensprobleme aus dem Zeitalter der Renaissance: Die Religion des Luigi Pulci, ihre Quellen und ihre Bedeutung* (Marburg: Elwert, 1926). Walser believes that in the *Morgante* Pulci expresses ideas that derive from Averroistic sympathies. Walser's work is pursued and refuted, to a degree, by Dieter Kremers, *Rinaldo und Odysseus: Zur Frage der Diesseitserkenntnis bei Luigi Pulci und Dante Alighieri* (Heidelberg: Winter, 1966). Kremers sees that Pulci's religious feeling is characterized by a spirit of religious toleration that he traces to the writings of Nicolas of Cusa and the influence on Pulci of Toscanelli. These studies are considered in detail in Chapter 4. Some critics believe that Pulci was, strictly speaking, heretical in his views; see, among others, Edoardo Lebano, "Note sulla religiosità di Luigi Pulci," *Forum Italicum* 4, 4 (1970): 517–32; and, with particular reference to the figure of the devil Astarotte, "I miracoli di Roncisvalle e la presunta ortodossia del diavoli-teologo Astarotte nel 'Morgante' di L. Pulci," *Italica* 46 (1969): 120–34. On the other hand, Pellegrini regards Pulci's *Confessione* as a genuine statement of religious belief, *Luigi Pulci*, pp. 40–42.

77. "Qui con certi alberelli et consigli di Salay mi governo"; "Non posso ad altro pensare che a tte e a Salay. . . ." Letters 7, 8, *Morgante*, pp. 950–53; see also 3, 4.

78. Letter 16, *Morgante*, p. 963.

79. "Pur Sallai a confessar fe'irti." Sonnet 47, p. 47.

80. "la Bibbia abbaia" (lit., the Bible barks). Sonnet 146, p. 146.

81. See Lucien Febvre, *Le Problème de l'incroyance au XVIe siècle: la religion de Rabelais* (Paris: Michel, 1942).

82. For the text of the "Confessione" see *Sonetti*, pp. 151–63; or Volpi, "Pulci," p. 55–64.

83. Marcel, *Marsile*, p. 432, note 4.

84. For an account of these editions see E. H. Wilkins, "On the Earliest Editions of the

*Morgante* of Luigi Pulci," *Papers of the Bibliographical Society of America* (1951): 1–21. Two important editions of the *Morgante,* that of Franco Ageno (1955) and that of Raffaello Ramat (1961) contain information on editions of the poem that appeared in Pulci's lifetime.

85. For Sanseverino's offer, see the letter from Pier Filippo Pandolfini to Lorenzo, quoted in Volpi, "Pulci," p. 27.

86. Antonio Gramsci, "The Formation of Intellectuals" in *The Modern Prince and other writings* (New York: International Publishers, 1959), pp. 118–25.

## Chapter 1. The Form of the Narrative

1. Bruni follows Villani in giving Charlemagne a major role in the reconstruction of Florence after the barbarian invasions. Yet he refrains from eulogy and even appears to be critical of the way in which the Emperor came to hold political power in Italy. On the question of the election of the Emperor in contrast to his appointment by the Pope he says: "Fuit praeterea disceptatio varia, cum alii veterem imperatorum seriem et antiquum succedendi morem servandum censerunt; alii etsi alienum a iure, tamen quia expediret, novum electionis exemplum a pontifice introductum probarent. Nobis autem plurimum videtur referre, populus romanus hortatu pontificis, an pontifex ipse iniussu populi imperatorem crearit. Constat enim nullius magis quam populi romani id munus esse. Nam pontificatus per illa tempora magis ab imperatoria auctoritate pendebat, nec quisquam praesidebat, nisi quem post senatus cleri et populi romani electionem, imperatoria comprobasset auctoritas. . . . Carolo certe ipsi, utcumque tandem electo, divina porro humanaque faverunt" ("Furthermore there was much debate; some persons wished to observe the old way [by election]; others, as an easier method (although illegal), approved the new way of appointment by the pope. Many of us considered whether the emperor should be chosen by the people through the agency of the pope, or by the pope without the will of the people. For it is agreed that this [office] is the gift of no one greater than the Roman people. For the pope in this period depended more on imperial authority, nor did anyone govern unless the imperial authority approved him, after election by the senate, the priests and people of Rome. . . . Divine and human factors favored Carlo, however he was elected. . . ."), *Historiarum florentini populi liber,* 1, p. 23. It is worth noting that Bruni cannot allow the matter of the relationship between the Emperor and his people, his 'constitutionality' as it were, to go without comment.

2. Were the first edition of the poem (1478) not lost, it might solve this problem; one could then determine in what ways if any its opening differed from that of the second (1483) edition.

3. For a study of the possibility that Pulci wrote the *Morgante* as a defense of Christian warfare against the infidel (Turks) in his own time, see Ruggero Ruggieri, *L'umanesimo cavalleresco italiano da Dante al Pulci* (Rome: Ateneo, 1962), pp. 199–223. In my view, Ruggieri's thesis overlooks the extent to which the enemy in the *Morgante* is not identified as a national or religious group. The poem portrays a conflict of a different and chiefly moral order, which threatens the integrity of chivalric society from within. Even when Pulci relates the story of Roncisvalle, the viciousness of the infidel is made effective against Christians only by the treachery of Gano and stupidity of Carlo. For Pulci's correspondence with Lorenzo concerning preparations in Naples for war against the Turks, see Letter 17, in *Morgante e lettere,* ed. De Robertis, p. 963–65; see also letters 19 and 21, pp. 967–68 and 971–72 respectively.

4. Rajna describes the sources for the *Morgante* in these articles: "La materia del 'Morgante' in un ignoto poema cavalleresco del sec. XV," *Il Propugnatore* 2, 1 (1869): 7–35, 220–52, 353–84; and "La rotta di Roncisvalle nella letteratura cavalleresca italiana," *Il*

*Propugnatore* 4, 1 (1871–72): 52–78, 330–80 and 2 (1871–72): 53–133. The *Orlando* is edited by Johannes Hübscher: *'Orlando,' Die Vorlage zu Pulcis 'Morgante,'* Ausgaben und Abhandlungen aus dem Gebiete der Romanischen Philologie, 60 (Marburg: Elwart, 1886). This edition contains a comparison of the texts of the *Orlando* and the *Morgante* and a description of the sources of the *Orlando*. Pulci's sources in Part 1 are discussed in detail by Domenico De Robertis, *Storia del Morgante* (Florence: Le Monnier, 1958), pp. 3–41. A useful discussion of the sources of Part 2 can be found in Angelo Gianni, *Pulci uno e due* (Florence: La Nuova Italia, 1967), and in Ruggieri, *L'umanesimo cavalleresco*, especially pp. 253–65.

5. "La congiunzione tra la prima e la seconda parte rimane pur sempre cosa di puramente esterno e accidentale." *Il Propugnatore* 4, 2 (1871–72): 94.

6. Rajna's conclusions, although based on historical evidence that has never been disputed, were not universally accepted, in large measure because for certain readers they contradicted the experience of reading the poem. Zingarelli's early challenge to Rajna's analysis of the *Morgante*'s structure is important chiefly because it testifies to that critic's sense of the poem as a totality. Zingarelli tried to prove that Part 1 contained significant references to events in Part 2, *notably* to Gano's treachery at Roncisvalle in canto 22, octaves 37 and to Orlando's death, octave 38. This evidence is, however, invalidated by facts that came to light after Zingarelli presented his argument. Unaware of the existence of the 1478 edition of Part 1, he thought that by the time Pulci had published the 1481 edition of Part 1 he must have had Part 2, in print only two years later in 1483, well in mind and perhaps even largely written. Hence his vision of the poem as the product of a single, continuous process of conception and composition. (The existence of the 1478 edition undermines Zingarelli's argument in another way too: it raises the possibility that the original canto 22 did not contain the references to Roncisvalle which the current version of 1481 possesses.) The octaves in canto 22 referring to action in subsequent cantos might have been added in 1481. Nicola Zingarelli, "La Composizione del 'Morgante' di Luigi Pulci," *Scritti di varia letteratura* (Milan: Hoepli, 1935), pp. 469–84. Certainly the differences between Parts 1 and 2 point to a major change in the poet's attitude toward his work and make it difficult to read the poem as Zingarelli would have us read it: unified according to a general plan in which the narrative elements of plot are arranged in a logical order and characters are developed with consistency. While it is probably safe to say that Pulci intended from the outset to write a poem about Charlemagne that would include Orlando's death at Roncevaux, he had in all likelihood no plan for the whole composition. Nevertheless Zingarelli's search for evidence to support his perception of the poem as unified is significant because it points to his intuitive understanding—shared by other readers—that the poem as a whole is in some way coherent. Ruggieri's interest in the "seriousness," "serietà," of the *Morgante*—in his view a matter of its political reference—reflects a similar experience of its narrativity. Gianni, too, perceives the poem to be unified after a fashion; for him it is a coherent expression of the poet's enthusiasm for his matter, the subject he gathers from his various sources, demonstrating what the critic calls a pure "epicità." *Pulci uno e due*, p. 147. Gianni's approach to the poem is evaluated in a thoroughly comprehensive review article by Remo Ceserani, "Studi sul Pulci," *Giornale storico della letteratura italiana* 146 (1969): 412–35, who argues that no simply linear reading of the *Morgante* is adequate and insists that it be analyzed as a multilevel narrative, p. 428. In an earlier work Ceserani explores from a stylistic perspective the ways in which Pulci transforms the *Orlando*, "L'Allegria fantasia di Luigi Pulci e il Rifacimento dell' *Orlando*," *Giornale storico della letteratura italiana* 135 (1958): 174–214.

7. Giovanni Getto, *Studio sul Morgante* (Como: Carlo Marzorati, 1944), p. 8. Getto further characterizes the form of the poem: "Poesia dunque senza dimensioni e senza sviluppi, e tutta tramata su veloci prove e assaggi svagati, poesia filologica, appunto, che si

celebra in un caratteristico ed accentuato gusto del dettaglio e del particolare minuto. Perciò come dev' essere scartata, quale illegittima istanza, ogni richiesta di una metodica azione, devendosi in fondo considerare il *Morgante* come un poema a tempo aperto e insieme ogni domanda di una distesa coerenza psicologica o comunque di un sistema di vaste concrezioni fantastiche, allo stesso modo ha da essere respinto ogni tentativo volto a segnare, nell'interno del poema, presunte modificazioni e momenti che articolano la fantasia del Pulci in un prima e un poi, in una storia o in uno sviluppo . . ." ("[It is] therefore a poetry without dimensions and without development, entirely organized as quick experiments and vague reflections; [it is] a philological poetry, precisely in that it calls attention to itself by its characteristic and accentuated love of detail and the particular. Therefore every search for a methodical action (which must end by considering the *Morgante* as a poem without a temporal element), and also every demand for a psychological coherence, or a system underlying these complicated fantasies, ought to be rejected as illegitimate. Moreover, every attempt to follow changes and moments which articulate the imagination of Pulci in a before and an after, in a history or a development, ought similarly to be dismissed. . . ."), pp. 178–79.

8. "Se c'è un fatto su cui la critica s'è trovato concorde, e che ha sempre dominato, scopertamento o incosapevolmente . . . il giudizio e l'interpretazione dell' arte del Pulci questo è l'inattitudine del poeta a "narrare," la nessuna "vena" narrativa: non l'incapacità . . . di svolgere il filo della vicenda, di condurre in porto in qualche modo . . . una data avventura, ma che non si abbia mai la sensazione di un più alto e ampio dominio, di una visione di insieme dei tanti casi, che non si riesca a cogliere un tono un tempo unico . . ." ("If there is one fact upon which critics agree and which has always dominated consciously or not . . . the assessment and interpretation of Pulci's art it is the poet's inability to "narrate," the absence of a narrative thread [in the poem]. [This is] not an inability to set forth a sequence of events, to conclude a given adventure in some fashion . . . but rather that the poet never has a perception of a higher and more ample scope, a vision of the whole, of the many events [he describes], that he does not succeed in establishing a single tone, a single temporality . . ."), De Robertis, *Storia*, p. 26.

9. "Pulci rappresenta un ineccepibile modello di attività poetica 'in assenza,' cioè assolutamente disancorata dalla realtà fattuale . . . la realtà è puramente letteraria, costituita da incastri, rielaborazioni, manomissioni tradizionali, una letteratura della letteratura" ("Pulci represents an unexceptionable model of poetic activity 'in absence,' that is absolutely unconnected with factual reality, in which . . . reality is purely literary, constituted by amplifications, elaborations, and tinkerings of tradition—a literature about literature"), Orvieto, *Pulci*, p. 321.

10. The connection between the development of perspective in the visual arts, where from a technical point of view discussion of the discovery belongs, and in historical writing, i.e. in relation to a sense of period, is put clearly by Erwin Panofsky: "No medieval man could see the civilization of antiquity as a phenomenon in itself, yet belonging to the past and historically detached from the contemporary world—as a cultural cosmos to be investigated and, if possible, reintegrated, instead of being a world of living wonders or a mine of information. . . . Just as it was impossible for the Middle Ages to elaborate the modern system of perspective, which is based on the realization of a fixed distance between the eye and the object and thus enables the artists to build up comprehensive and consistent images of things, just as impossible was it for them to evolve the modern idea of history, which is based on the realization of an intellectual distance between the present and the past, and thus enables the scholar to build up comprehensive and consistent concepts of bygone periods." "Introductory," *Studies in Iconology* (New York: Harper and Row, 1962), pp. 27–28.

11. On amplification in medieval romance see William W. Ryding, *Structure in Medieval Narrative* (Hague: Mouton, 1971), pp. 66–114, and Eugene Vinaver, *The Rise of Romance* (New York: Oxford University Press, 1973).

12. "Un centro da cui si springionino . . . immagini e motivi poetici." Getto, *Studio*, p. 18.

13. "Ciascun brano presenta una sort di circolarità conclusa. . . ." Although these units resemble each other they lack a comprehensive order—an "iter programmatico." But they are developed according to certain typical functions: the insult, the message, the duel, and so forth. It is the organizing effect of these functions, represented in each portion of the narrative and analyzable in terms of a "substruttura" ("substructure"), that gives Part 1 its coherence. Part 2, in contrast, abandons the "struttura evenemenziale" ("eventualizing structure"), which gives Part 1 the effect of a collage, and imitates the form of the chronicle in being open-ended: "seguendo un processo che in teoria potrebbe essere dilatato all'infinito." In this case, analysis must go beyond that of individual episodes—no longer conceived as discrete units—and be directed to their causal arrangement. To evaluate the narrativity of the poem as a whole, Orvieto asks for a structuralist study to be pursued along the lines suggested by Propp, Todorov, and Dorfman. Orvieto, *Pulci*, pp. 244–50.

14. The concept of a "function" in relation to the structure of narrative is first described by Vladimir Propp, *Morphology of the Folktale*, trans. Laurence Scott (Austin: University of Texas Press, 1968). I use the term without claiming for it the structural status Propp gives it.

15. For narratives on the matter of France see particularly Eugene Dorfman, *The Narreme in the Medieval Romance Epic* (Toronto: University of Toronto Press, 1969) pp. 80–127 (on the structure of the *Chanson*), and Françoise Voigt, *Roland-Orlando dans l'epopée Française et Italienne* (Leiden: E. J. Brill, 1938). For Arthurian narrative see Rosemond Tuve, *Allegorical Imagery: Some Medieval Books and Their Posterity* (Princeton: Princeton University Press, 1966), esp. pp. 345–58.

16. The bibliography on this subject is vast and I limit my references to works which are now practically classics or to those which are specifically concerned with medieval narrative. Roland Barthes, "Introduction to the Structural Analysis of Narratives," in *Image, Music, Text*, trans. Stephen Heath (New York: Hill and Wang, 1977), pp. 79–124, is a seminal essay on the application of structuralist analysis to literary texts. For critical discussions of structuralist approaches to narrative fiction see Jonathan Culler, "Poetics of the Novel," in *Structuralist Poetics* (Ithaca: Cornell University Press, 1975), pp. 189–238; and Tzevtan Todorov, *The Poetics of Prose*, trans. Richard Howard (Ithaca: Cornell University Press, 1977). A most thorough critique of structuralist assumptions is to be found in Cesare Segre's "Analysis of the Tale, Narrative Logic, and Time," in *Structures and Time: Narration, Poetry, Models*, trans. by John Meddemmen (Chicago: University of Chicago Press, 1979), pp. 1–56. See also Barbara Herrnstein Smith, "Narrative Versions, Narrative Theories," *Critical Inquiry* 7, 1 (1980): pp. 213–36. For critiques of structuralist approaches to medieval narrative in particular, see Joan M. Ferrante, "Some Thoughts on the Application of Modern Critical Methods to Medieval Literature," *Yearbook of Comparative and General Literature* (1980): 5–9, and Evelyn Birge Vitz, "Narrative Analysis of Medieval Texts: *La Fille du Comte de Pontieu*," *Modern Language Notes* 92 (1977): 645–90, and "Desire and Causality in Medieval Narrative," *Romanic Review* 71, 3 (1980): 213–43.

17. Segre, *Structures and Time*, pp. 37–40.

18. Dorfman, in *The Narreme*, terms the unit he uses in his analysis of medieval romance epic a "narreme"; it resembles a Proppian "function" in that it implies an agent and describes relations of cause and effect. Schemes which reflect a paramount concern for the narrative as a system of signs depend on a conceptually different kind of unit, i.e., one that conveys more than an idea of narrative action. Cf. Barthes's concept of the "lexie."

19. Roland Barthes, *S/Z*, trans. Richard Miller (New York: Hill and Wang, 1974); Gerard

Genette, *Narrative Discourse: An Essay on Method*, trans. Jane N. Lewin (Ithaca: Cornell, University Press, 1980); Tzvetan Todorov, *Le Grammaire du Decameron* (The Hague: Mouton, 1969). Claude Bremond offers a critique of Propp's concept of a function because it fails adequately to record possibilities of choice that develop in the course of narrative action; see *Logique du Reçit* (Paris: Seuil, 1973). esp. pp. 15–48. For a reply to Bremond's objections, see Culler, *Structuralist Poetics*, pp. 208–12.

20. Cesare Segre, *Semiotics and Literary Criticism* (The Hague: Mouton, 1973), p. 65; see also "Analysis of the Tale, Narrative Logic, and Time," in *Semiotics*, pp. 10–14. Cf. Paul Ricoeur, "Narrative Time," in *Critical Inquiry* 7, 1 (1980): 169–90, esp. 174–75.

21. For a study of Pulci's reworking of his sources in this canto see Ruggieri, "Da Baligante ad Antea e da Roncisvalle a Parigi," in *L'umanesimo cavalleresco*, pp. 253–65.

22. Pulci takes "Lattanzio's" account from the *Reali di Francia*; I have not yet identified what historian, if any, he intends to refer to (the Christian apologist Lanctantius died in 340). "Alcuin's" account Pulci takes from Acciaiuoli's *Vita Caroli Magni*; Alcuin was popularly thought to have been the author of the *Vita Karoli*, completed in 828 by Eginhard. For more on these histories and their relation to the text of the *Morgante*, see Luigi Pulci, *Morgante*, ed. Franca Ageno, pp. 1074–1105 and footnotes; see also Chapter 4.

23. For a discussion of Pulci's use of pastoral, see Chapter 4.

24. Vitz, "Narrative Analysis" pp. 658–66.

25. Ramat, "Introduzione," in Luigi Pulci, *Il Morgante*, pp. 24–25.

## *Chapter 2. Models of Chivalry*

1. For a summary of the developing representation of love in narratives of the matter of France, see Françiose Voigt, *Roland-Orlando*, pp. 59–60; 68–69; 104–12.

2. Rosemond, Tuve. *Allegorical Imagery*, p. 348. For a study of the kinds of conflicts between kings and their vassals that are common in epic, see W. T. H. Jackson, *The Hero and the King: an Epic Theme* (New York: Columbia University Press, 1982), especially pp. 54–78 on the *Chanson de Roland* and related medieval poems on the matter of France.

3. Fellowship and worship are both terms used to describe notions fundamental to the understanding of the chivalric order. In the *Morgante*, the idea of the court as a collectivity of worthy vassals, especially as it is exemplified in the selected group of twelve paladins, is expressed by the term "compagnia" (e.g., 7. 9 ff). Worship, a term denoting in English narrative the honor a knight wins in combat, is in the *Morgante* the equivalent of "fama," or reputation. This is an indispensible measure of value in adventures which have an erotic interest: conventionally ladies respond to a knight's worship or a paladin's "fama" rather than to his person or character.

4. Here Orlando and Gano have some of the attributes they have in the *Chanson* where Gano, Orlando's stepfather, is provoked to treachery by the hero's malice. Gianni suggests that in the *Chanson* Roland is moved by jealousy; *Pulci uno e due*, pp. 416–19.

5. For a study of the Proteus figure in Renaissance literature, see A. Bartlett Giamatti, "Proteus Unbound: Some Versions of the Sea God in the Renaissance" in *The Disciplines of Criticism*, ed. P. Demetz, T. Greene, and L. Nelson, Jr. (New Haven: Yale University Press, 1965), pp. 437–75.

6. In the *Timaeus*, Plato declares that the creator "sought to make the universe eternal, so far as might be." As this proved impossible, he created the heavens so that they moved "according to number" and thus became a "moving image of eternity": "And yet there is no difficulty in seeing that the perfect number of time fulfils the perfect year when all the eight revolutions, having their relative degrees of swiftness, are accomplished together and attain their completion at the same time, measured by the rotation of the same and equally

moving. After this manner and for these reasons, came into being such of the stars as in their heavenly progress received reversals of motion to the end that the created heaven might imitate the eternal nature. . . ." *The Dialogues of Plato*, trans. B. Jowett, (New York: Random House, 1937), 37–39; 2, pp. 18–21. Aristotle, asserting that time was the motion of the spheres, concluded: "And this is the reason of our habitual way of speaking, for we say that human affairs and those of all other things that have natural movement and become and perish seem to be in a way circular, because all these things come to pass in time and have their beginning and end as it were 'periodically,' for time itself is conceived as 'coming round' and this again because time and such a standard rotation mutually determine each other." *Physics*, trans. Philip Wicksteed and Francis Cornford (Cambridge, Mass.: Harvard University Press, The Loeb Library, 1957), 4, 14, 223 b; Vol. 1, p. 425.

7. "Eadem [fate] nascentia occidentiaque omnia per similes fetuum seminumque renovate progressus. Haec actus etiam fortunasque hominum indissolubili causarum conexione constringit, quae cum ab immobilis providentiae proficiscatur exordiis, ipsas quoque immutabiles esse necesse est"; *De Consolatione Philosophiae* 4. 6; ed. Adrian Scuto and George D. Smith (London: Burns Oates and Washburn, 1925), p. 126.

8. For these brief characterizations of classical and medieval historiographies I am indebted to two studies: Robert W. Hanning, *The Vision of History in Early Britain* (New York: Columbia University Press, 1966), esp. pp. 20–32; and J. G. A. Pocock, *The Machiavellian Moment: Florentine Political Thought and the Atlantic Republican Tradition* (Princeton: Princeton University Press, 1975), esp. pp. 3–48.

9. Attilio Momigliano, in his essay on the Margutte episode in canto 18, stresses Morgante's bestiality and sees that his death is the height of the "material grotesque." *L'indole e riso di Luigi Pulci* (Rocca S. Casciano, Indagine di storia letteraria e artistica, no. 7, 1907), p. 284; see also "Il 'Morgante' " in *Studi di poesia* (Bari: Laterza, 1938), pp. 33–39. I would prefer to augment this conception of the giant's character to include a psychological dimension: the instinctive, irrational nature of bestial thought and behavior.

10. Cf. St. Paul: "Dearly beloved, avenge not yourselves, but rather give place unto wrath: for it is written, Vengeance is mine; I will repay, saith the Lord." Rom. 12:19. See also *Paradiso* 4. 67–69.

11. "Omnis fortuna est bona," *De consolatione* 4. 7 (Scuto and Smith, p. 133); cf. "Si disponentem providentiam spectes, nihil usquam mali esse perpendas." ("If you contemplate providential order, you will consider nothing to be bad anywhere.") 4. 6; p. 130.

12. Cf. St. Paul on God's selective purpose in history and the irrelevance to it of the deeds of men: "What shall we say then? Is there unrighteousness with God? God forbid." Rom. 9:14. See also Rom. 1:18 and *Paradiso* 3. 70–87.

13. Villani declares: "E prima diremo, onde fu il cominciamento della detta nostra città, sequendo per li tempi infino che Iddio ne concedera di grazia . . ." ("And first we will say whence our city began, following through the times as long as God gives it grace . . ."), *Istorie fiorentine* (Milan, 1802), 1. 1; p. 2. And Dati: "Però che niuno bene si può acquistare sanza la grazia di Dio, la quale è apparecchiata a tutti coloro che la cercano là ov'elle si può trovare e ella abita intra le virtú e intra le buone operazioni . . . ; puossi dire ancora per fortuna, perché i beni del mondo sono nelle mani di lei e non sono sicuri che ella non gli possa torre, ma e' pare che le virtú abbino potenza di tenerla legata . . ." ("For no good can be acquired without God's grace, which is apparent to all those who look for it there where it can be found. And it is to be found among the virtues and good works . . .; one can even say through fortune, for although the goods of the world are in her hands and are not so secure that she can not take them away, it seems that the virtues are able to hold her in check . . ."), *Istoria di Firenze* (Norcia, 1904), p. 60; quoted in Claudio Varese, *Storia e politica nella prosa del quattrocento* (Turin: Einaudi, 1961), p. 77.

14. Landino's fortune arbitrarily disposes of goods: "La quale pigliando giuoco di

gl'huomini spesso gli toglie a chi gli merita e dagli a chi non gli merita . . ." ("Playing with human beings, [it] often takes them from him who is deserving and gives them to him who is not . . ."). But fortune is governed by "providentia": "una somma ragione di dio, la quale tutte le chose ordine e dispone. . . ." ("the highest reason of God, which orders and disposes of all things. . . .") Fate is similarly governed: it is "[una] certa dispositione nelle chose mobili, per la quale la providentia conlege e compone ciascuna chosa per certo ordine. . . ." ("It is a certain disposition in changing things through which Providence links and combines each thing in a certain order"), *Comento di Christophforo Landino Fiorentino sopra la comedia di Danthe Alighieri poeta fiorentino* (Florence: Nicholo di Lorenzo della Magna, 1481), sig. E8, E8v. On Brutus Landino remarks: "Et certamente sarebbe stato inaudita crudelta e altutto aliena dalla doctrina e equita di tanto poeta porre in eterno si grave supplicio quegli equali per ardentissima carita si missono alla morte per liberare la patria dal giogo della servitu per la quale se fussino stati christiani harrebono honoratissima sedia nel supremo cielo acquistato. Non niego Cesare essere stato ornato di molte varie e excellentissime virtu: ma subito che in lui nacque si esserata impieta che per speranza doccupare la tyrannide passo e fiume rubicone: dhuomo excellentissimo divenne immanissima fiera. Et con questa sola scellerateza sobmerse e extinse tutti ebeneficii de quali Roma si confessava allui debetrice" ("And certainly it would have been an unspeakable cruelty and altogether foreign to the teaching and sense of fairness of so great a poet to have punished so severely for eternity those who from the most ardent love underwent death to free their country from the yoke of that servitude, [a deed] which, had they been Christian, would have earned them a most honorable place in the highest heavens. I do not deny that Caesar was made glorious by many varied and most excellent virtues: but [I would assert] that suddenly there was born in him so grievous a treachery (lit. impiety) that, hoping to become a tyrant, he crossed the Rubicon: from a most excellent man he became a most inhuman beast. And with that crime alone were cancelled all the debts which Rome acknowledged she owed him"), *Inferno* 34, sig. r8. Baron compares Landino's treatment of Dante's Caesar with that of Bruni, on which it draws for inspiration, and concludes that the later historian is the more conservative—a conclusion one might expect given the political situations in which each wrote: "The one element different from Bruni's arguments is a greater openness of mind toward the Christian-medieval aspect of the Empire concept, an aspect of which the pioneer generation of the early Quattrocento had lost sight so completely that Dante's treatment of Caesar had seemed to Bruni nothing but an arbitrary product of a poet's fancy." *Crisis*, p. 51.

15. "La forza accompagnata dalla ragione debbe sempre vincere. . . . Però che niuno bene si può acquistare senza la grazia di Dio, la quale è apparechiata a tutti coloro che la cercano là ov'ella si può trovare e ella abita intra le virtú e intra le buone operazioni. . . ." Dati, *Istoria*, p. 131; in Varese, *Storia e politica*, p. 79; see also note 12.

16. See Barbara R. Hanning, "Glorious Apollo: Poetic and Political Themes in the First Opera," *Renaissance Quarterly* 32, 4 (1979): 485–513.

17. See especially 3. 5. 25.

18. Coluccio Salutati, *De laboribus Herculis*, ed. B. L. Ullman (Zurich: Thesaurus Mundi, 1951), 3. 5, p. 176; 3. 42, pp. 417–22; 4. 1, pp. 484–86.

19. *Libri rerum familiarum*, ed. Enrico Bianchi in *Prose* (Milan: Ricciardi, 1955), 16 (10, 3), pp. 918–919; see also *De vita solitaria*, 1. 3, pp. 332, 33. For a summary of the various changes in the mythological significance of Hercules, see F. Gaeta, "L'avventura di Ercole," *Rinascimento* 5, 2 (1954): 227–60.

20. Aristotle claims that the lion keeps his eyes open when asleep; on the lion and serpent symbolism, see Weinstein, "Myth of Florence," pp. 35–38. Orvieto identifies the lion as Christ but this is, I think, to misunderstand the animal's function and its relation to Rinaldo's reasonable character. Orvieto, *Pulci*, p. 242.

21. For associations of water creatures with error, see James Nohrnberg, *The Analogy of the Faerie Queene* (Princeton: Princeton University Press, 1976), pp. 140–42.

22. The episode contains a curious crux. When Rinaldo orders the dragon's head mounted on the city walls, Corbante insists that its history be carved there as well, including the names of the paladins who killed it (4. 79). Later, however, Pulci adds that Corbante does not disclose the names of the paladins because Rinaldo wants them hidden from "Il popol folle" (4. 102), who, presumably, are capable of turning against even their benefactors.

23. For a survey of allusions to Dante's poety in the *Morgante*, see Giuseppe Rotondi, "Reminiscenze Dantesche nel Pulci," *Convivium* (1936): 422–24.

24. For a neoplatonic version of the relationship of love and death, see Pico della Mirandola on the Orpheus myth in the *Commento sopra una canzone de amore composta da Girolamo Benivieni* where, referring to the mystery of the myth as it is expressed in the *Symposium*, he sees that Orpheus's failure to keep from looking back is tantamount to a refusal truly to die to this world. Edgar Wind, who analyzes these passages with reference to the relationship between Amor and death, states that the doctrine that the "vita amorosa proceeds from death" was widely accepted in the Medici circle. See "Amor as a God of Death" in *Pagan Mysteries in the Renaissance* (New York: W. W. Norton, 1968), pp. 156–57.

25. The image of the *Venus armata* usually symbolizes the union of martial and amiable spirits. A medal depicting the goddess was struck for Giovanna Tornabuoni which may have been known to her daughter Lucrezia. Further elaborated in the image of the couple Mars and Venus, the oxymoron of love-hate is also represented in their daughter Harmonia (or *discordia concors*), especially with reference to the cosmos. See Wind, *Pagan Mysteries*, pp. 81–96. In both the *De rerum natura* and the *Metamorphoses*, the conflict of love is the source of new life; originally expressed in the *Theogony*, this idea is also represented in Plutarch's *Moralia*, Cicero's *De natura deorum*, in the *De consolatione philosophiae* (where the concord of Mars and Venus rules the elements and seasons, Book 4, Poema 6), and most familiarly in the *Filostrato*. For useful background on the *Venus armata* in ancient epic and history, see Phillip Elliot Parrotti, "The Female Warrior in Renaissance Epic" (Ph.D. diss., University of New Mexico, 1972).

26. Getto correctly sees Rinaldo as the most "mutable" of the characters in the *Morgante*: he can be reasonable, but he is also, on occasion, a thief, a pilgrim, a usurper, as well as Carlo's defender. His protean personality may owe something to the considerable transformations it underwent in the process of becoming part of the Italian cycles of the matter of France. *Studio*, p. 90. Hübscher notes the particularly important role Rinaldo plays in these narratives, in contrast to his relatively obscure place in the French *chansons de geste*. In fact, for Italian (and especially Tuscan) narrators, Rinaldo became a kind of folk hero, a leader of rebels against oppressive authorities. Hübscher, *"Orlando"* p. lxiii.

27. "Legitimum principem et mundanarum rerum iustissimum monarcham in Caesare finxit." ("He [Dante] portrayed in Caesar a legitimate prince and most just monarch.") *Dialogi*, ed. Klette, pp. 76f.; ed. Garin, pp. 88f.; quoted in Baron, *Crisis*, pp. 473–74.

28. *Ethics*, 5, 10; 1137a34–1138a ll.

29. Salutati continues: ". . . it ought to have been preferable to endure not only the life of a Caesar who, we read, exercised extreme clemency, but even the lives of a Sulla and a Marius who could not get their fill of the citizens' blood", 4. 9–10; quoted in Baron, *Crisis*, p. 163.

## Chapter 3. Typical Adventures

1. "Tempus edax rerum, tuque, invidiosa vetustas, / omnia destruitis" ("Time is the devourer of all things and you also, envious age, destroy everything") 15. 234, 35; "nec

perit in toto quicquam, mihi credite, mundo, / sed variat faciemque novat . . ." ("for nothing in the world disappears entirely, believe me/but it changes and presents a new appearance . . .") 15. 254, 55.

2. See Michael Murrin, *The Veil of Allegory* (Chicago: University of Chicago Press, 1969), esp. pp. 32–53.

3. Malory concludes: "Yet som men say in many partys of Inglonde that kynge Arthure ys nat dede, but had by the wyll of oure Lorde Jesu into another place; and men say that he shall com agayne, and he shall wynne the Holy Crosse. Yet I woll nat say that het shall be so, but rather I wolde sey: here in thys worlde he chaunged hys lyff. And many men say that there ys wrytten uppon the tumbe thys.

HIC IACET ARTHURUS, REX QUONDAM REXQUE FUTURUS." *Works*, ed. Eugene Vinaver (London: Oxford University Press, 1971), p. 717.

4. "Proles Hippolyti . . . Virbius" ("Virbius, son of Hippolytus") 7. 761, 762; "solus . . . aevum exigeret . . . versoque ubi nomine Virbius esset" ("Hippolytus might live out his years alone . . . and take the altered name of Virbius") 7. 774–76.

5. "Sed Diana Hippolytum revocatum ab inferis in Aricia nymphae commendavit Egeriae et eum Virbium quasi bis virum iussit vocari: cuius nunc filium cognominem dicit in bellum venire. Adeo omnia ista fabulosa sunt. nam cum castus ubique inductus sit et qui semper solus habitaverit, habuisse tamen fingitur filium. Virbius est numen coniunctum Dianae . . ." ("But Diana committed Hippolytus, who had been called back from the underworld, to the care of the nymph Egeria in Aricia and ordered him to be called Virbius as a twice-born man: now he [Vergil] declares that the son of that name went into battle. All this is fiction. For since he [Hippolytus] was chaste and would always have lived alone, Vergil made up the son. Virbius is the divinity linked to Diana . . ."), Servius *Commentarii in Vergilii Carmina*, ed. George and Hermann Hegen (Leipzig: Teubner, 1883), 2, p. 193.

6. 7. 764; Servius, 2, p. 193.

7. I reproduce the text and its gloss:

> iamque dies aderat, profugis cum regibus aptum
> fumat Aricinum Triviae et face multa
> conscius Hippolyti splendet lacus. . . .
>
> (3. 1. 55–57)

now the day comes when smoke arises in the grove of Trivia at Aricina, refuge of runaways kings, and the lake, aware of the secret of Hippolytus, glitters from [the light of] many torches.

Domitius on *lacus conscius Hippolyti:* "Nam revocatum ab inferis ope Asculapii Hippolytum Diana occultavit in nemore Aricino, unde equi arcentur quoniam ab his olim fuerat discerptus. Putaturque illic vivere in occulto, et appellant Virbius" ("For, called back from the underworld by the craft of Asculapius, Hippolytus was hid by Diana in the Aricinian grove, where horses are prevented from entering, since he had been torn apart by them once. He is thought to live there in hiding and they call him Virbius"), Statius, *Opera cum observationibus ac cum commentariis* (Paris, 1618). sig. Qq iii, iii^v.

8. "Nam Hippolytus licet discerptus in vitam secundum fabulas redierit, tamen mortis conditionem evadere non potuit" ("For according to legend, Hippolytus, having been dismembered, was allowed to return to life; nevertheless he could not have escaped death"), *Scriptores Rerum Mythicarum Latini Tres*, ed. Georgius Henricus Bode (Celle: E. H. C. Schulze, 1834), 2, 129; p. 118.

9. See especially "morte carent animae . . ." 158–59; "nihil interit . . ." 165; see also above note 1.

10. Servius, 2, p. 105. See especially the commentary on 1. 745 and the concept of purgatory, where Servius declares that those who inhabit the Elysian fields ("laeta arva")

do so for a long time but not forever: "Merentur enim temporis multi, non perpetuitatis."

11. "Sedet aeternumque sedebit/infelix Theseus" ("he sits and will sit forever / unhappy Theseus") 6. 617–18. Servius, glossing this line, relates the story of Hercules' descent and rescue of Theseus. Servius, 2, p. 87.

12. Cf. *The Homeric Hymn to Demeter.*

13. See Servius's gloss to *Georgics*, 1. 39; Servius, 3, p. 143. For the mythographers see *Scriptores*, 1, 7, p. 3; 2, 15, p. 78, 79; and esp. 3: "Hanc [Ceres] ideo frumenti deam confingunt, quia ubi plenitudo sit fructuum, ibi abundent gaudia necesse est. Proserpinam vero quasi segetum [cornfield] voluerunt, id est per terram radicibus *proserpentem.* . . . Hanc a Plutone raptam, id est in terra satam, cum lampadibus Ceres inquirere dicitur; unde et lampadarum dies Cereri dedicantur, illa videlicet ratione, quod tempore messis cum lampadibus, id est solis fervore, fructus ad metendum cum gaudio requirantur. . . . Sane Ceres a Jove meruit, ut Proserpina sex esset mensibus in caelo cum matre, sex apud inferos cum marito; quod fictum dicimus sive quia post sationem tantundem temporis quasi latent gramina priusquam fructus producant, sive quia, ut dicit Servius, ipsa est eadem quae et Luna, quae toto anno VI mensibus crescit, VI deficit . . ." ("Therefore they pretended that this woman [Ceres] was the goddess of grain, because where there is much fruit there must also be great rejoicing. Moreover they wished Proserpina to signify a cornfield, that is, a snaking though the earth with roots. . . . Snatched by Pluto, that is, in a planted field, it is said that Ceres sought her with torches; why torchlike days were sacred to Ceres may be seen thus: at the time of the harvest, its fruits are sought with torches, that is, by the heat of the sun, to be harvested with rejoicing. . . . Ceres was justly rewarded by Jove, when [he decreed that] Proserpina would remain six months in heaven with her mother, six months below with her husband. We relate this fiction either because after sowing the fields lie dormant for just so much time before they produce grain, or because, as Servius says, she is identical with the moon, who in all grows for six months and wanes for six months . . ."), 3, 7. 1–2, pp. 197–98. The mythographer later identifies Proserpina as moisture: "Per Plutonem enim terra, cui praeest, per Proserpinam humor terram fecundans significatur; quae ut aiunt, bene Proserpina quasi *proserpendo nata* dicitur, quod humor per herbas vel arbores crescentes insensibiliter de terra surgat et iis incrementum conferat. Quod Ceres, quae dea est frugum, Proserpinam quaerere dicitur, fruges, ut perhibent, significat nimiae siccitatis tempore humorem desiderare . . ." ("Therefore the earth is signified by Pluto, who presides over it, and the moisture making the earth fertile by Proserpina; they say these things correctly for it is said that Proserpina was born creeping as it were, since moisture arises from the earth through grass or tress growing imperceptibly and brings them growth. That Ceres, who is the goddess of the harvest, is said to seek Proserpina, the harvest, as they say, signifies that moisture is desired in a time of drought"), 3, 7. 4, p. 199.

14. A second and specifically Christian allegorization of the myth ignores its references to the seasons and exploits Ovid's hints of Proserpina's youthful indiscretions. Prompted by her lascivious mind, she is snatched by the devil and only restored to earth by Ceres, the prelate burning with *caritas* and also a figure of Christ. See Petrus Berchorius, *Reductorium morale, Liber XV*, cap. ii–xv, "Ovidius Moralizatus" (Utrecht: Instituut voor Laat Latijn der Rijksuniversiteit, 1962), pp. 94–95.

15. Boccaccio, *Genealogie Deorum Gentilium Libri*, ed. Vincenzo Romano (Bari, Laterza, 1951), 8. 4; 1, p. 397, ll. 6–7.

16. Grain does not grow when the ground is overcultivated, "ob nimium frequentatam sationem," *Genealogie* 8. 4; 1, p. 397, ll. 28–29.

17. "Hinc turbata Ceres, id est agricultores, qui terrei dici possunt homines, strumenta frangit ruralia, id est frustra operata cognoscit et negligit, et ululatu femineo, id est agricultorum querela, incensis facibus, id est exustione agrorum, per quam humores

adversi, qui sunt circa terre superficiem, exalant, et utiles ab inferiori terra evocantur in altum . . ." ("Here angry Ceres, that is, the farmers, who may be called men of the earth, breaks the tools of the country, that is, she realizes that she has used them in vain, and she scorns them, and with womanly shrieks, that is, with the laments of the farmers, she lights the torches, that is, she burns the brush and stubble of the fields, [an act] by which the noxious humors that are on the surface of the earth are exhaled, and the beneficial ones returned upward from the lower earth . . ."), *Genealogie* 8.4; 1, p. 397, ll. 31–36.

18. "Per quam quietem intermissio culture intelligenda est, ut possit terra ob intermissionem emunctos humores reassummmere," *Genealogie* 8. 4; 1, p. 198, ll. 2–4.

19. It is impossible to know the extent of Pulci's knowledge of medieval and Renaissance mythography. I have assumed he had a general knowledge of the most common interpretations of popular myths—the sort of material contained in the work of Hyginus, Berchorius, and the Vatican mythographers. I find it hard to imagine he did not know Boccaccio's *Genealogie*, although there is no direct evidence that he did. I refer to these mythographies by way of comparison and to establish a general background for Pulci's use of myth. The most important identifications—Antea as Echo and fame, Rinaldo as Hercules and a figure of earthly glory—Pulci's narrative itself confirms.

20. Boccaccio, for example, relies on etymology to explain that *Hera* means the earth and *Cleos* glory; thus Hercules in one who achieves earthly glory ("gloriosus in terra") *Genealogie* 13. 1; 1, p. 638, 11. 11. See also Vat. Myth 3: Hercules is "gloria virorum fortium." *Scriptores*, 3, p. 246.

21. *Hyginus, Fabularum Liber* (Basle: Heragiana, 1570), sig. el.

22. *Scriptores*, 1, 48, p. 18.

23. *Scriptores*, 2, 133, p. 120.

24. On Theseus: "Illique comes ad Inferos usque ad rapiendam Proserpinam ivit, sed minus feliciter ex hoc illi successit, nam Perythoo a Tricerbero Orci cane trucidato, mortis ipse in periculo fuit, ni forte supervenisset Hercules, qui illum a discrimine liberavit et reduxit ad superos" ("Then, as a comrade [of Pirithoos] he went to the underworld to seize Proserpina, but events went less than happily, for Pirithoos was eaten by Tricerberus, the dog of the underworld, and he was himself in danger of death, except for the chance arrival of Herculus who freed him from danger and led him back to earth"), *Genealogie* 10. 49; 2, p. 521, ll. 13–17. On Castor and Pollux: "Et sic dum descendit ad Inferos unus, occidens scilicet primo tanquam mortalis, alter tanquam divinus apud Superos adhuc consistit, et econverso, dum ascendit unus ad Superos, divinus esse videtur, stante adhuc altero aliquantisper apud Inferos tanquem mortali" ("And thus when one descends to the underworld, that is to say, falls just as a mortal, the other as a divinity is with heavenly beings, and in reverse, while one ascends to heaven and seems to be divine, so the other remains for a time as a mortal in the underworld"), *Genealogie* ll. 7; 2, p. 547, ll. 27–31.

25. For a study of the image of the horse and horseman in Italian Renaissance epic, see A. Bartlett Giamatti, "Headlong horses, headless horsemen: an essay on the chivalric epics of Pulci, Boiardo, and Ariosto" in *Italian Literature: roots and branches: Essays in honor of Thomas Goddard Bergin,* ed. Giose Rimanelli and Kenneth John Atchity (New Haven: Yale University Press, 1976), pp. 265–307.

26. "Eum predoctum multis . . .", *Genealogie* 4. 14; 1, p. 172, 11–13.

27. "Nam per Echo, que nil dicit nisi post dictum, famam ego intelligo, que unumquenque mortalium diligit, tanquam rem, per quam consistit. Hanc multi fugiunt et parvi pendunt, et in aquis, id est in mundanis deliciis, non aliter quam aqua labilibus se ipsos, id est suam gloriam, intuentur et adeo a suis voluptatibus capiuntur, et spreta fama post paululum tamquam non fuissent, moriuntur; et si forsan aliquid nominis superest, in florem vertitur, qui mane pupureus et splendens est, sero autem languidus factus marcescit, et in nichilum solvitur" ("For by Echo, who says nothing that has not already been

said, I understand fame, which delights every mortal as that by which he lasts and is remembered. She is avoided by many who value her little, and see their fame in water, that is, in worldly delights no less changeful than water, and thus they are seized by their pleasures; having dismissed fame, they die after a little while as if they had not lived; and if by chance something of their name remains, it is changed into a flower, which in the morning is a lovely purple, in the evening withers and dissolves into nothing"), *Genealogie* 7. 59; 1, p. 381, ll. 1–10.

28. For a summary of the controversy, see especially Alberto Tenenti, "Il mito della gloria" In *Il senso della morte e l'amore della vita nel Rinascimento* (Turin: Einaudi, 1957), pp. 22–43.

29. Petrarch's "Fama" appears like the morning star: "un amorosa stella / sul venir d'oriente innanzi al Sole . . .", "Trionfo della fama" (10–12) in *Rime sparse e i trionfi*, ed. Ezio Chiorboli (Bari: Laterza, 1930), p. 343, ll. 10–11.

30. See, for example, Boccaccio: "Perseum equo Pegaso vectum fame cupidine tractum demonstrat." ("Perseus carried by Pegasus represents one led by desire of fame"), *Genealogie* 12. 25; 2, p. 595, ll. 32–33.

31. Orvieto sees Chiariella as a figure of Christ. This is to limit her to a positive function. Actually she is both good and bad: she helps Orlando from prison but she detains him with love after he is released. Orvieto, *Pulci*, p. 289.

32. That Orlando is susceptible to Chiariella's charm is a logical consequence of the fact that he too is powerless against Antea, who fights (like Orlando himself) with enchanted arms. Her strength may in fact reflect his own love of fame, for on taking the field against him she says: "I have been of a strange mind / to defeat a man with so much worship" ("Io ero in un pensiero strano/d'abbatter un tal uom, c'ha tanta fama"), 16. 77. For Orlando, desire for fame is bound up with his role as heroic martyr and with an aspect of his character that he experiences finally as a powerful temptation to be the consort of a divine creature. For a brilliant study of the ways in which the notion of a "homecoming" is connected to the epic hero's dissociation from an "immortal" in early Greek epic, see Douglas Frame, *The Myth of Return in Early Greek Epic* (New Haven: Yale University Press, 1978), pp. x; 34–80. The connection persists in later redactions of the Circe story and its allegorizations where Ulysses is made to perceive his return home in relation to his rejection of a divine lady. This is sometimes further moralized to include a rejection of the sexuality she offers her lovers, i.e., the opportunity to become purely physical or bestial.

33. Cf. the army Marsilio and Luciana gave Rinaldo and the army Vergante's people promise him for his help in ridding them of their tyrant king: "Noi sian tutti omai / sempre tuoi servi e schiavi in sempiterno" ("We will always be your servants"), 14. 28.

34. Orvieto traces Margutte to two celebrated archetypes, the pseudo-Homeric Margite in *Margite* and the demons in the Cercopi, in *Pulci*, pp. 171–72.

35. Boccaccio discusses fate with reference to Cicero, who, he says, speaks as follows: "Fatum id appello quod Greci imarmenidem, id est ordinem seriemque causarum, cum causa causam gignat, ea est ex omni eternitate fluens veritas sempiterna. Quod cum ita sit, nichil est futurum, cuius non causas id ipsum efficientes natura contineat. Ex quo intelligitur ut Fatum sit non id quod supersititose, sed id quod phylosophice dicitur, causa eterna rerum cur et ea que preterierint facta sunt, et que instant fiant et que sequuntur futura sint" ("I call fate what the Greeks call order, the sequence of causes, the cause which brings forth cause; it is eternal truth flowing from all eternity. Since it is thus, nothing lies in the future whose efficient causes it does not contain in itself. From this it is understood that Fate is not a superstition but [rather] what it is termed philosophically, the eternal cause of things that have been in the past, that are in the present, and that will be in the future"), *Genealogie* 1. 5; 1, p. 27, ll. 17–24. By defining *fatum* as *causa eterna causarum*, he links fate to divine will and so identifies it as Providence.

36. "Formas vero, quas eum sumere consuetum aiunt, et abicere, eas existimo pas-
siones, quibus anguntur homines . . ." ("Indeed those forms, which they say he [Proteus]
assumed and then relinquished, I judge to be the passions which torment men . . ."),
*Genealogie* 7. 9; 1, p. 345, 11. 10–12.

## Chapter 4. Poetry and History

1. On Carlo see 24. 37; 25. 6, 7, 114; 27. 167, 168, 185.
2. On the Passion see 26. 7, 22; 152. On Gano see 25. 4, 13, 65, 69, 114; 26. 25; 27. 167.
On the Apocalypse see 25. 72–74; 27. 254–74.
3. Both Gianni and Orvieto read Part 2 as evidence of Pulci's loss of confidence in his
poetic abilities and purpose. In one sense this is doubtless the case. In reworking the
*Orlando,* he enjoyed a certain immunity from self-questioning. In composing a poem
which drew on several sources, by contrast, he was confronted with a kind of freedom he
had not had earlier. That Part 2 should express his concerns over questions relating not to
his matter, the history of Carlo, but rather to his part in presenting it, his poetics, is not
surprising. In many respects Part 2 is a richly poetic work; it introduces to the poem a
debate on questions of authority, on illusionism in art, on the purpose of poetry; in a less
theoretical vein, it reveals an understanding of human psychology—in its portraits of
Gano and Antea—absolutely foreign to the allegorical expositions of character in Part 1.
None of these features suggests that Pulci was experiencing a sense of his own limitations
as a poet. That he was engaged in questioning the presumption of epic he had initially
entertained is a different matter and not in doubt.
4. For a study of Pulci's adaptation of various motifs from this literature see Gaetano
Mariani, *Il Morgante e i cantari trecenteschi* (Florence: Le Monnier, 1953).
5. In a fine recent study of the idea of the source in Renaissance literature, David Quint
refers to the opening lines of the *Morgante* and finds that "With their direct quotation of the
beginning of the gospel of John, [they] reverse the poet's position of dependence upon the
Word and assert his creative freedom. The Christian Word is now authorized by Pulci's
'parere,' which is both an assertion of faith and of poetic control . . .", *Origin and Originality in Renaissance Literature: Versions of the Source* (New Haven: Yale University Press,
1983), p. 81. The creative freedom Quint discerns in the *Morgante* is certainly there, but, I
think, not all at once; nor is it consistently displayed. Pulci *always* embellishes what he
finds in the *Orlando,* but until he begins to work with multiple sources he does not really
compare, criticize, and fully determine the ideological content of what he writes. Spitzer
also sees Pulci's poem as an example of language that is "autonomous," no longer serving
as an aggregate of signs that indicate a "real" and transcendent world. See "Linguistics and
Literary History," in *Linguistics and Literary History* (Princeton: Princeton University Press,
1948), p. 21.
6. I use Richmond Lattimore's translations of both poems: *The Iliad of Homer* (Chicago:
University of Chicago Press, 1967), and *The Odyssey of Homer* (New York: Harper and Row,
1968).
7. Access to the Muse did not always guarantee the truth to the poet of ancient epic:
the Muses tell Hesiod that they can also make "convincing lies," *Theogony* 26, 27. But in any
case, the poet's invocation of the Muse registers his claim to the truth. For a study of the
relationship of images of praise to the figure of the Muse, see Gregory Nagy's appendix on
the *kleos apthiton* formula in *Studies in Greek and Indic Metre* (Cambridge, Mass.: Harvard
University Press, 1974). For this reference I am indebted to Amy Johnson. In the introduction to his seminal study of the figure of the poet in Renaissance epic, Robert Durling
sketches the development of the epic poet (in his capacity as "Narrator") in relation to the

"matter" of his poem; he makes a fundamental distinction between the poet as he functions in Homeric epic, that is, as one who receives a divine truth, and as he comes to function later in the novel, that is, as "a natural man, limited to natural powers. . . ." He perceives the crisis in the development of this poetics in the Renaissance epics of Boiardo, Ariosto, and Spenser; *The Figure of the Poet in Renaissance Epic* (Cambridge, Mass.: Harvard University Press, 1965), pp. 8–10.

8. √irgil, *Eclogues, Georgics, Aeneid I–VI* (Cambridge, Mass: Harvard University Press, Loeb Classical Library, 1967).

9. The crucial difference in Hellenic culture between an understanding of history based on an oral education and that based on a reading knowledge of literary texts is discussed by Eric Havelock, *Preface to Plato* (Cambridge, Mass.: Harvard University Press, 1953). The first method constitutes history as a repository of cultural and moral values, the second as a subject on which to exercise and develop critical and moral faculties. Insofar as the Renaissance continued to foster in some degree elements of oral culture, it too can be seen to exhibit symptoms of the conflict first waged in fourth-century Athens.

10. See G. W. Pigman III, "Versions of Imitation in the Renaissance," *Renaissance Quarterly* 33, 1 (1980): esp. pp. 3–9.

11. Given Pulci's preoccupation with Dante, this distinction appears particularly suggestive. Dante—the pilgrim in the *Paradiso*—sees the truth, "l'alta luce che da se è vera," but his vision is not matched by his ability to remember or express in words what he has seen, 33. 52–57. Pulci's artist, on the other hand, has an acute moral vision but is powerless to do more than construct, for his audience, a representation of choices analagous to those it must, in fact, make on its own. Dante is concerned with the verbalization of what is categorically ineffable, Pulci with the didactic function of the artist.

12. Marsilio's description of the soul at birth is a diabolical parody of that of Dante's Marco Lombardo: Marco declares that the soul ("l'anima") at birth is childish and knows nothing—"l'anima semplicetta che sa nulla"; it therefore requires the discipline of law; *Purg.* 16. 88. This doctrine, with its implied reference to the *tabula rasa*, derives from the *De anima*, 3. See *The Divine Comedy, Purgatorio*, 2, ed. Charles S. Singleton, (Princeton: Princeton University Press, 1973), pp. 358–59, note 88.

13. Kremers accepts Marsilio's characterization of the origin of faith as an expession of Pulci's own views and argues that the poet advocates religious toleration, *Rinaldo und Odysseus*, pp. 54–55. It is difficult to see why Pulci would choose Marsilio as his mouthpiece; I think it much more likely that he intended to show the error in Marsilio's views. Ageno notes a resemblance between Marsilio's anecdote and the story of the three rings of religion in *Dec.* 1, 3; ed. Ageno, note 44, 1–2, p. 846.

14. See, for example, Sir Thomas Malory's account of Balin le Sauvage, whose fate is sealed when he passes beyond a certain cross. Malory's source is the French *Roman de Balain; Works*, pp. 55–56.

15. Cf. Petrarch, *Rime*, 323, 25–36. The poet complains of being deprived of his happy plant, the laurel, and, consequently, of his sorrowful life. If Pulci has these lines in mind, he may well be alluding to a comparable disappointment he experiences with regard to his "laurel," that is, Lorenzo. I suggest, however, that the image also refers to his growing doubt that any poetry can be truly eternal, that is, that it can continue to function authoritatively for all generations of poets.

16. On the interpretation of the character of Astarotte critics are in frequent disagreement. Gianni criticizes de Sanctis for seeing in Astarotte the spirit of the new age and argues that the devil is a representative of Ficinian orthodoxy (drawn originally from Macabel in the *Spagna maggiore*) and that, echoing Ficino's *De christiana religione*, he is designed both to reassure and to scandalize Lorenzo; *Pulci uno e due*, pp. 392–400, esp. 395. Orvieto also sees that Astarotte both imitates and parodies Ficino; Pulci is, in other words,

writing against his will; *Pulci*, pp. 259–65. Astarotte certainly is, by virtue of his origins and his function, an ambivalent character. Damned yet in the service of Malagigi, his captivity is significant in the context of Pulci's representation of history as Providential—the view of history the poem has presented from canto 22 when Gano is released from Creonta's prison. Because Astarotte is so closely associated with Rinaldo, his parodic aspect I find difficult to discern. That Pulci was both intrigued and alarmed at the prospect of what Astarotte recommended, that is, adventuring beyond the limits prescribed by orthodoxy, is obvious. Whether or not he associates this adventuresomeness with Ficino is another matter. The frequency with which the image of transgression appears suggests Pulci's interest in the problem. Astarotte plays a role in an essentially Faustian drama, but in this case the seeker after knowledge is not damned nor is the devil wholly Satanic, because both are constrained and controlled by a moral purpose.

17. Pulci may be remembering Boccaccio's description of the dwelling place of the Muses in *Genealogie* 14, 11, where Boccaccio excuses and explains why poets seek to live in the country not the city. It is tempting, moreover, to see in these lines a reference to Callimachus's prologue to his *Aitia,* where Apollo says to the poet: " 'This too I bid you: tread a path which carriages do not trample; do not drive your chariot upon the common tracks of others, nor along a wide road, but on unworn paths, though your course be more narrow. For we sing among those who love the shrill voice of the cicada and not the noise of asses' ", 1.1.17–32. Steele Commager argues that this text was familiar to Alexandrian and Latin poets as a source for the opposition of epic and pastoral style; *The Odes of Horace* (Bloomington, Ind.: Indiana University Press, 1967), pp. 36–38. But in what form it might have come to Pulci, if at all, is uncertain. In any case, it appears to herald the independence he finally achieves at the conclusion to the *Morgante* when he discusses the possibilities of pastoral rather than epic.

18. For a useful discussion of the varieties of interpretation of the Ulysses episode in the *Inferno,* see Kremers, *Rinaldo,* pp. 106–120. He discerns two principal interpretations: that which regards Ulysses' breach of the limits set by the pillars as an example of an intellectual pride comparable to that of the rebellious angels, presented by, among others, B. Nardi, "La tragedia d'Ulisse," *Studi danteschi* 20 (1931): 5–15; and that which regards the hero's death as a sign that pagans (unlike Christians) cannot receive the gift of eternal life, presented in Natalino Sapegno's edition of the *Inferno* (Florence, 1955); see Kremers, *Rinaldo,* pp. 110–14. Mazzotta, in an extended commentary on this episode, sees that Dante condemns a specific form of intellectual pride—that exemplified in the political rhetoric of Cicero; *Dante: Poet of the Desert* (Princeton: Princeton University Press, 1979) pp. 66–106. For a study of Dante's sources in Cicero, see Barbara Reynolds, who specifically refers to the *De officiis* 3, 97, and the *De finibus* 5, 18–19, in "Dante's Tale of Ulysses," *Annali,* Sezione romanza 2, 1 (1960): 49–65. In the latter text, Cicero encourages the reader to pursue knowledge for its own sake (precisely, I think, what Dante discourages) although he does caution against a "miscellaneous omniscience" as indicative of "curiosity": "Atque omnia quidem scire cuiuscumquemodi sint cupere curiosorum . . ." 5. 18; Cicero, *De finibus bonorum et malorum* (Cambridge, Mass.: Harvard University Press, Loeb Classical Library, 1971), pp. 450–51. This warning is forcefully echoed by Augustine, who insists that knowledge which is not useful to human beings is dangerous: "It is to satisfy this unhealthy curiosity that freaks and prodigies are put on show in the theatre, and for the same reason men are led to investigate the secrets of nature, which are irrelevant to our lives, although such knowledge is of no value to them and they wish to gain it merely for *the sake of knowing*" (my italics); *The Confessions,* 10, trans. R. S. Pine Coffin (Harmondsworth: Penguin, 1978), p. 242. This text appears to have been definitive for Petrarch in the *De ignorantia;* see below, note 20.

19. The Divine Comedy, *Inferno,* 1, ed. Singleton, pp. 276–77.

20. Rinaldo simply rectifies Ulysses' mistake and so corrects his own tendency, expressed earlier, to endorse that hero's course of action. On the proper regard for pure science in contrast to moral knowledge, cf. Petrarch: "Nam quid, oro, naturas, belvarum et volucrum et piscium et serpentum nosse profuerit, et naturam hominum, ad quid nati sumus, unde et quo pergimus, vel nescire vel spernere?" ("For what, I ask, does it serve to know the natures of beasts and birds, and fish, and reptiles, and not to know or to care about the nature of man, for what we are born, whence we have come and whither we go?"), *Prose*, pp. 714–15. See Giuseppe Rotondi, "Rileggendo il 'Morgante,'" *Convivium* (1936): 392, note 1.

21. Pulci has had Astarotte indicate earlier the relative power of knowledge that derives from experience in contrast to abstract reasoning; the devil proposes to transport Rinaldo back to France by means of an herb that will render him invisible for, he says: "Where reason and knowledge are lacking, experience is enough for the wise man" ("dove manca ragione o sci̇enzia, / basta al savio veder la speri̇enzia", 25. 204). (Cf. Montaigne: "Quand la raison nous faut, nous y employons l'experience. . . ."; "De l'experience," *Essais*, 3.) For a summary of contemporary thought on the existence of the Antipodes, see Kremers, *Rinaldo*, pp. 79–85. When Columbus first proposed his journey to the west, the bishops to whom Queen Isabella referred the case denied that it was possible, since Augustine had so declared: "But as to the fable that there are Antipodes, that is to say, men on the opposite side of the earth . . . that is on no ground credible"; *The City of God* 16. 9, trans. Marcus Dods (New York: Random House, 1950), p. 532. See Vincent Cronin, *Florentine Renaissance* (New York: Dutton, 1967), pp. 141–42, which cites *The Journal of Christopher Columbus*, trans. C. R. Markham (London: The Hakluyt Society, 1893).

22. Cf. "Nemo, quantunque moralibus et intellectualibus virtutibus et secundum habitum et secundum operationem perfectus, absque fide salvari potest, dato quod nunquam aliquid de Christo audiverit" ("No one, however perfect in moral and intellectual virtues, both in his habits and his works, can be saved without faith, even though he has never heard anything about Christ"), *Monarchia*, ed. Pier Giorgio Ricci (Verona: Mondadori, 1965), 2. 7. 5.

23. See *The City of God*, esp. 5. 12, 15.

24. See Chapter 3, note 32.

25. Astarotte's extension ironically contains more traditional bestiary material than Luciana's symbolic structure; it is based entirely on Book 8 of Pliny's *Historia naturalis*, and Books 23 and 25 of Albertus Magnus's *De animalibus*. Landino had just translated Pliny's work, published in Venice in 1476; Albertus Magnus's bestiary had been even more recently published in Rome in 1487 and again in Mantua in 1479. Pulci draws on them in the context of a discussion of discoveries in science because he believes them to be representative of the most up-to-date information. For a study of the bestiary material represented in both versions of Luciana's tent see D. De Robertis, "Un' topos della tradizione dei cantari e una lacuna nell'Orlando' Laurenziano," *Atti dell' Accade. delle Scienze di Torino* 89 (1954–55): 187–203; F. Ageno, "Ancora su i bestiari del *Morgante*," *Studi di Filologia Italiana* 14 (1956): 485–94. Ageno points out that Pulci's first bestiary includes information on birds of prey he derives from his own experience, whereas the second, Astarotte's additions, carefully follows sources; *Studi* 14, 487.

26. For a study of Toscanelli see Eugenio Garin, "Ritratto di Paolo dal Pozzo Toscanelli," in *La Cultura Filosofica del Rinascimento Italiano* (Florence: Sansoni, 1961), pp. 312–34. For Renaissance cartography in general, see Walter Oakeshott, "Some Classical and Medieval Ideas in Renaissance Cosmography" in *Fritz Saxl: 1890–1948*, ed. D. J. Gordon (London: Thomas Nelson, 1957), pp. 245–60.

27. Kremers suggests that Cusa also influenced Pulci's idea of religious toleration; *Rinaldo*, pp. 58–67. I do not myself find the principal concern in the Antipodes episode to

be the expression of religious toleration but rather the proper place and function of pure knowledge, or knowledge for its own sake. This is, after all, what is at issue in the work from which the episode takes its inspiration and to which the *Morgante* is constantly referring in one way or another.

28. *Purgatorio*, 1, ed. Singleton, p. 328–29.

29. For a study of the "formula" of the golden age, see E. H. Gombrich, "Renaissance and Golden Age," *Journal of the Warburg and Courtauld Institutes* 24 (1961), esp. pp. 307–309.

30. It has been assumed that Pulci here refers to the poem he has just written as pastoral; see, for example, notes to 28.141, *Il Morgante*, ed. Ramat, p. 1238.

31. "Io ti promissi, o mio dilectissimo Laurentio, che ritornando ad me con le mie compagnuzze muse, di loro et di me ti farei parte." Letter 6, *Morgante e Lettere,* p. 950.

32. "Staromi qualche di ancora con teco tra questi boschi, et ragionerò con le mie più domestiche muse di te. . . ." Letter 8, p. 952.

33. *Ciriffo Calvaneo . . . Con la Giostra. . . .* (Florence, 1572), p. 81.

34. Virgil, *Eclogues. Georgics. Aeneid I–VI* (Cambridge, Mass: Harvard University Press, Loeb Classical Library, 1967).

35. For a study of the order of Vergil's *Eclogues* see John Van Sickle, *The Design of Virgil's Bucolics* (Romeo: Atence and Bizzari, 1978), pp. 187–205.

## Afterword. The Three 'Orlando' Poets

1. Michael Murrin makes a strong case for understanding several episodes of the *Orlando Innamorato* as historical allegory. As a whole, however, the poem does not admit this kind of interpretation. See Michael Murrin, *The Allegorical Epic: Essays in its Rise and Decline* (Chicago: University of Chicago Press, 1980), pp. 74–85.

2. Matteo Maria Boiardo, *Orlando Innamorato* ed. Giuseppe Anceschi (Milan: Garzanti, 1978), 1; 1. 1. 1.

3. Ludovico Ariosto, *Orlando Furioso*, ed. Lanfranco Caretti (Turin: Einaudi, 1966), 43. 171; 19. 31.

4. "Come suol fuor de la nube il sole / scoprir la faccia limpida e serena . . ." ed. Caretti, (32. 80); cf. "ut sol, qui tectus aquosis / nubibus ante fuit, victis e nubibus exit . . ." *Met.* (5. 570–71).

# BIBLIOGRAPHY

Acciajolo, Donato. *Vita Caroli Magni*. In *Scriptores Rerum Germanicarum*, 1. Edited by J. B. Mencke. Leipzig, 1728.

Ageno, F. "Ancora su i bestiari del *Morgante.*" *Studi di Filologia Italiana* 14 (1956): 485–94.

Ariosto, Ludovico. *Orlando Furioso*. Edited by Lanfranco Caretti. Turin: Einaudi, 1966.

Aristotle. *Physics*. Translated by Philip Wicksteed and Francis Cornford. Cambridge, Mass.: Harvard University Press, Loeb Classical Library, 1957.

Augustine. *City of God*. Translated by Marcus Dods. New York: Random House, 1950.

———. *Confessions*. Translated by R. S. Pine-Coffin. Harmondsworth: Penguin, 1978.

Baron, Hans. *Crisis of the Early Italian Renaissance*. 2d rev. ed. Princeton: Princeton University Press, 1966.

Barthes, Roland. *S/Z*. Translated by Richard Miller. New York: Hill and Wang, 1974.

———. *Image, Music, Text*. Translated by Stephen Heath. New York: Hill and Wang, 1977.

Berchorius, Petrus. *Reductorium Morale, Liber XV*. Utrecht: Instituut voor Laat Latijn der Rijksuniversiteit, 1962.

Boccaccio, Giovanni. *Genealogie Deorum Gentilium Libri*. Edited by Vincenzo Romano. Bari: Laterza, 1951.

Boethius. *De Consolatione Philosophiae*. Edited by Adrian Scuto and George D. Smith. London: Burns Oates and Washburn, 1925.

Boiardo, Matteo Maria. *Orlando Innamorato*: Edited by Giuseppe Anceschi. 2 Vols. Milan: Garzanti, 1978.

Bremond, Claude. *Logique du Récit*. Paris: Seuil, 1973.

Brown, Alison. "The Humanist Portrait of Cosimo de'Medici, *Pater Patriae.*" *Journal of the Warburg and Courtauld Institutes* 24 (1961): 186–221.

———. *Bartolomeo Scala, 1430–1497: Chancellor of Florence.* Princeton: Princeton University Press, 1979.

Bruni, Lionardo. *Historiarum Florentini populi liber.* Edited by Emilio Santini. Rerum Italicarum Scriptores, vol. 19, pt. 3. Citta di Castello: Lapi, 1914.

Castiglione, Baldesar. *Il Libro del cortegiano.* Edited by Bruno Maier. Turin: Unione, 1964.

Ceserani, Remo. "L'Allegria fantasia di Luigi Pulci e il Rifacimento dell'*Orlando.*" *Giornale storico della letteratura italiana* 135 (1958): 174–214.

———. "Studi sul Pulci," *Giornale storico della letteratura italiana* 146 (1969): 412–35.

Cicero. *De finibus bonorum et malorum.* Cambridge, Mass.: Harvard University Press, Loeb Classical Library, 1971.

Commager, Steele. *The Odes of Horace.* Bloomington, Ind.: Indiana University Press, 1967.

Cronin, Vincent. *Florentine Renaissance.* New York: Dutton, 1967.

Culler, Jonathan. *Structuralist Poetics.* Ithaca: Cornell University Press, 1977.

Dante Alighieri. *Monarchia.* Edited by Pier Giorgio Ricci. Verona: Mondadori, 1965.

———. *The Divine Comedy.* Translated by Charles S. Singleton. 6 vols. Bollingen Series 80. Princeton: Princeton University Press, 1977.

De Robertis, Domenico. "Un' topos della tradizione dei cantari e una lacuna nell'Orlando' Laurenziano." *Atti dell'Accade. delle Scienze di Torino* 89 (1954–55): 187–203.

———. *Storia del Morgante.* Florence: Le Monnier, 1958.

Dorfman, Eugene. *The Narreme in the Medieval Romance Epic.* Toronto: University of Toronto Press, 1969.

Durling, Robert. *The Figure of the Poet in Renaissance Epic.* Cambridge, Mass.: Harvard University Press, 1965.

Febvre, Lucien. *Le Problème de l'incroyance au XVIe siècle: la religion de Rabelais.* Paris: Michel, 1942.

Ferrante, Joan M. "Some Thoughts on the Application of Modern Critical Methods to Medieval Literature." *Yearbook of Comparative and General Literature* (1980): 5–9.

Frame, Douglas. *The Myth of Return in Early Greek Epic.* New Haven: Yale University Press, 1978.

Garin, Eugenio. "Ritratto di Paolo dal Pozzo Toscanelli." In *La Cultura Filosofica del Rinascimento Italiano*, 312–34. Florence: Sansoni, 1961.

Gaeta, F. "L'avventura di Ercole." *Rinascimento* 5, 2 (1954): 227–60.

Getto, Giovanni. *Studio sul Morgante*. Como: Marzorati, 1944.

Giamatti, A. Bartlett. "Proteus Unbound: Some Versions of the Sea God in the Renaissance." In *The Disciplines of Criticism*, ed. P. Demetz, T. Greene, and L. Nelson, Jr., 437–75. New Haven, Yale University Press, 1965.

———. "Headlong horses, headless horsemen: an essay on the chivalric epics of Pulci, Boiardo, and Ariosto." In *Italian Literature: roots and branches: Essays in Honor of Thomas Goddard Bergin*, edited by Giose Rimanelli and Kenneth John Atchity, pp. 265–307. New Haven: Yale University Press, 1976.

Gianni, Angelo. *Pulci uno e due*. Florence: La Nuova Italia, 1967.

Gombrich, E. H. "Renaissance and Golden Age." *Journal of the Warburg and Courtauld Institutes* 24 (1961): 307–9.

Gramsci, Antonio. "The Formation of Intellectuals." In *The Modern Prince and other writings*, pp. 118–25. New York: International Publishers, 1959.

Gutkind, Carl. *Cosimo de' Medici, 1389–1464*. Oxford: Clarendon Press, 1938.

Hale, John. *Florence and the Medici: the Pattern of Control*. London: Thames and Hudson, 1977.

Hanning, Barbara. "Glorious Apollo: Poetic and Political Themes in the First Opera." *The Renaissance Quarterly* 32, 4 (1979): 485–513.

Hanning, Robert W. *The Vision of History in Early Britain*. New York: Columbia University Press, 1966.

Havelock, Eric. *Preface to Plato*. Cambridge, Mass.: Harvard University Press, 1953.

Homer. *The Iliad*. Translated by Richmond Lattimore. Chicago: University of Chicago Press, 1967.

———. *The Odyssey*. Translated by Richmond Lattimore. Chicago: University of Chicago Press, 1968.

Hyginus. *Fabularum Liber*. Basle, 1570.

Jackson, W. T. H. *The Hero and the King: an Epic Theme*. New York: Columbia University Press, 1982.

Kremers, Dieter. *Rinaldo und Odysseus: Zur Frage der Diesseitserkenntnis bei Luigi Pulci und Dante Alighieri*. Heidelberg: Winter, 1966.

Landino, Cristoforo. *Comento . . . sopra la comedia di Danthe Alighieri poeta fiorentino*. Florence, 1481.

Lazzari, Alfonso. *Ugolino e Michele Verino*. Turin, 1897.

Lebano, Edoardo. "I miracoli di Roncisvalle e la presunta ortodossia del diavoli-teologo Astarotte nel 'Morgante' di L. Pulci." *Italica* 46 (1969): 120–34.

———. "Note sulla religiosità di Luigi Pulci." *Forum Italicum* 4, 4 (1970): 517–32.

————. "Luigi Pulci and Late Fifteenth-Century Humanism in Florence." *The Renaissance Quarterly* 27, 4 (1974): 489–98.

Marcel, Raymond. *Marsile Ficin*. Paris: Les Belles Lettres, 1958.

Malory, Sir Thomas. *Works*. Edited by Eugene Vinaver. London: University Press, 1971.

Mariani, Gaetano. *Il Morgante e i cantari trecenteschi*. Florence: Le Monnier, 1953.

Martines, Lauro. *The Social World of Florentine Humanists: 1390–1460*. Princeton: Princeton University Press, 1969.

Mazzotta, Giuseppe. *Dante: Poet of the Desert*. Princeton: Princeton University Press, 1979.

Medici, Lorenzo de'. *Lettere (1460–1474)*. Edited by Riccardo Fubini. Florence: Giunti, 1977.

————. *Lettere (1474–1478)*. Edited by Riccardo Fubini. Florence: Giunti, 1977.

————. *Lettere (1478–1479)*. Edited by Nicolai Rubinstein. Florence: Giunti, 1977.

Momigliano, Attilio. *L'indole e riso di Luigi Pulci*. Rocca S. Casciano, Indagine di storia letteraria e artistica, no. 7. 1907.

————. "Il 'Morgante.'" In *Studi di poesia*, pp. 33–39. Bari: Laterza, 1938.

Murrin, Michael. *The Veil of Allegory*. Chicago: University of Chicago Press, 1969.

————. *The Allegorical Epic: Essays in its Rise and Decline*. Chicago: University of Chicago Press, 1980.

Nagy, Gregory. *Studies in Greek and Indic Metre*. Cambridge, Mass.: Harvard University Press, 1974.

Nigro, Salvatore. *Pulci e la cultura medicea*. Bari: Laterza, 1972.

Nohrnberg, James. *The Analogy of the Faerie Queene*. Princeton: Princeton University Press 1976.

Oakeshott, Walter. "Some Classical and Medieval Ideas in Renaissance Cosmography." In *Fritz Saxl: 1890–1948*. Edited by D. J. Gordon, pp. 245–60. London: Thomas Nelson, 1957.

*'Orlando,' Die Vorlage zu Pulcis 'Morgante*. Edited by Johannes Hübscher. Ausgaben und Abhandlungen aus dem Gebiete der Romanischen Philologie, no. 60. Marburg, 1886.

Orvieto, Paolo. *Pulci medievale*. Rome: Salèrno, 1978.

Ovid. *Metamorphoses*. 2 vols. Cambridge, Mass.: Harvard University Press, Loeb Classical Library, 1968.

Palmieri, Matteo. *Della vita civile*. Edited by Felice Battaglia. Scrittori Politici Italiani, no. 14. Bologna: Zanichelli, 1944.

Panofsky, Erwin. *Studies in Iconology*. New York: Harper and Row, 1962.

Parotti, Phillip Elliot. "The Female Warrior in Renaissance Epic." Ph.D. dissertation, University of new Mexico, 1972.

Pellegrini, Carlo. *Luigi Pulci: L'uomo e l'artista*. Pisa: Nistri, 1912.

Petrarca, Francesco. *Rime sparse e i trionfi*. Edited by Ezio Chiroboli. Bari: Laterza, 1930.

———.*Prose*. Milan: Ricciardi, 1955.

Pigman, G. W. III. "Versions of Imitation in the Renaissance." *The Renaissance Quarterly* 33, 1 (1980): 3–9.

Plato. *The Dialogues*. Translated by B. Jowett. New York: Random House, 1937.

Pocock, J. G. A. *The Machiavellian Moment: Florentine Political Thought and the Atlantic Republican Tradition*. Princeton: Princeton University Press, 1975.

Propp, Valdimir. *Morphology of the Folktale*. Translated by Laurence Scott. Austin: University of Texas Press, 1968.

Pulci, Luigi. *Ciriffo Cavalneo di Luca Pulci, Gentil'huomo fiorentino. Con la Giostra del Magnifico Lorenzo de Medici*. Florence, 1572.

———. *Sonetti di Matteo Franco e di Luigi Pulci*. Lucca?, 1759.

———. *Il Morgante*. Edited by Franca Ageno. Milan: Ricciardi, 1957.

———. *Il Morgante*. Edited by Raffaello Ramat. Milan: Rizzoli, 1961.

———. *Morgante e Lettere*. Edited by D. De Robertis. Florence: Sansoni, 1962.

Rajna, Pio. "La materia del 'Morgante' in un ignoto poema cavalleresco del sec. XV." *Il Propugnatore* 2, 1 (1869): 7–35, 220–52, 353–84.

———. "La rotta di Roncisvalle nella letteratura cavalleresca italiana." *Il Propugnatore* 4, 1 (1871–72): 52–78, 330–80; and 2 (1871–72): 53–133.

Reynolds, Barbara. "Dante's Tale of Ulysses." *Annali*, Sezione romanza 2, 1 (1960): 49–65.

Ricoeur, Paul. "Narrative Time." *Critical Inquiry* 7, 1 (1980): 169–90.

*Ricordi di Firenze Dell'Anno 1459 di Autore anonimo*. Edited by G. Volpi. Rerum italicarum scriptores, vol. 27, pt. 1. Città di Castello: Muratori, 1907.

Rizzo, Anna Padoa. *Benozzo Gozzoli, pittore fiorentino*. Florence: Edam, 1972.

Rochon, André. *La jeunesse de Laurent de Medicis*. Paris: Les Belles Lettres, 1963.

Rotondi, Guiseppe. "Rileggendo il 'Morgante.' " *Convivium* (1936): 392.

———. "Reminiscenze Dantesche nel Pulci." *Convivium*, (1936): 422–24.

Rubinstein, Nicolai. "The Beginnings of Political Thought in Florence." *Journal of the Warburg and Courtauld Institutes* 5 (1942): 198–227.

———. *The Government of Florence under the Medici*. Oxford: Oxford University Press, 1966.

———. "Florentine Constitutionalism and Medici Ascendancy in the Fifteenth Century." In *Florentine Studies, Politics and Society in Renaissance Florence*. Edited by Nicolai Rubinstein, pp. 442–62. Evanston, Ill: Northwestern University Press, 1968.

Ruggieri, Ruggero. *L'umanesimo cavalleresco italiano da Dante al Pulci*. Rome: Ateneo, 1962.

Ryding, William. *Structure in Medieval Narrative*. Hague: Mouton, 1971.

Quint, David. *Origin and Originality in Renaissance Literature: Versions of the Source*. New Haven: Yale University Press, 1983.

Salutati, Coluccio. *De laboribus Herculis*. Edited by B. L. Ullman. Zurich: Thesaurus Mundi, 1951.

*Scriptores Rerum Mythicarum Latini Tres*. Edited by Georgius Henricus Bode. Celle: E. H. C. Schulze, 1834.

Segre, Cesare. *Semiotics and Literary Criticism*. The Hague. Mouton, 1973.

———. *Structures and Time: Narration, Poetry, Models*. Translated by John Meddemmen. Chicago: Chicago University Press, 1979.

Seigel, Jerrold. *Rhetoric and Philosophy in Renaissance Humanism: The Union of Eloquence and Wisdom, Petrarch to Valla*. Princeton: Princeton University Press, 1968.

Servius. *Servii Grammatici Commentarii in Vergilii Carmina*. Edited by George and Hermann Hegen. Leipzig: Teubner, 1883.

Shumaker, Wayne. *The Occult Sciences in the Renaissance*. Berkeley and Los Angeles: University of California Press, 1972.

Smith, Barbara Herrnstein. "Narrative Versions, Narrative Theories." *Critical Inquiry* 7, 1 (1980): 213–36.

Spitzer, Leo. *Linguistics and Literary History*. Princeton: Princeton University Press, 1948.

Statius. *Opera cum observationibus ac cum commentariis*. Paris, 1618.

Struever, Nancy K. *The Languages of History in the Renaissance*. Princeton: Princeton University Press, 1970.

Tenenti, Alberto. *Il senso della morte e l'amore della vita nel Rinascimento*. Turin: Einaudi, 1957.

Todorov, Tzevtan. *The Poetics of Prose*. Translated by Richard Howard. Ithaca: Cornell University Press, 1977.

Torre, Arnaldo della. *Storia dell'Accademia Platonica di Firenze*. Florence: Carnesecchi, 1902.

Trexler, Richard C. *Public Life in Renaissance Florence*. New York: Academic Press, 1980.

Tuve, Rosemond. *Allegorical Imagery: Some Medieval Books and Their Posterity*. Princeton: Princeton University Press, 1966.

Vallese, G. "Il 'Morgante' e l'antihumanesimo del Pulci." *Italica* 30 (1953): 81–86.

Valeri, Nino. *L'Italia nell'età dei principati dal 1343 al 1516*. Milan: Mondadori, 1949.

Van Sickle, John. *The Design of Virgil's Bucolics*. Rome: Atence and Bizzari, 1978.

Varese, Claudio. *Storia e politica nella prosa del quattrocento*. Turin: Einaudi, 1961.

Virgil. *Eclogues. Georgics. Aeneid*. 2 Vols. Cambridge Mass.: Harvard University Press, Loeb Classical Library, 1967.

Villani, Giovanni. *Istorie Fiorentine*. Milan. Societa tipografica de' classici italiani, 1802.

Vinaver, Eugene. *The Rise of Romance*. New York: Oxford University Press, 1973.

Vitz, Evelyn Birge. "Narrative Analysis of Medieval Texts: *La Fille du Comte de Pontieu.*" *Modern Language Notes* 92 (1977): 645–90.

———. "Desire and Causality in Medieval Narrative." *Romanic Review* 71, 3 (1980): 213–43.

Volpi, G. "Luigi Pulci: Studio Biografico." *Giornale storico della letteratura italiana* 22 (1893): 1–64.

Voigt, Françoise. *Roland-Orlando dans l'epopée Française et Italienne*. Leiden: E. J. Brill, 1938.

Walker, D. P. *Spiritual and Demonic Magic from Ficino to Campanella*. London: The Warburg Institute, 1958.

Walser, Ernst. *Lebens- und Glaubensprobleme aus dem Zeitalter der Renaissance: Die Religion des Luigi Pulci, ihre Quellen and ihre Bedeutung*. Marburg: Elwert, 1926.

Weinstein, Donald. "The Myth of Florence." In *Florentine Studies: Politics and Society in Renaissance Florence*. Edited by Nicolai Rubinstein, pp. 15–44. Evanston, Ill: Northwestern University Press, 1968.

Welliver, Warman. *L'impero fiorentino*. Florence: La Nuova Italia, 1957.

White, Hayden. "The Value of Narrativity in the Representation of Reality." *Critical Inquiry* 7, 1 (1980): 5–27.

Wilcox, D. *The Development of Florentine Humanist Historiography in the Fifteenth Century*. Cambridge, Mass: Harvard University Press, 1969.

Wilkins, Ernest H. "On the Dates of Composition of the *Morgante* of Luigi Pulci." *PMLA* 66 (1951): 244–50.

———. "On the Earliest Editions of the *Morgante* of Luigi Pulci." *Papers of the Bibliographical Society of America* (1951): 1–21.

Wind, Edgar. *Pagan Mysteries in the Renaissance*. New York: W. W. Norton, 1968.

Zingarelli, Nicola. "La Composizione del 'Morgante' di Luigi Pulci." In *Scritti di varia letteratura*, pp. 469–84. Milan: Hoepli, 1935.

# INDEX